# Garfield
## hits the big time

BY: JIM DAVIS

**BALLANTINE BOOKS · NEW YORK**

Copyright © 1993 United Feature Syndicate, Inc.
GARFIELD Comic Strips © 1992, 1993 United Feature
Syndicate, Inc.

All rights reserved under International and Pan-American Copyright
Conventions. Published in the United States by Ballantine Books, a
division of Random House, Inc., New York, and simultaneously in
Canada by Random House of Canada Limited, Toronto.

Library of Congress Catalog Card Number: 93-90003

ISBN: 0-345-38332-X

Manufactured in the United States of America

First Edition: October 1993

10 9 8 7 6 5 4 3

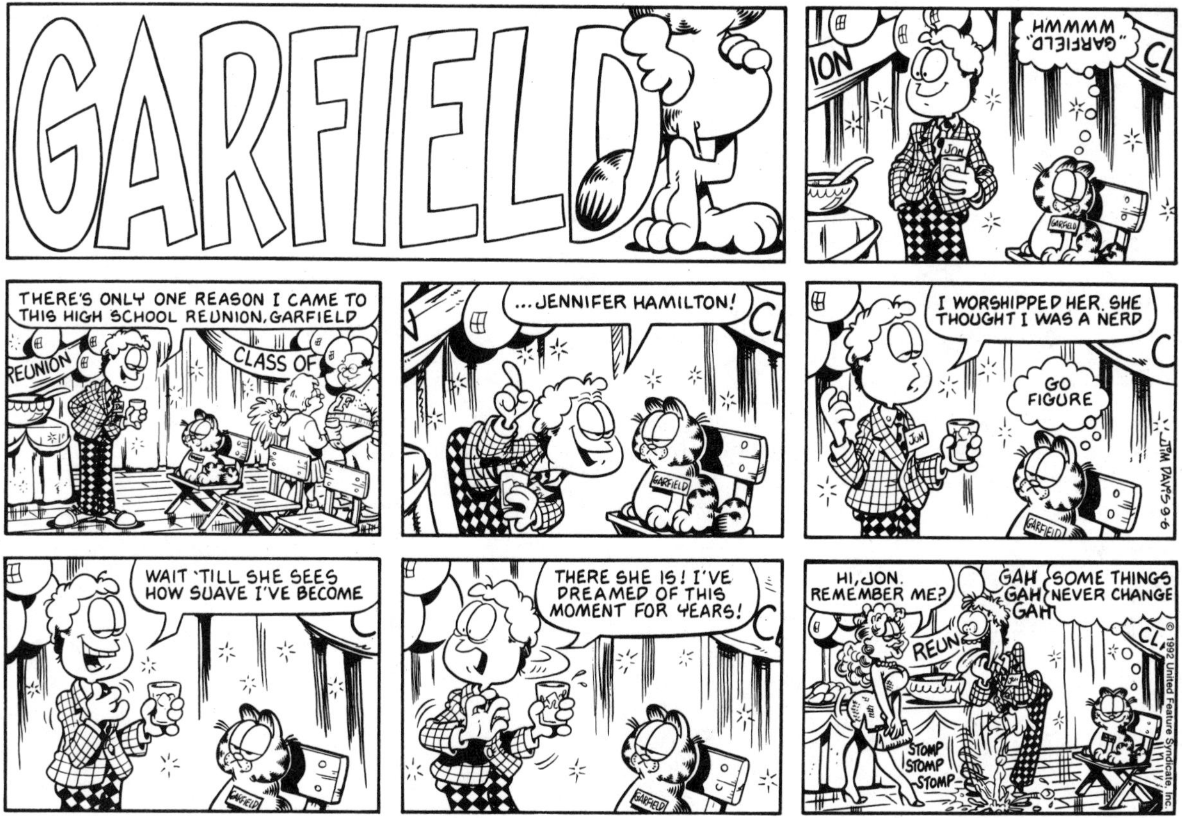
GARFIELD
"GARFIELD," HMMMM
JON
GARFIELD
THERE'S ONLY ONE REASON I CAME TO THIS HIGH SCHOOL REUNION, GARFIELD
REUNION
CLASS OF
...JENNIFER HAMILTON!
I WORSHIPPED HER. SHE THOUGHT I WAS A NERD
GO FIGURE
JON
JIM DAVIS 9-6
WAIT 'TILL SHE SEES HOW SUAVE I'VE BECOME
THERE SHE IS! I'VE DREAMED OF THIS MOMENT FOR YEARS!
HI, JON. REMEMBER ME?
GAH GAH GAH
SOME THINGS NEVER CHANGE
STOMP STOMP STOMP
© 1992 United Feature Syndicate, Inc.

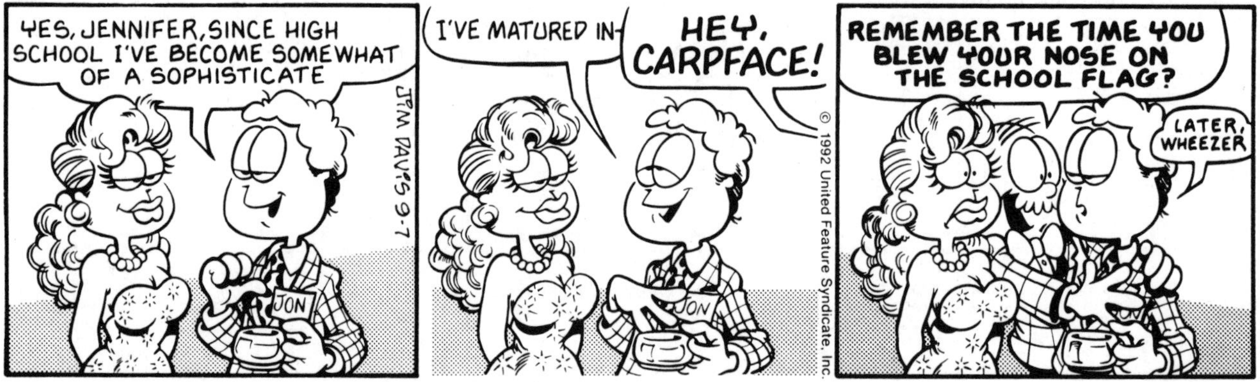
YES, JENNIFER, SINCE HIGH SCHOOL I'VE BECOME SOMEWHAT OF A SOPHISTICATE
JIM DAVIS 9-7
I'VE MATURED IN-
HEY, CARPFACE!
© 1992 United Feature Syndicate, Inc.
REMEMBER THE TIME YOU BLEW YOUR NOSE ON THE SCHOOL FLAG?
LATER, WHEEZER
JON

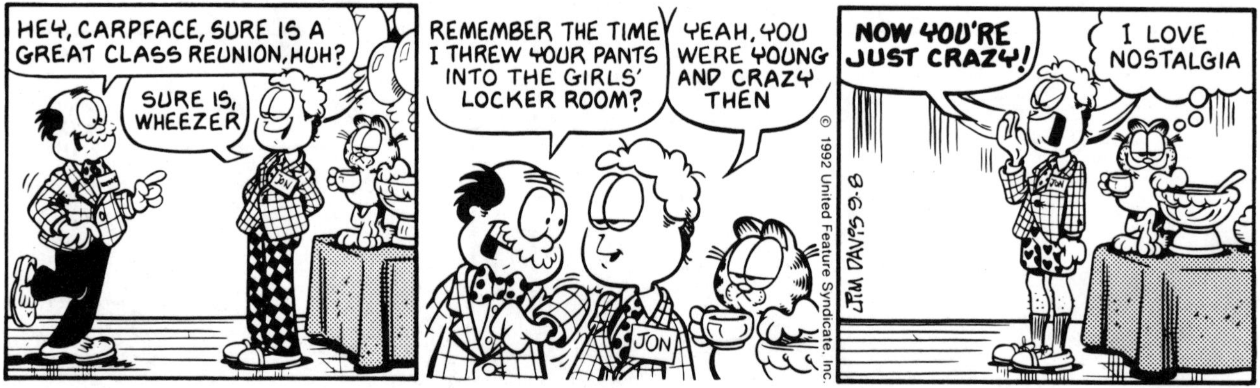
HEY, CARPFACE, SURE IS A GREAT CLASS REUNION, HUH?
SURE IS, WHEEZER
REMEMBER THE TIME I THREW YOUR PANTS INTO THE GIRLS' LOCKER ROOM?
YEAH, YOU WERE YOUNG AND CRAZY THEN
© 1992 United Feature Syndicate, Inc.
JIM DAVIS 9-8
NOW YOU'RE JUST CRAZY!
I LOVE NOSTALGIA
JON

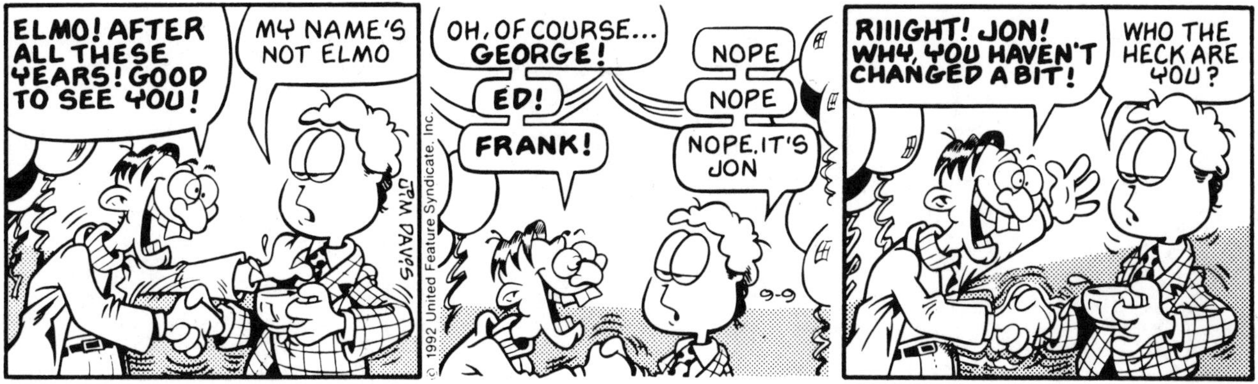
ELMO! AFTER ALL THESE YEARS! GOOD TO SEE YOU!
MY NAME'S NOT ELMO
JIM DAVIS
© 1992 United Feature Syndicate, Inc.
OH, OF COURSE... GEORGE!
NOPE
ED!
NOPE
FRANK!
NOPE, IT'S JON
9-9
RIIIGHT! JON! WHY, YOU HAVEN'T CHANGED A BIT!
WHO THE HECK ARE YOU?

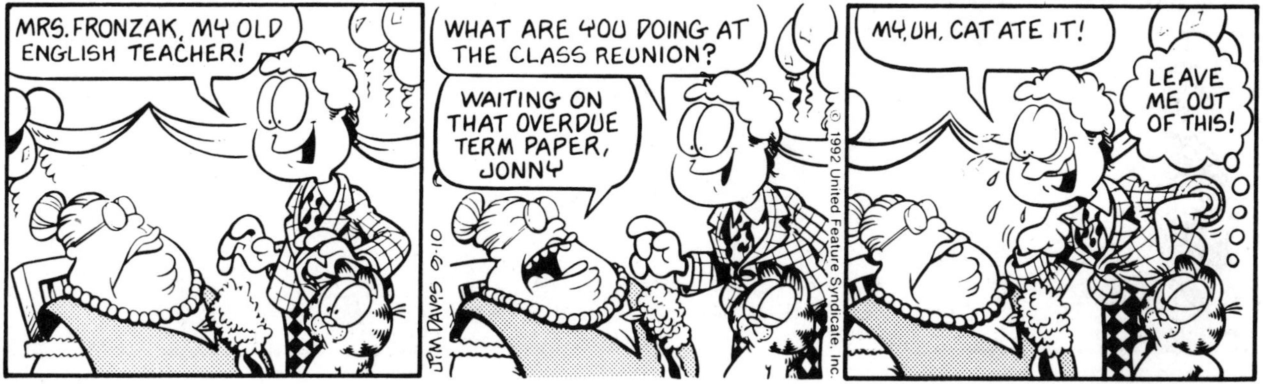
MRS. FRONZAK, MY OLD ENGLISH TEACHER!
JIM DAVIS 9-10
WHAT ARE YOU DOING AT THE CLASS REUNION?
WAITING ON THAT OVERDUE TERM PAPER, JONNY
© 1992 United Feature Syndicate, Inc.
MY, UH, CAT ATE IT!
LEAVE ME OUT OF THIS!

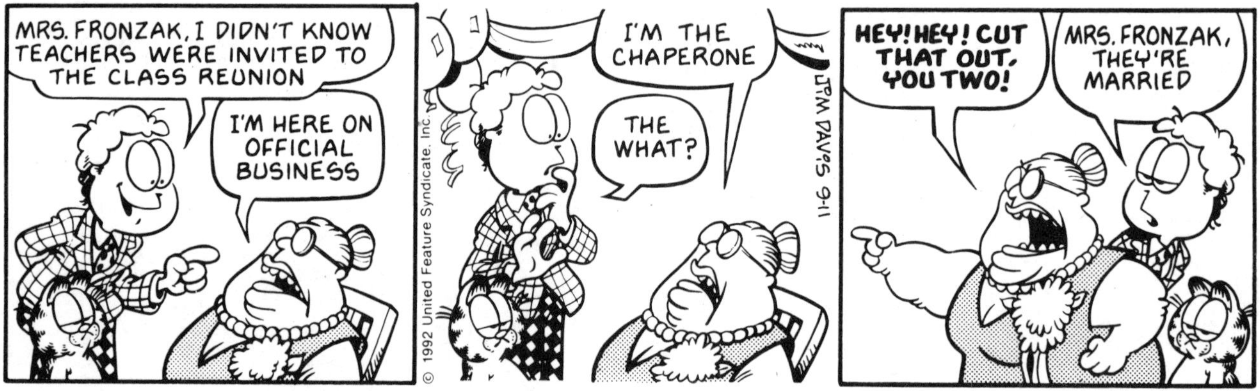
MRS. FRONZAK, I DIDN'T KNOW TEACHERS WERE INVITED TO THE CLASS REUNION
I'M HERE ON OFFICIAL BUSINESS
I'M THE CHAPERONE
THE WHAT?
HEY! HEY! CUT THAT OUT, YOU TWO!
MRS. FRONZAK, THEY'RE MARRIED
© 1992 United Feature Syndicate, Inc.
JIM DAVIS 9-11

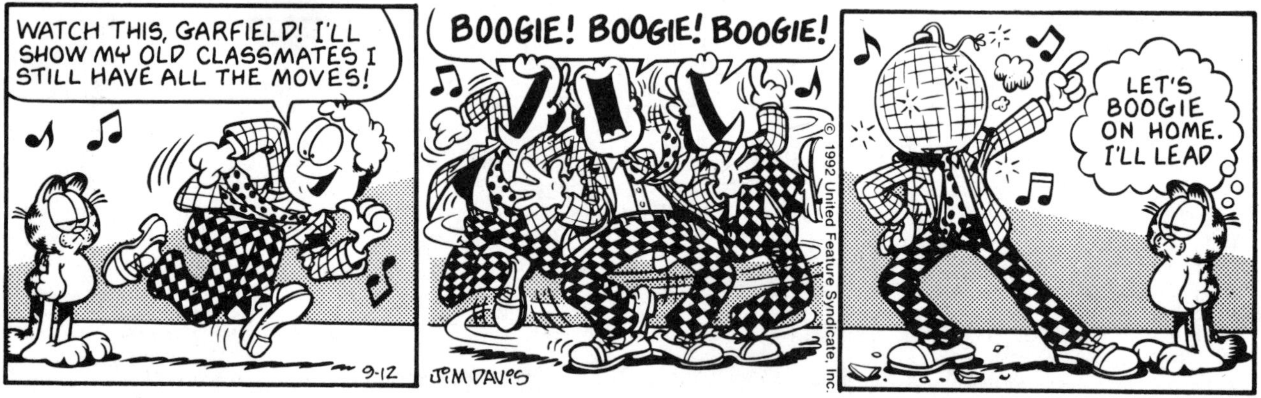
WATCH THIS, GARFIELD! I'LL SHOW MY OLD CLASSMATES I STILL HAVE ALL THE MOVES!
BOOGIE! BOOGIE! BOOGIE!
LET'S BOOGIE ON HOME. I'LL LEAD
9-12
JIM DAVIS
© 1992 United Feature Syndicate, Inc.

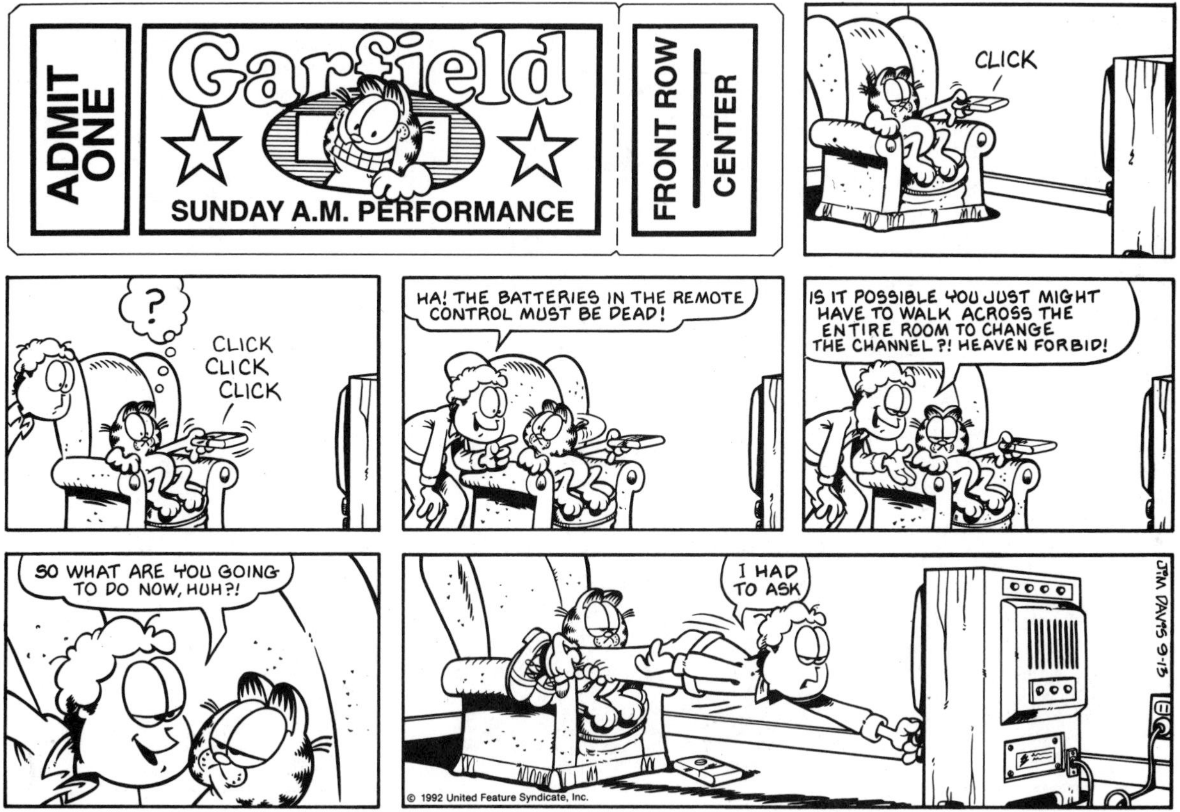

ADMIT ONE
Garfield
SUNDAY A.M. PERFORMANCE
FRONT ROW
CENTER
CLICK
?
CLICK CLICK CLICK
HA! THE BATTERIES IN THE REMOTE CONTROL MUST BE DEAD!
IS IT POSSIBLE YOU JUST MIGHT HAVE TO WALK ACROSS THE ENTIRE ROOM TO CHANGE THE CHANNEL?! HEAVEN FORBID!
SO WHAT ARE YOU GOING TO DO NOW, HUH?!
I HAD TO ASK
JIM DAVIS 9-13
© 1992 United Feature Syndicate, Inc.

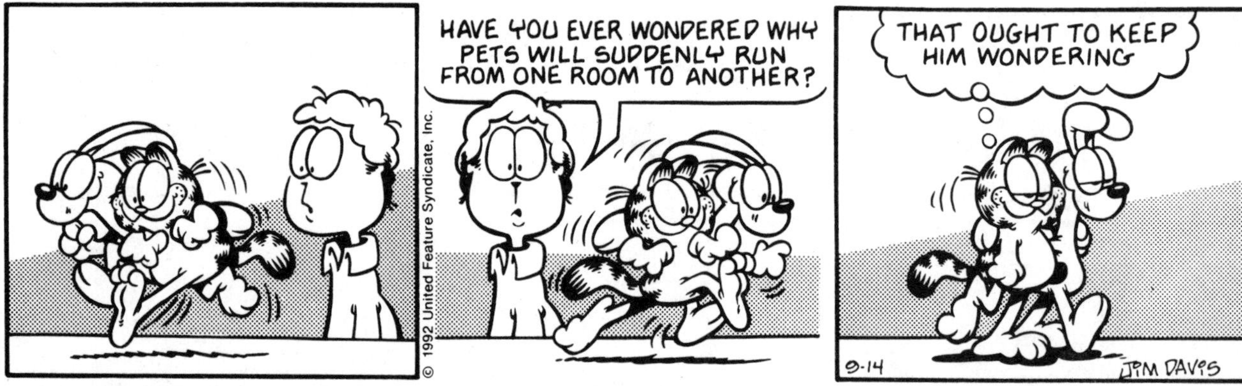
© 1992 United Feature Syndicate, Inc.
HAVE YOU EVER WONDERED WHY PETS WILL SUDDENLY RUN FROM ONE ROOM TO ANOTHER?
THAT OUGHT TO KEEP HIM WONDERING
9-14
JIM DAVIS

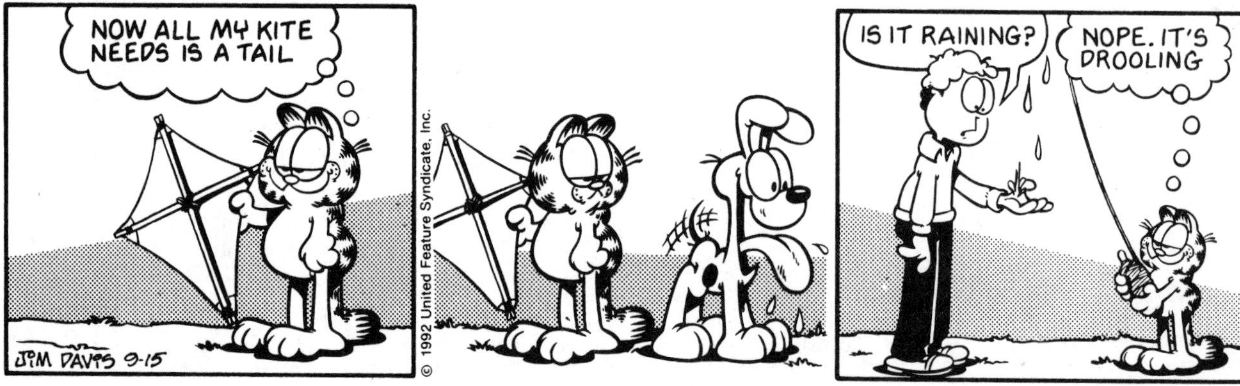
NOW ALL MY KITE NEEDS IS A TAIL
JIM DAVIS 9-15
© 1992 United Feature Syndicate, Inc.
IS IT RAINING?
NOPE. IT'S DROOLING

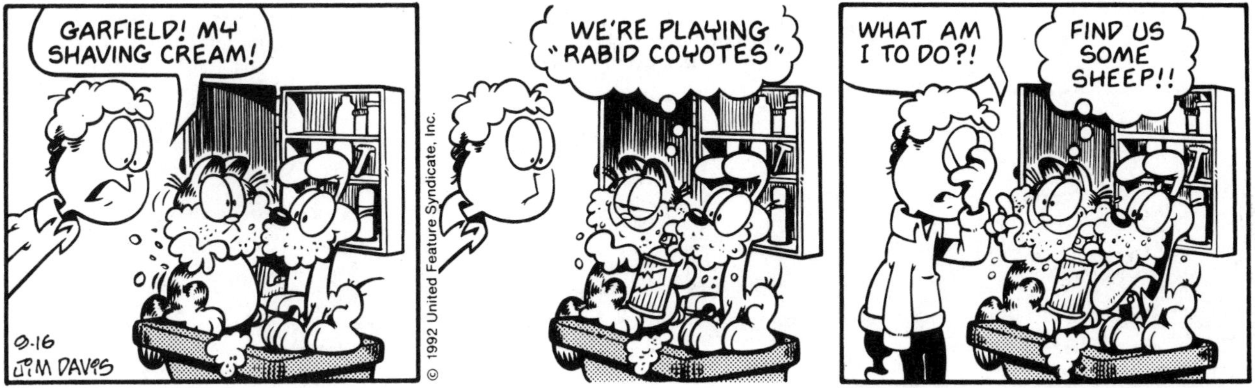
GARFIELD! MY SHAVING CREAM!
9-16
JIM DAVIS
© 1992 United Feature Syndicate, Inc.
WE'RE PLAYING "RABID COYOTES"
WHAT AM I TO DO?!
FIND US SOME SHEEP!!

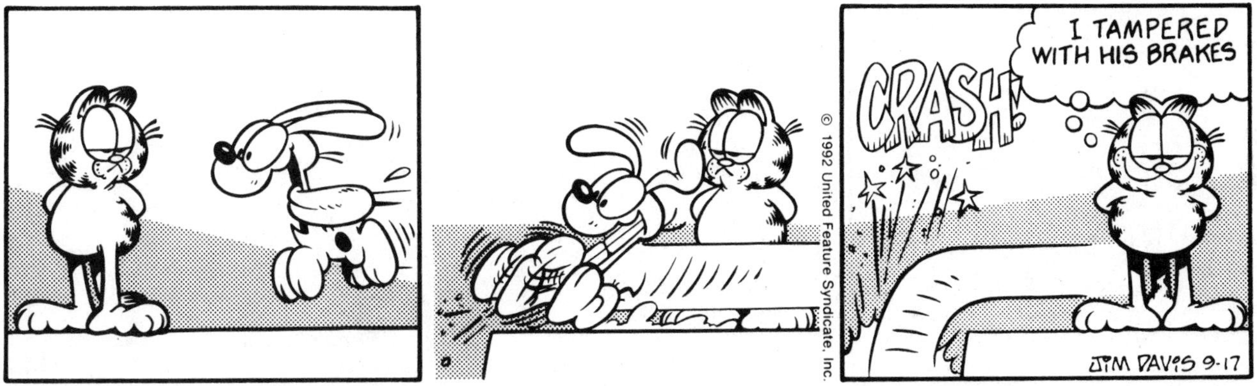
© 1992 United Feature Syndicate, Inc.
CRASH!
I TAMPERED WITH HIS BRAKES
JIM DAVIS 9-17

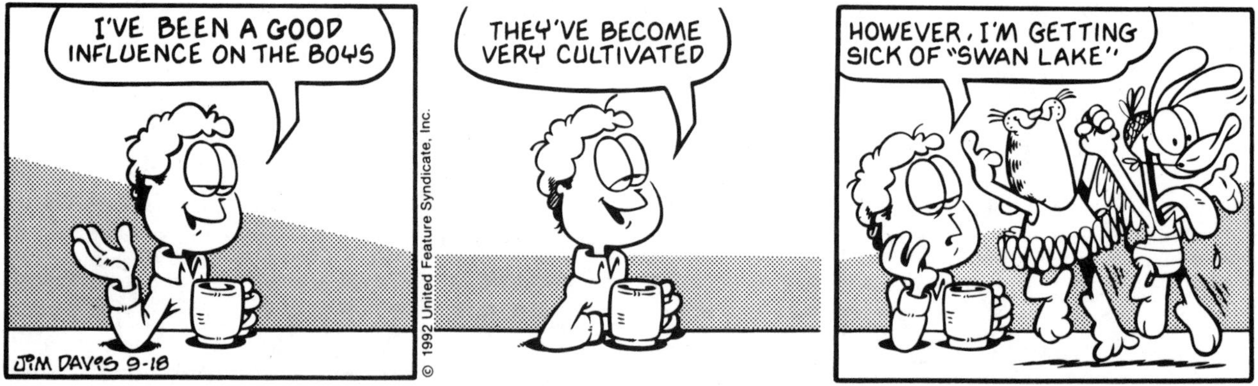
I'VE BEEN A GOOD INFLUENCE ON THE BOYS
JIM DAVIS 9-18
THEY'VE BECOME VERY CULTIVATED
HOWEVER, I'M GETTING SICK OF "SWAN LAKE"



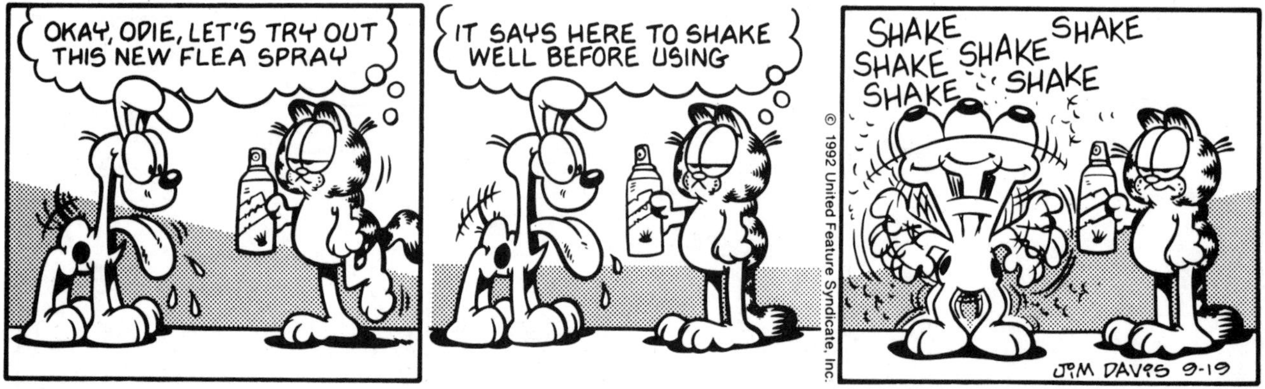
OKAY, ODIE, LET'S TRY OUT THIS NEW FLEA SPRAY
IT SAYS HERE TO SHAKE WELL BEFORE USING
SHAKE
SHAKE
SHAKE
SHAKE
SHAKE
SHAKE
JIM DAVIS 9-19

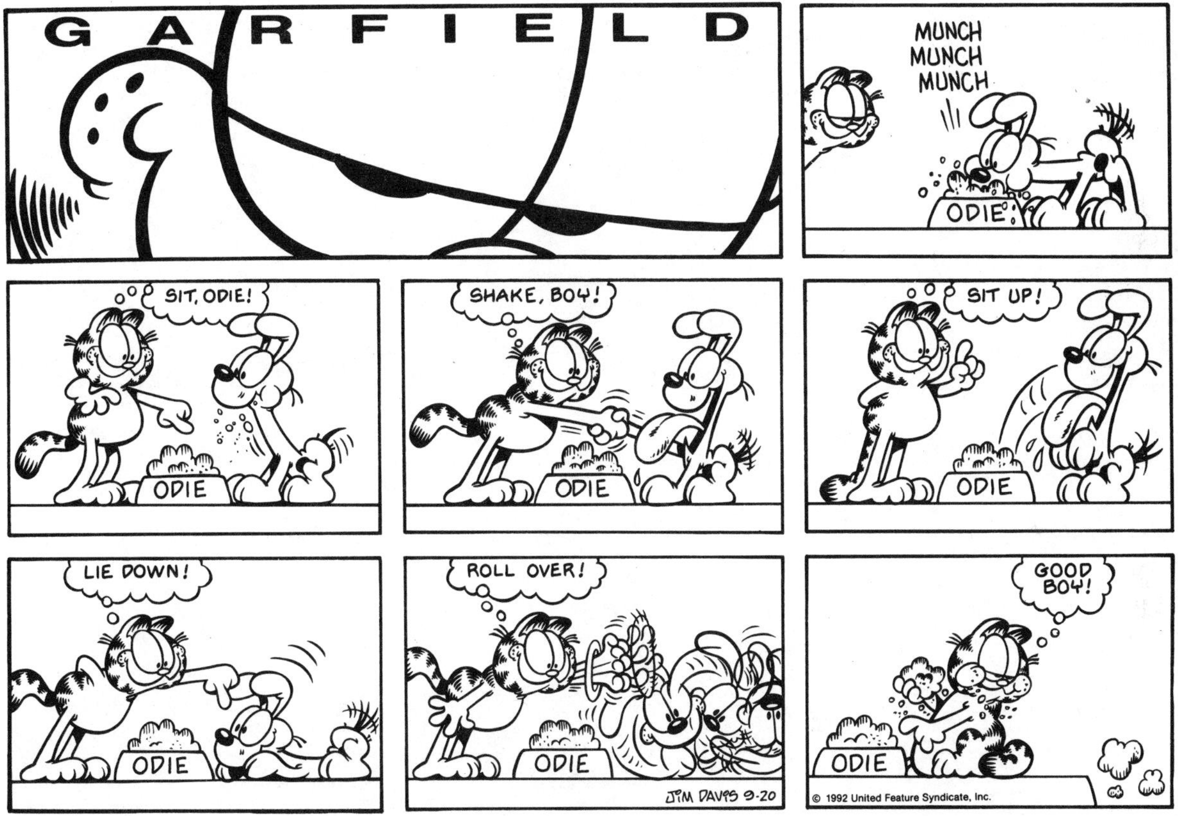
GARFIELD
MUNCH
MUNCH
MUNCH
ODIE
SIT, ODIE!
ODIE
SHAKE, BOY!
ODIE
SIT UP!
ODIE
LIE DOWN!
ODIE
ROLL OVER!
ODIE
JIM DAVIS 9-20
GOOD BOY!
ODIE
© 1992 United Feature Syndicate, Inc.

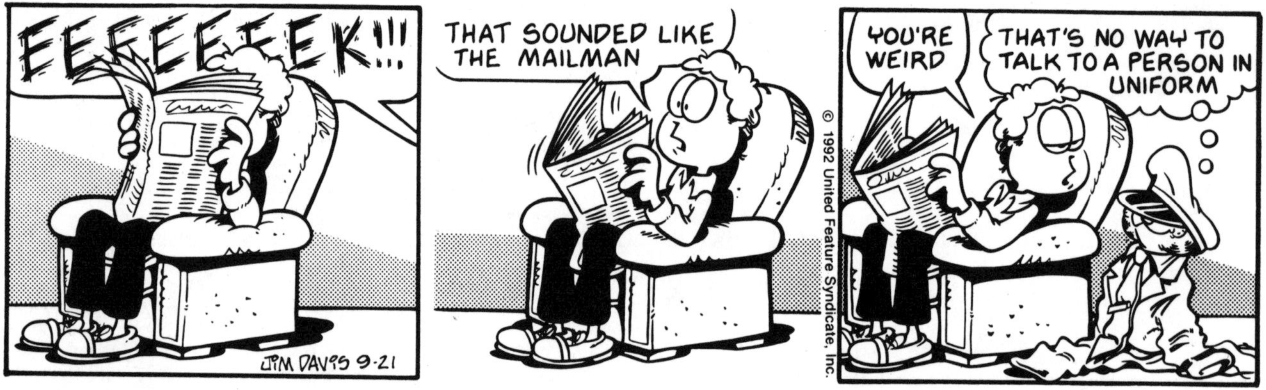
EEEEEEEEK!!!
JIM DAVIS 9-21
THAT SOUNDED LIKE THE MAILMAN
© 1992 United Feature Syndicate, Inc.
YOU'RE WEIRD
THAT'S NO WAY TO TALK TO A PERSON IN UNIFORM

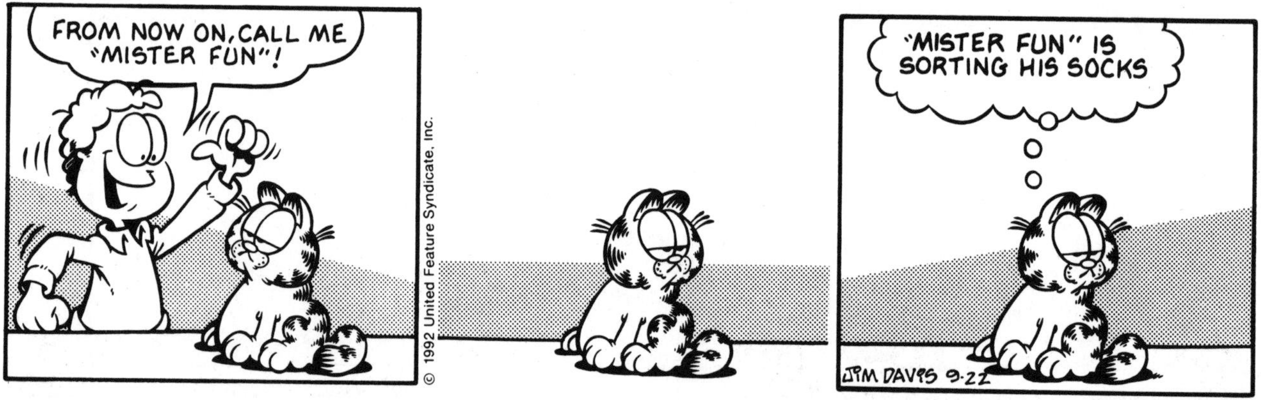
FROM NOW ON, CALL ME "MISTER FUN"!
© 1992 United Feature Syndicate, Inc.
"MISTER FUN" IS SORTING HIS SOCKS
JIM DAVIS 9-22

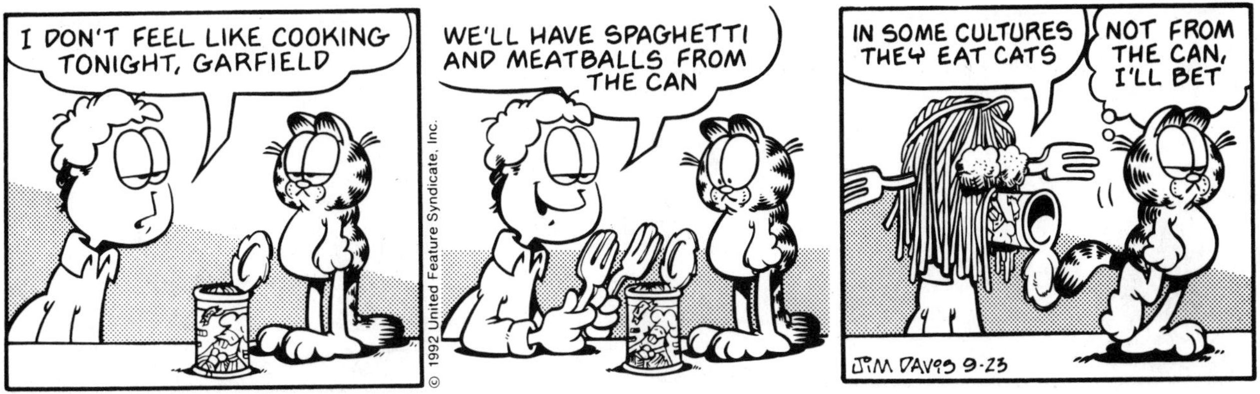
I DON'T FEEL LIKE COOKING TONIGHT, GARFIELD
WE'LL HAVE SPAGHETTI AND MEATBALLS FROM THE CAN
© 1992 United Feature Syndicate, Inc.
IN SOME CULTURES THEY EAT CATS
NOT FROM THE CAN, I'LL BET
JIM DAVIS 9-23

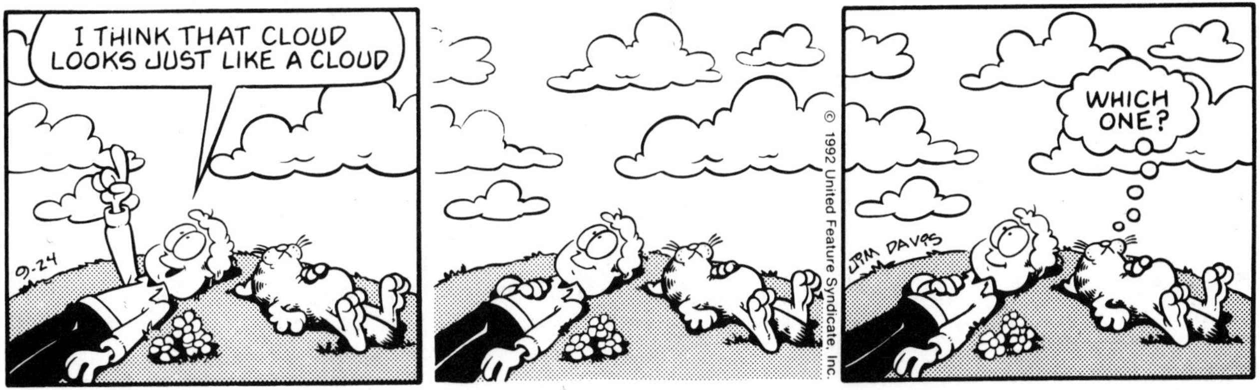
9-24
I THINK THAT CLOUD LOOKS JUST LIKE A CLOUD
© 1992 United Feature Syndicate, Inc.
JIM DAVIS
WHICH ONE?

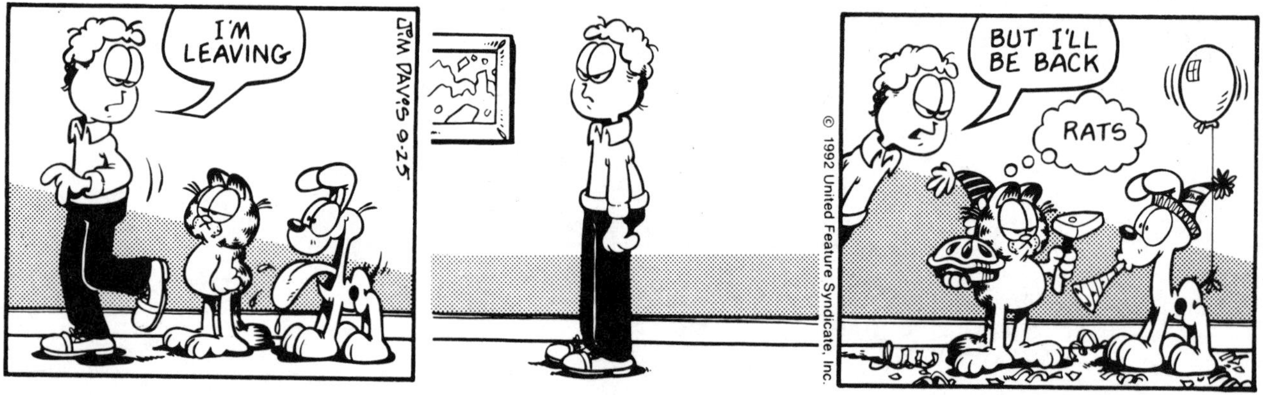
JIM DAVIS 9-25
I'M LEAVING
BUT I'LL BE BACK
RATS


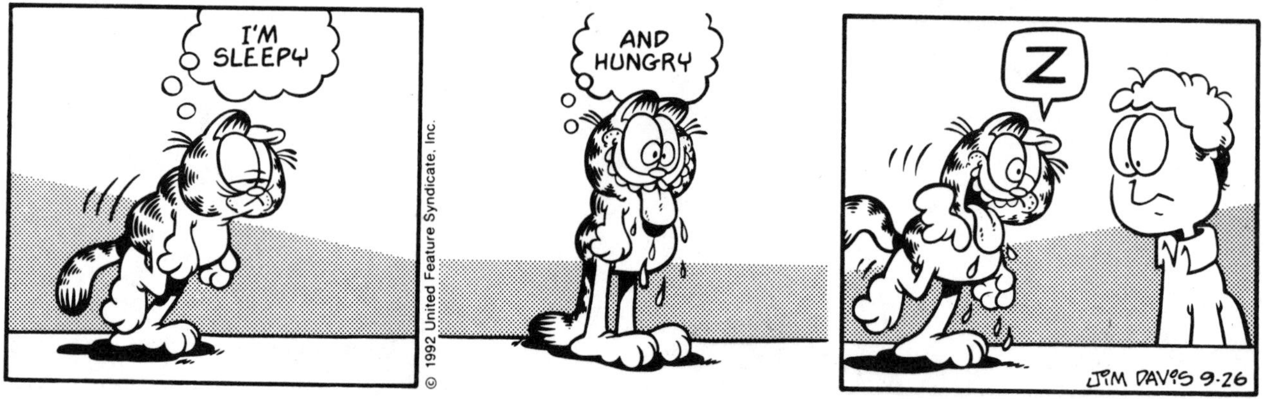
I'M SLEEPY
AND HUNGRY
Z
JIM DAVIS 9-26

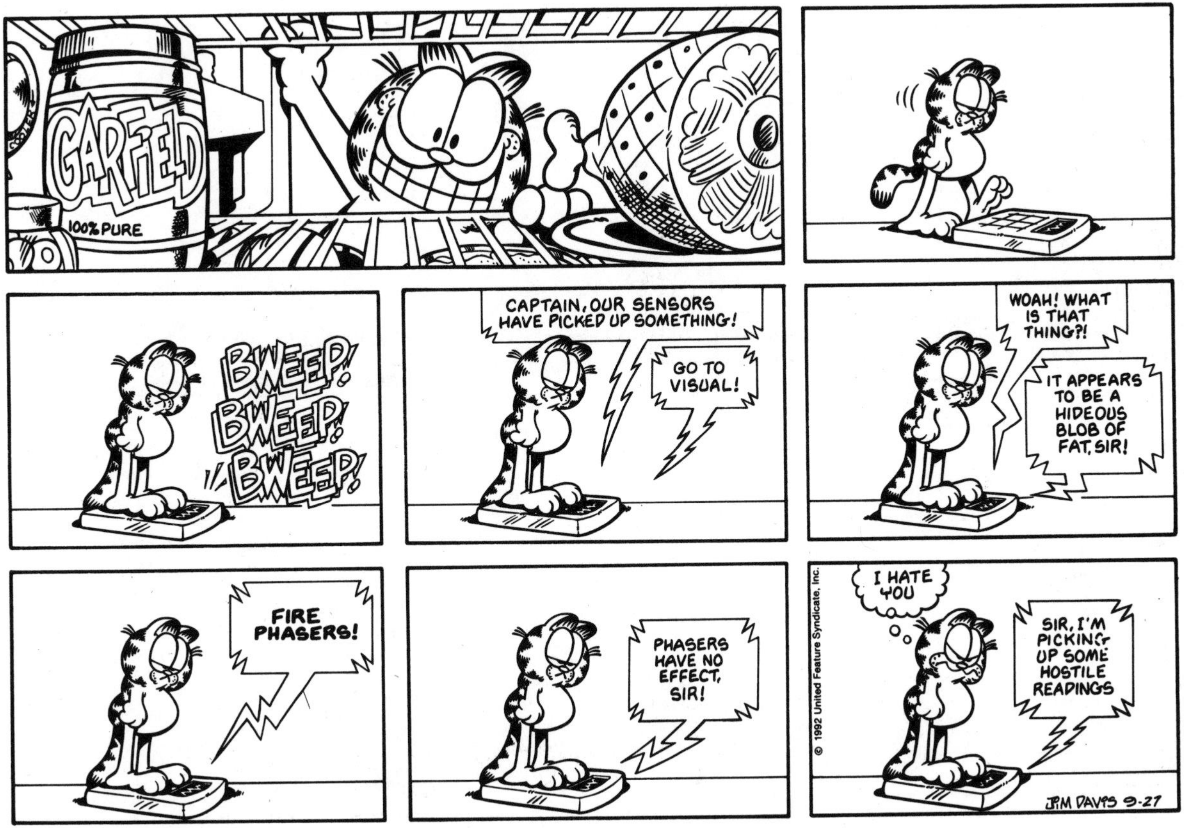
GARFIELD
100% PURE
BWEEP! BWEEP! BWEEP!
CAPTAIN, OUR SENSORS HAVE PICKED UP SOMETHING!
GO TO VISUAL!
WOAH! WHAT IS THAT THING?!
IT APPEARS TO BE A HIDEOUS BLOB OF FAT, SIR!
FIRE PHASERS!
PHASERS HAVE NO EFFECT, SIR!
I HATE YOU
SIR, I'M PICKING UP SOME HOSTILE READINGS
© 1992 United Feature Syndicate, Inc.
JIM DAVIS 9-27

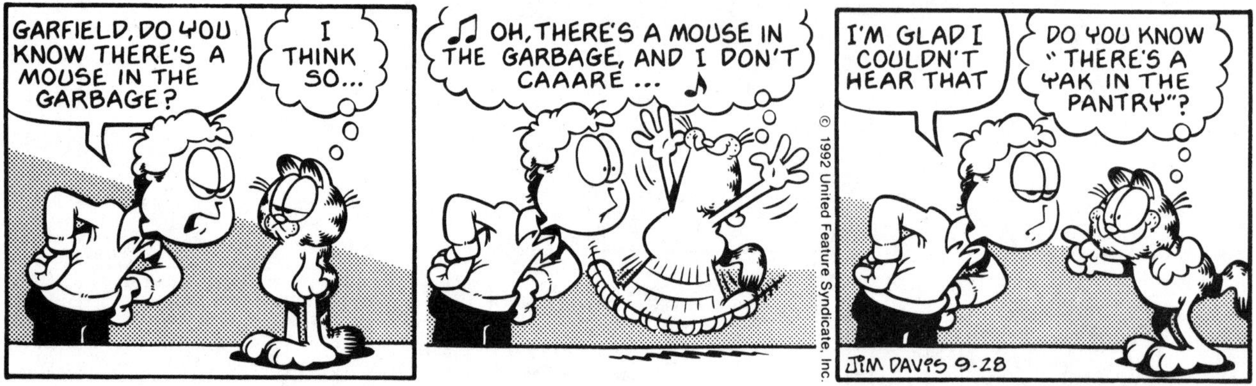
GARFIELD, DO YOU KNOW THERE'S A MOUSE IN THE GARBAGE?
I THINK SO...
♫ OH, THERE'S A MOUSE IN THE GARBAGE, AND I DON'T CAAARE ... ♪
I'M GLAD I COULDN'T HEAR THAT
DO YOU KNOW "THERE'S A YAK IN THE PANTRY"?
JIM DAVIS 9-28
© 1992 United Feature Syndicate, Inc.

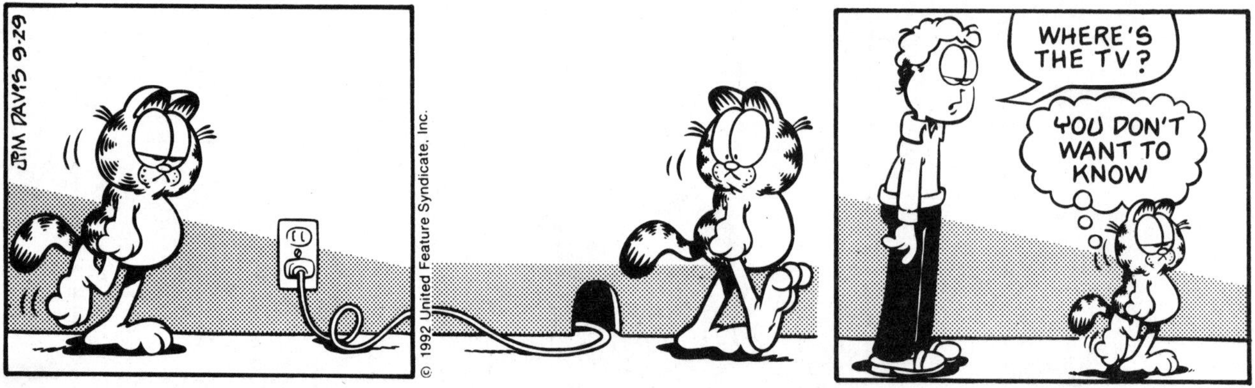
JIM DAVIS 9-29
© 1992 United Feature Syndicate, Inc.
WHERE'S THE TV?
YOU DON'T WANT TO KNOW

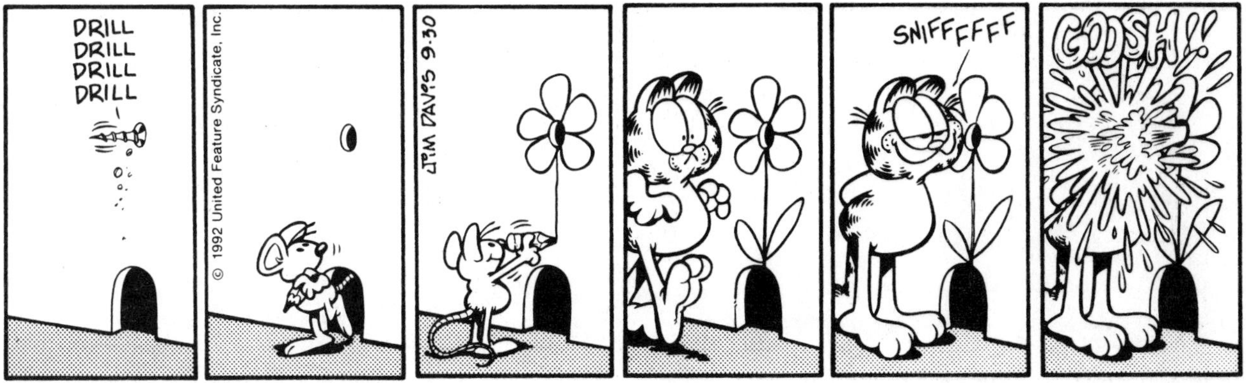
DRILL
DRILL
DRILL
DRILL
© 1992 United Feature Syndicate, Inc.
JIM DAVIS 9-30
SNIFFFFFF
GOOSH!!

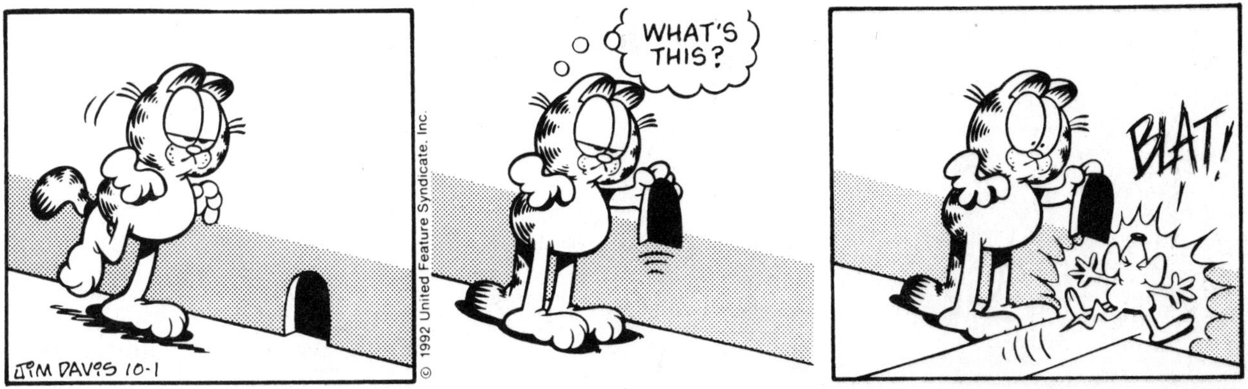
JIM DAVIS 10-1
© 1992 United Feature Syndicate, Inc.
WHAT'S THIS?
BLAT!

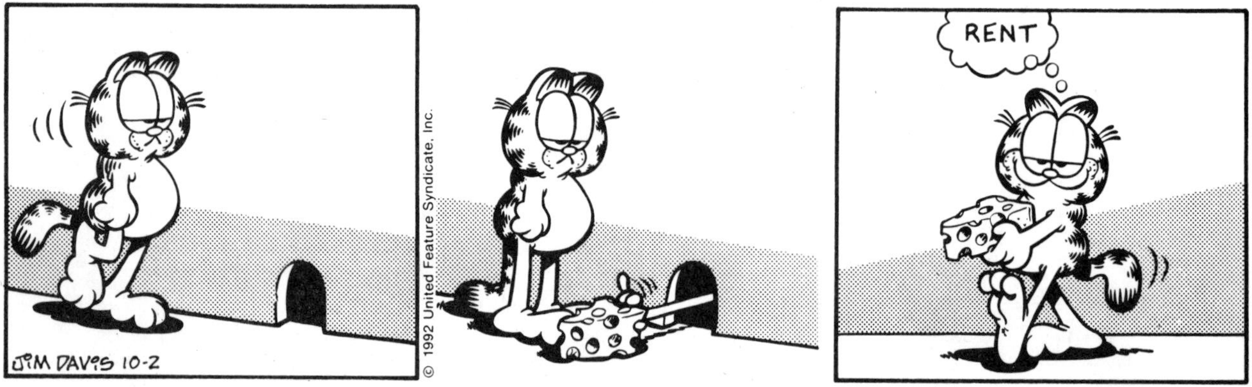
JIM DAVIS 10-2
RENT


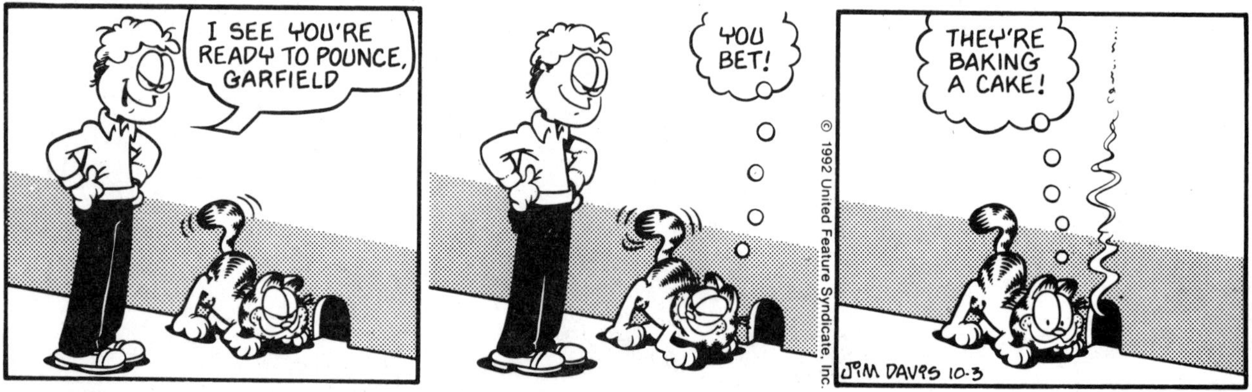
I SEE YOU'RE READY TO POUNCE, GARFIELD
YOU BET!
THEY'RE BAKING A CAKE!
JIM DAVIS 10-3

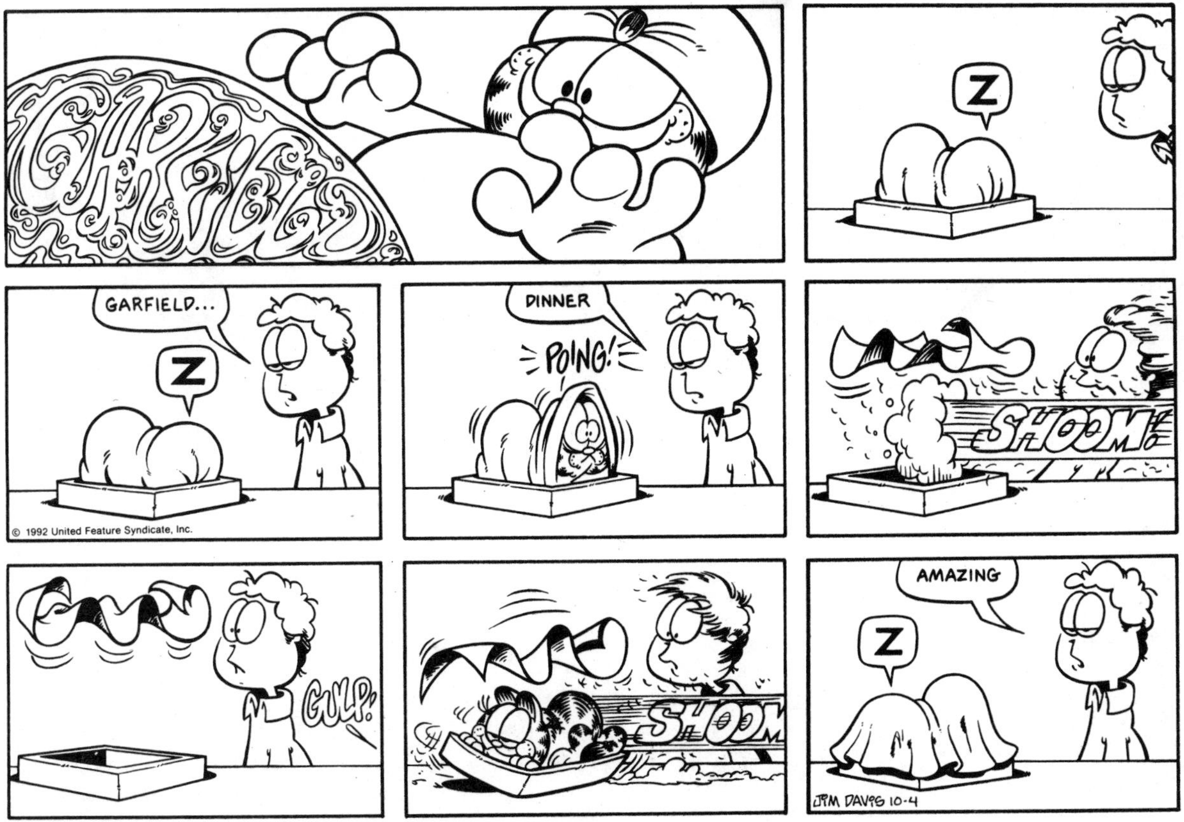
GARFIELD
Z
GARFIELD...
Z
DINNER
POING!
SHOOM!
GULP!
SHOOM
AMAZING
Z
© 1992 United Feature Syndicate, Inc.
JIM DAVIS 10-4

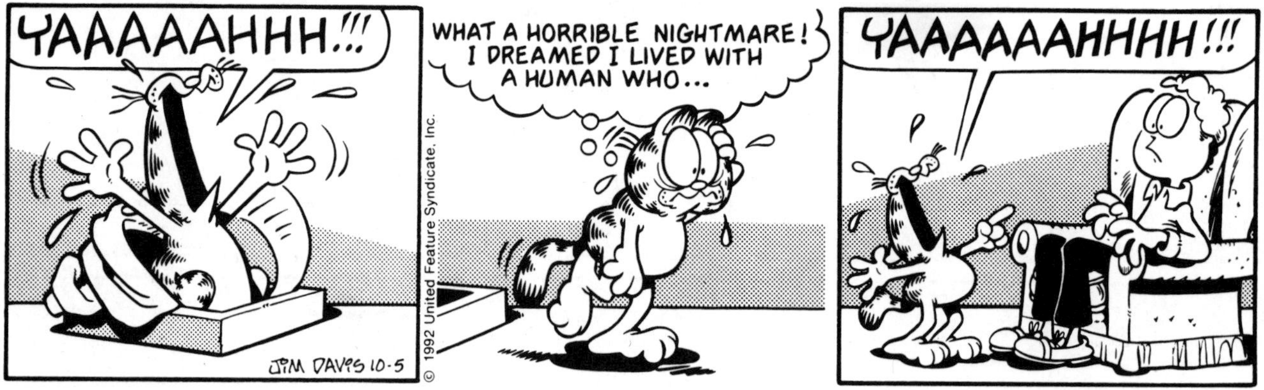
YAAAAAHHH!!!
JIM DAVIS 10-5
© 1992 United Feature Syndicate, Inc.
WHAT A HORRIBLE NIGHTMARE! I DREAMED I LIVED WITH A HUMAN WHO...
YAAAAAAHHHH!!!

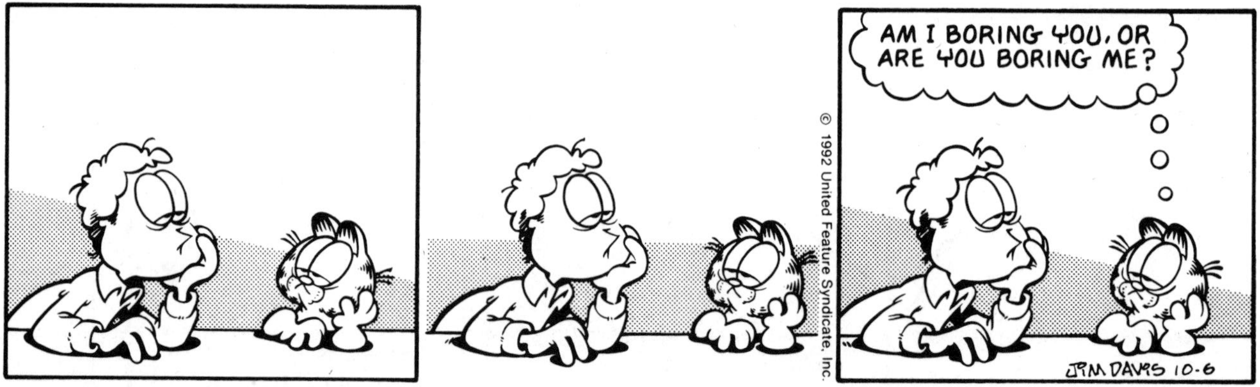
© 1992 United Feature Syndicate, Inc.
AM I BORING YOU, OR ARE YOU BORING ME?
JIM DAVIS 10-6

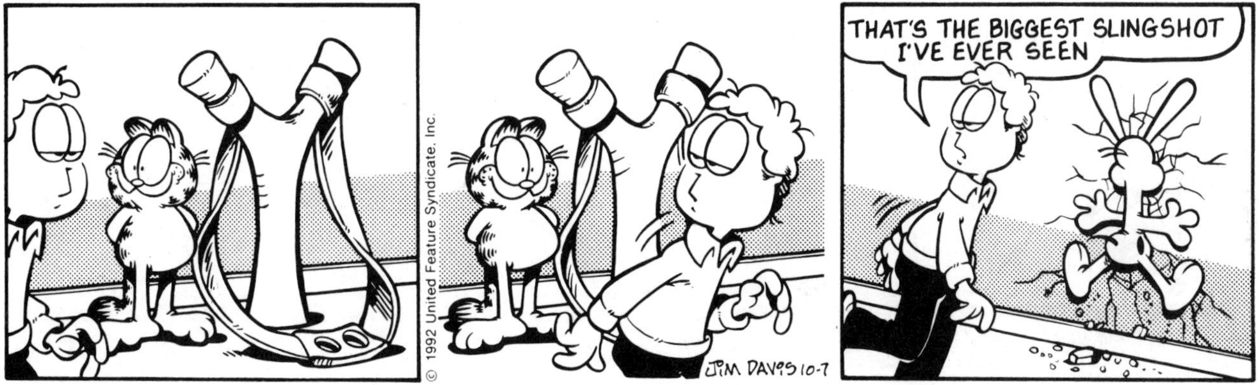
© 1992 United Feature Syndicate, Inc.
JIM DAVIS 10-7
THAT'S THE BIGGEST SLINGSHOT I'VE EVER SEEN

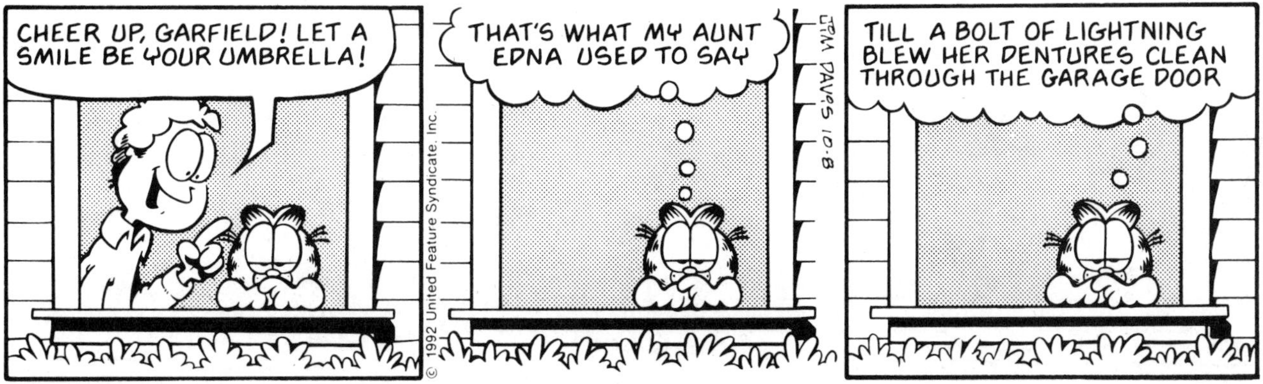
CHEER UP, GARFIELD! LET A SMILE BE YOUR UMBRELLA!
© 1992 United Feature Syndicate, Inc.
THAT'S WHAT MY AUNT EDNA USED TO SAY
JIM DAVIS 10-8
TILL A BOLT OF LIGHTNING BLEW HER DENTURES CLEAN THROUGH THE GARAGE DOOR

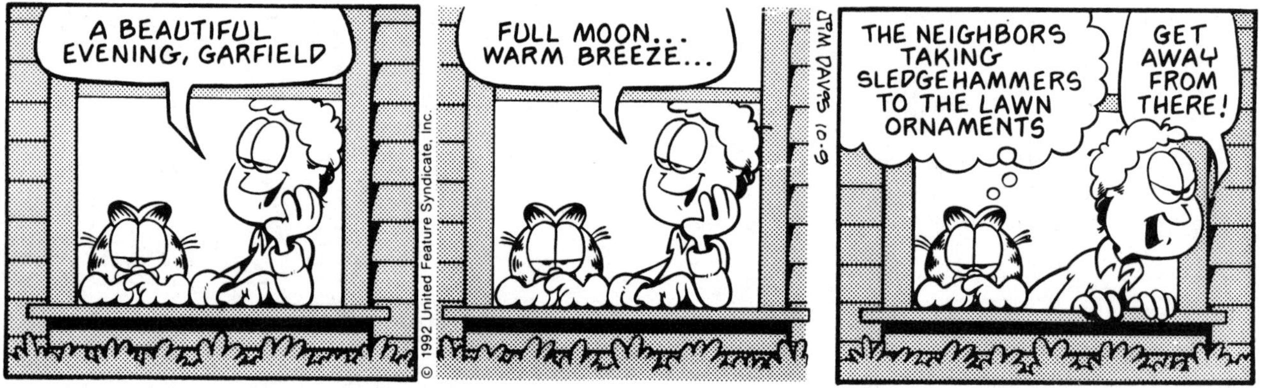
A BEAUTIFUL EVENING, GARFIELD
© 1992 United Feature Syndicate, Inc.
FULL MOON... WARM BREEZE...
JIM DAVIS 10-9
THE NEIGHBORS TAKING SLEDGEHAMMERS TO THE LAWN ORNAMENTS
GET AWAY FROM THERE!

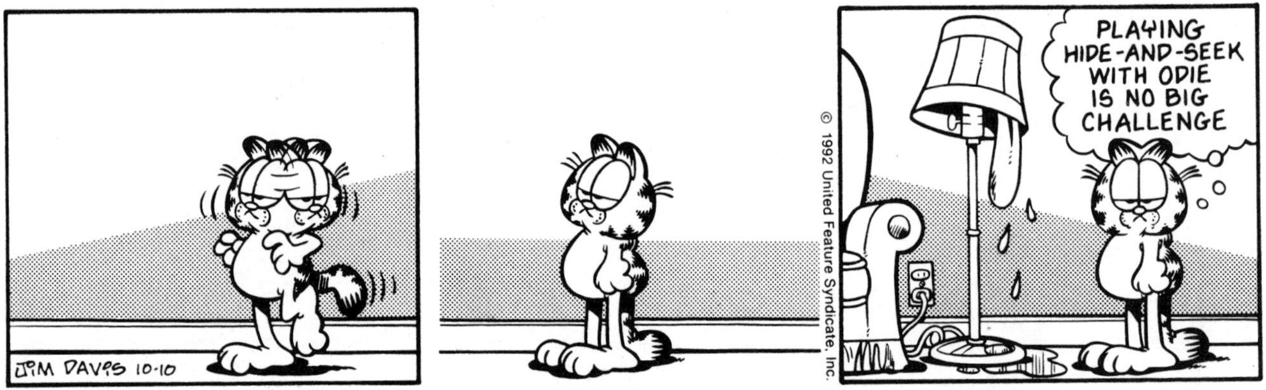
JIM DAVIS 10-10
© 1992 United Feature Syndicate, Inc.
PLAYING HIDE-AND-SEEK WITH ODIE IS NO BIG CHALLENGE

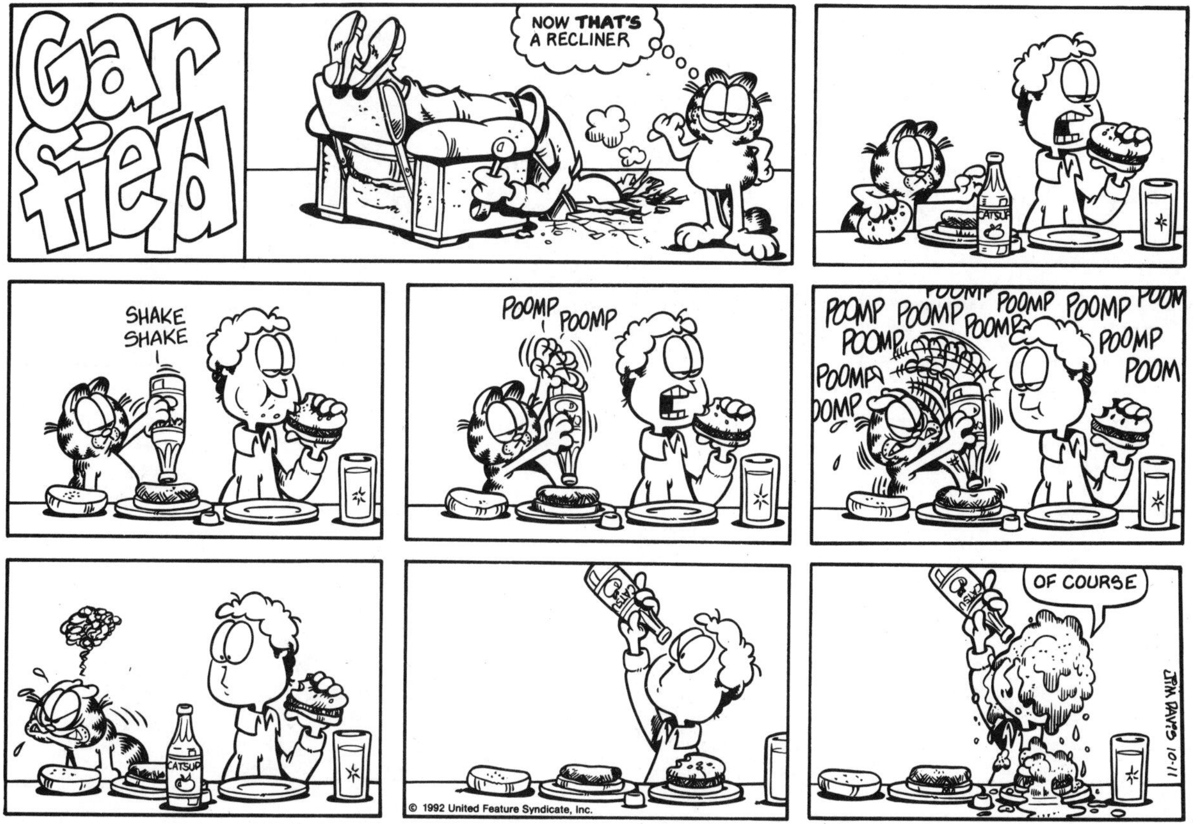
Garfield
NOW THAT'S A RECLINER
CATSUP
SHAKE SHAKE
POOMP POOMP
POOMP POOMP POOMP POOMP POOMP POOMP POOMP POOMP POOMP POOM POOM
CATSUP
© 1992 United Feature Syndicate, Inc.
OF COURSE
JIM DAVIS 10-11

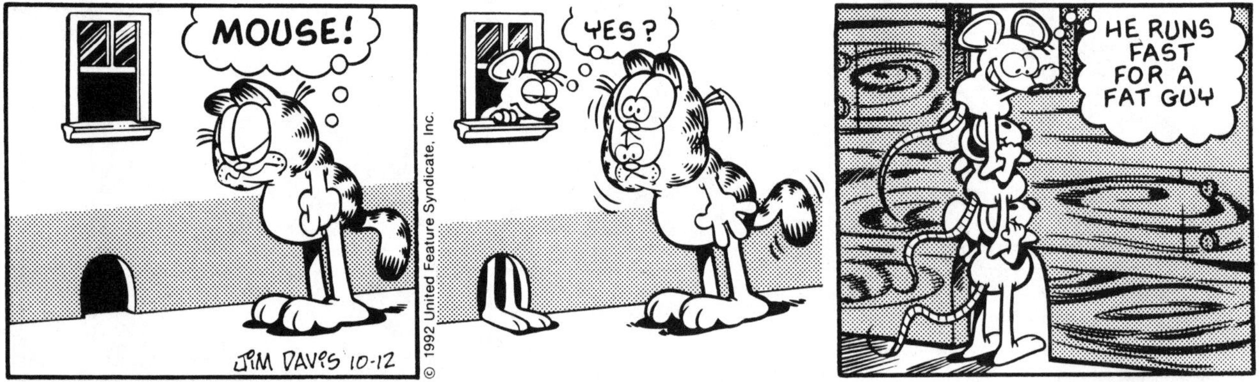
MOUSE!
JIM DAVIS 10-12
YES?
HE RUNS FAST FOR A FAT GUY


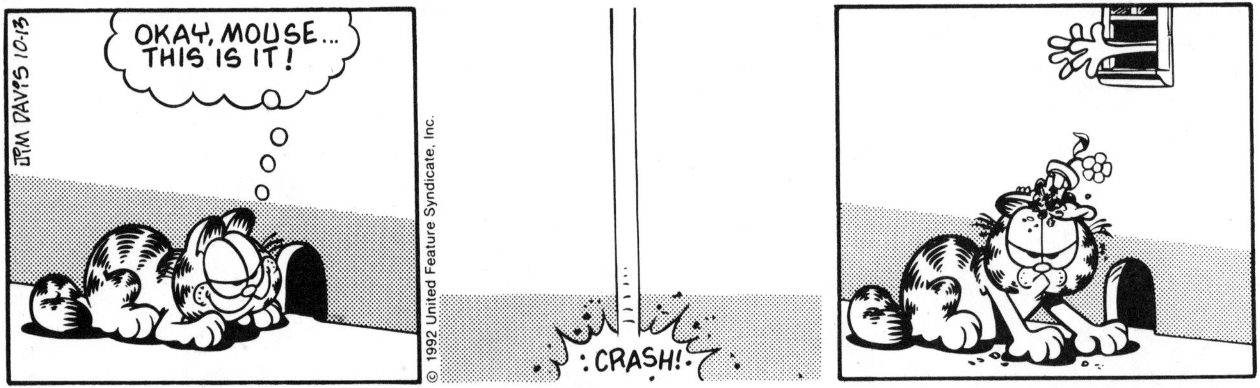
JIM DAVIS 10-13
OKAY, MOUSE... THIS IS IT!
CRASH!

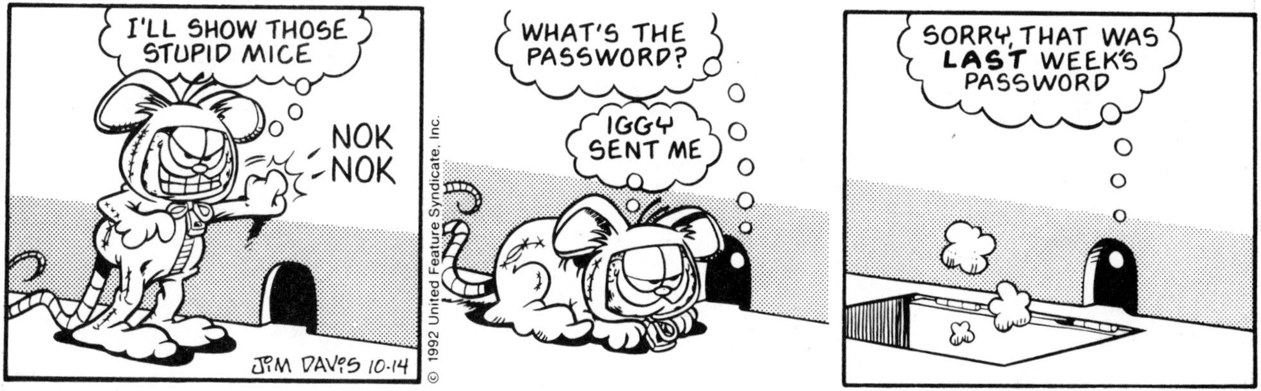
I'LL SHOW THOSE STUPID MICE
NOK NOK
JIM DAVIS 10-14
© 1992 United Feature Syndicate, Inc.
WHAT'S THE PASSWORD?
IGGY SENT ME
SORRY, THAT WAS **LAST** WEEK'S PASSWORD

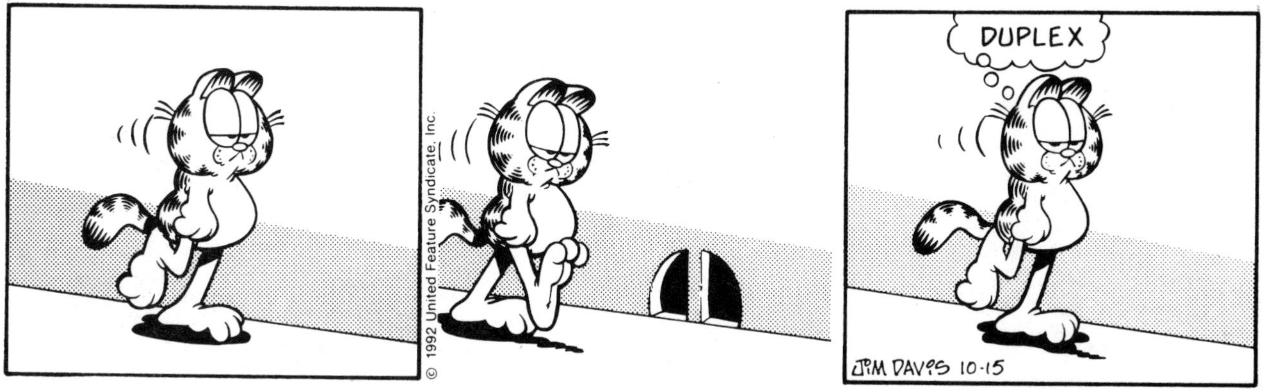
© 1992 United Feature Syndicate, Inc.
DUPLEX
JIM DAVIS 10-15

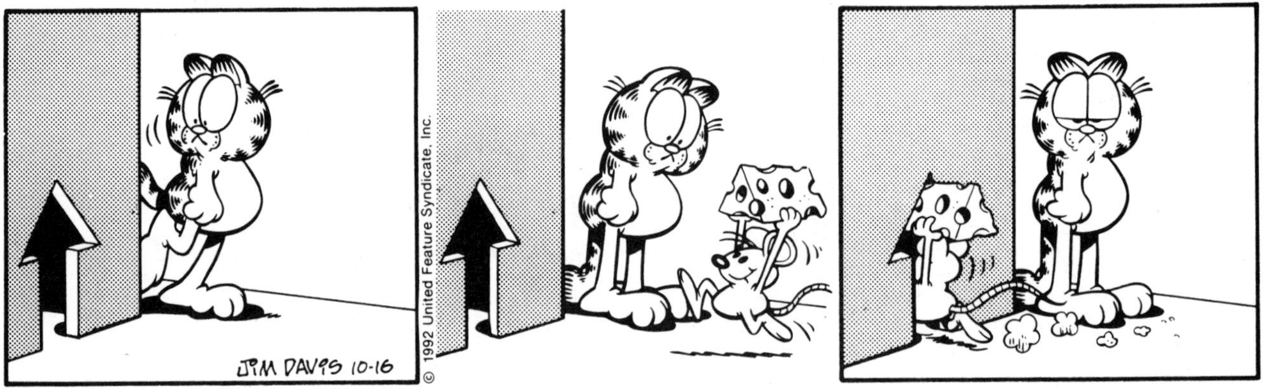
JIM DAVIS 10-16
© 1992 United Feature Syndicate, Inc.

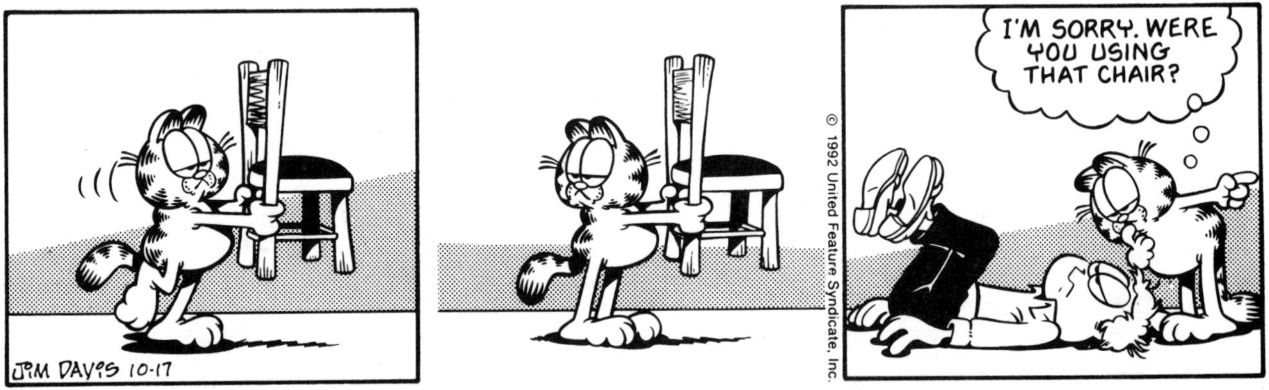
JIM DAVIS 10-17
© 1992 United Feature Syndicate, Inc.
I'M SORRY. WERE YOU USING THAT CHAIR?

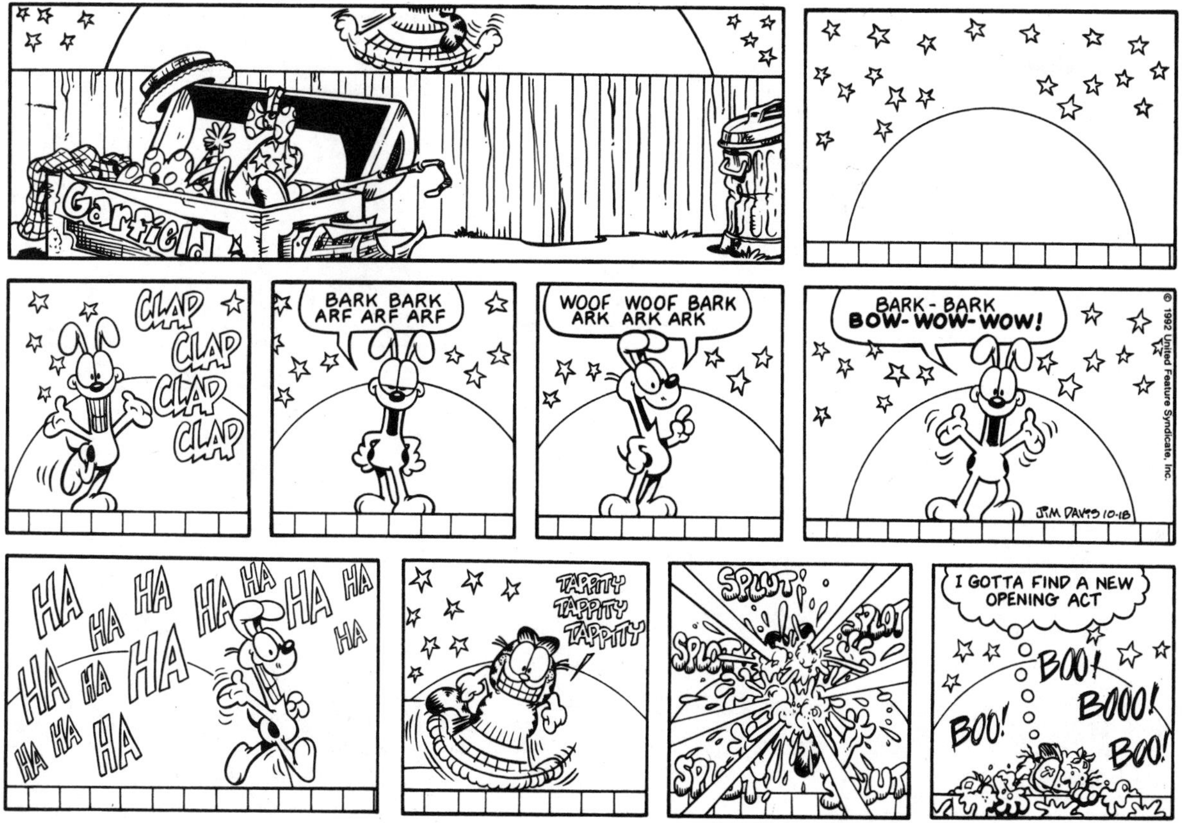
Garfield
CLAP CLAP CLAP CLAP
BARK BARK ARF ARF ARF
WOOF WOOF BARK ARK ARK ARK
BARK - BARK BOW-WOW-WOW!
© 1992 United Feature Syndicate, Inc.
JIM DAVIS 10-18
HA HA HA HA HA HA HA HA HA HA HA HA HA HA HA HA
TAPPITY TAPPITY TAPPITY
SPLUT SPLOT SPLOT SPLUT SPLUT
I GOTTA FIND A NEW OPENING ACT
BOO! BOO! BOOO! BOO!

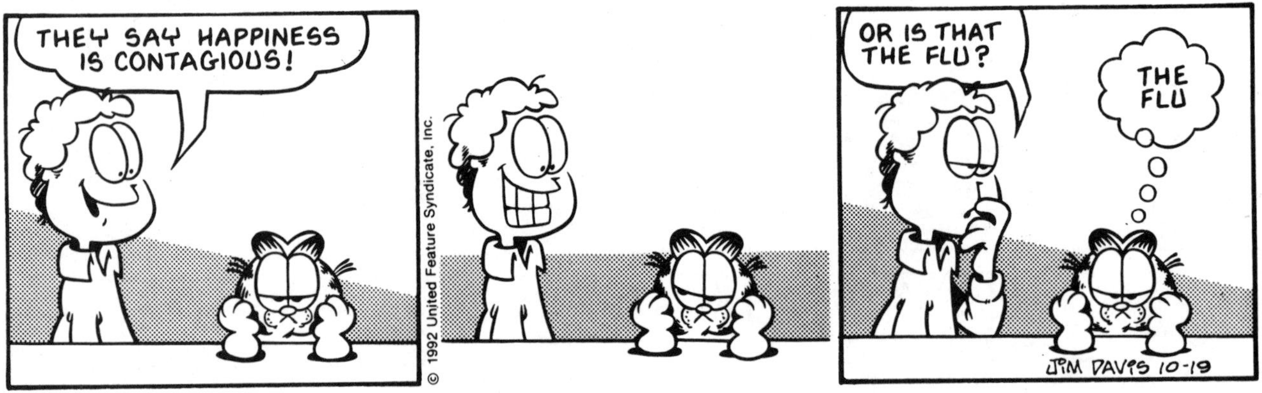
THEY SAY HAPPINESS IS CONTAGIOUS!
OR IS THAT THE FLU?
THE FLU
JIM DAVIS 10-19


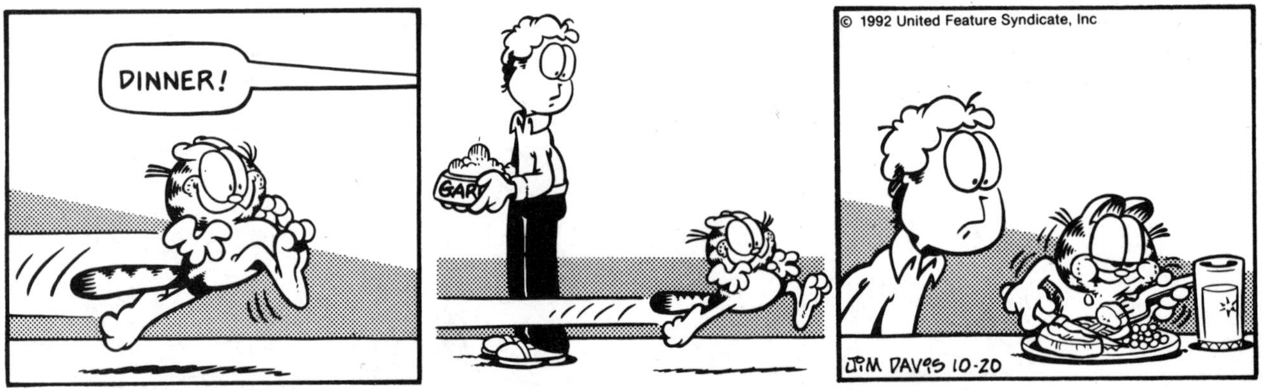
DINNER!
GARF
JIM DAVIS 10-20

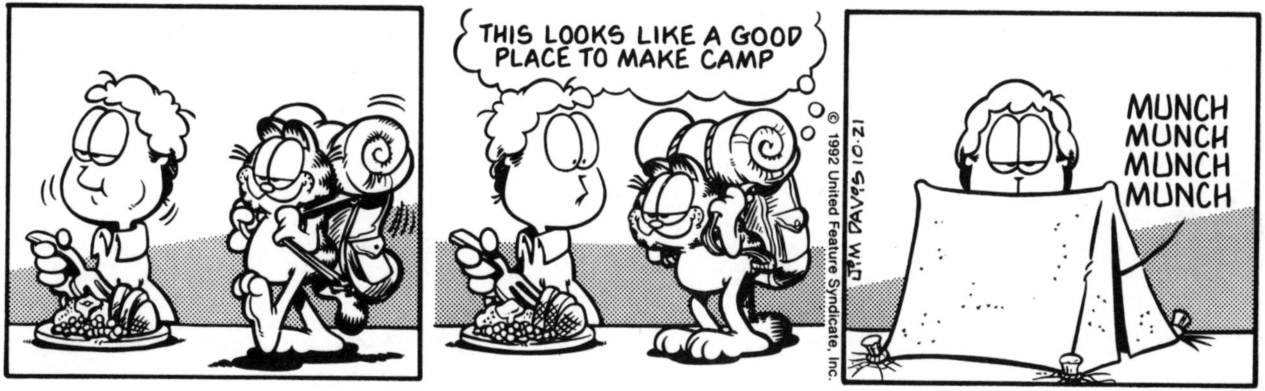
THIS LOOKS LIKE A GOOD PLACE TO MAKE CAMP
© 1992 United Feature Syndicate, Inc.
JIM DAVIS 10-21
MUNCH
MUNCH
MUNCH
MUNCH

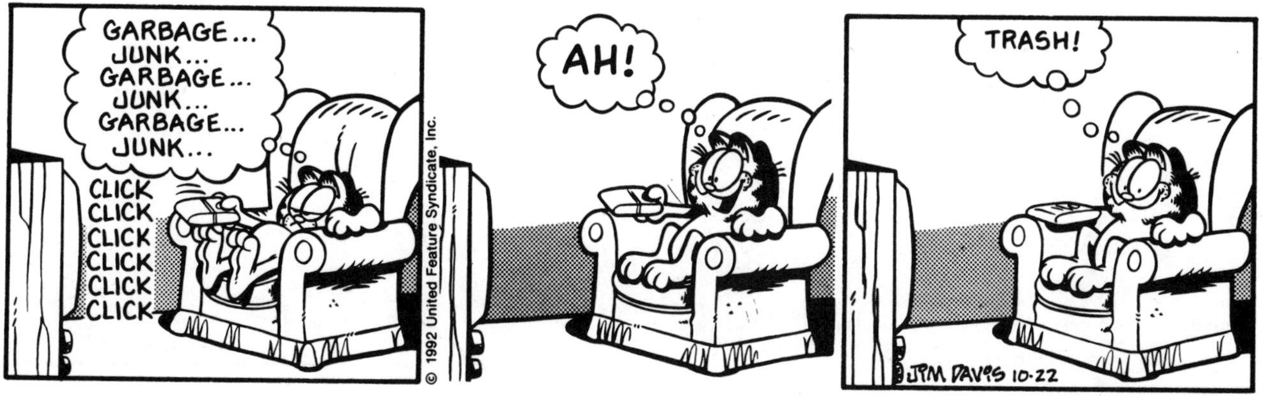
GARBAGE... JUNK... GARBAGE... JUNK... GARBAGE... JUNK...
CLICK CLICK CLICK CLICK CLICK CLICK CLICK
© 1992 United Feature Syndicate, Inc.
AH!
TRASH!
JIM DAVIS 10-22

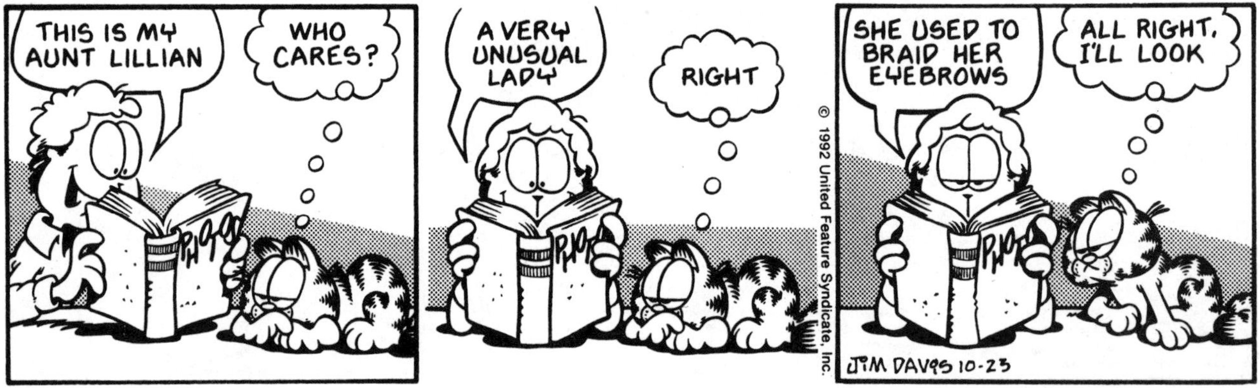
THIS IS MY AUNT LILLIAN
WHO CARES?
A VERY UNUSUAL LADY
RIGHT
SHE USED TO BRAID HER EYEBROWS
ALL RIGHT, I'LL LOOK
© 1992 United Feature Syndicate, Inc.
JIM DAVIS 10-23

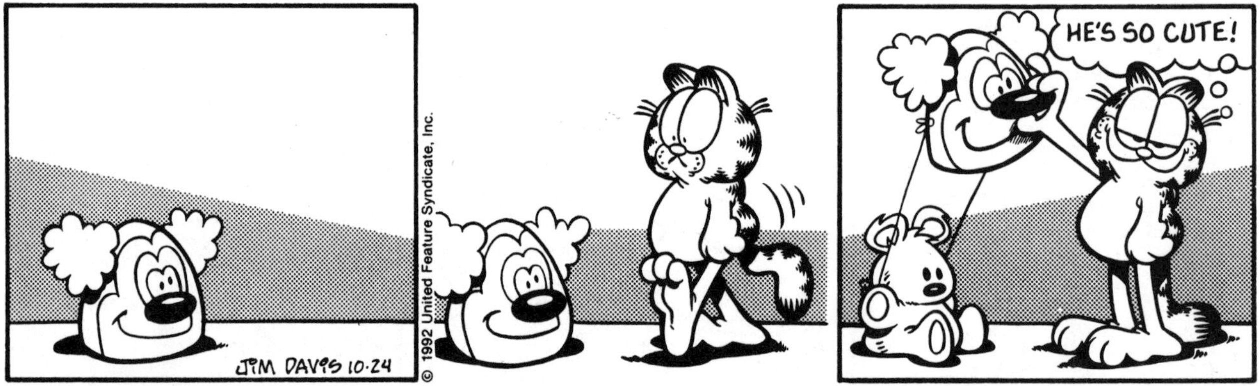
JIM DAVIS 10-24
© 1992 United Feature Syndicate, Inc.
HE'S SO CUTE!

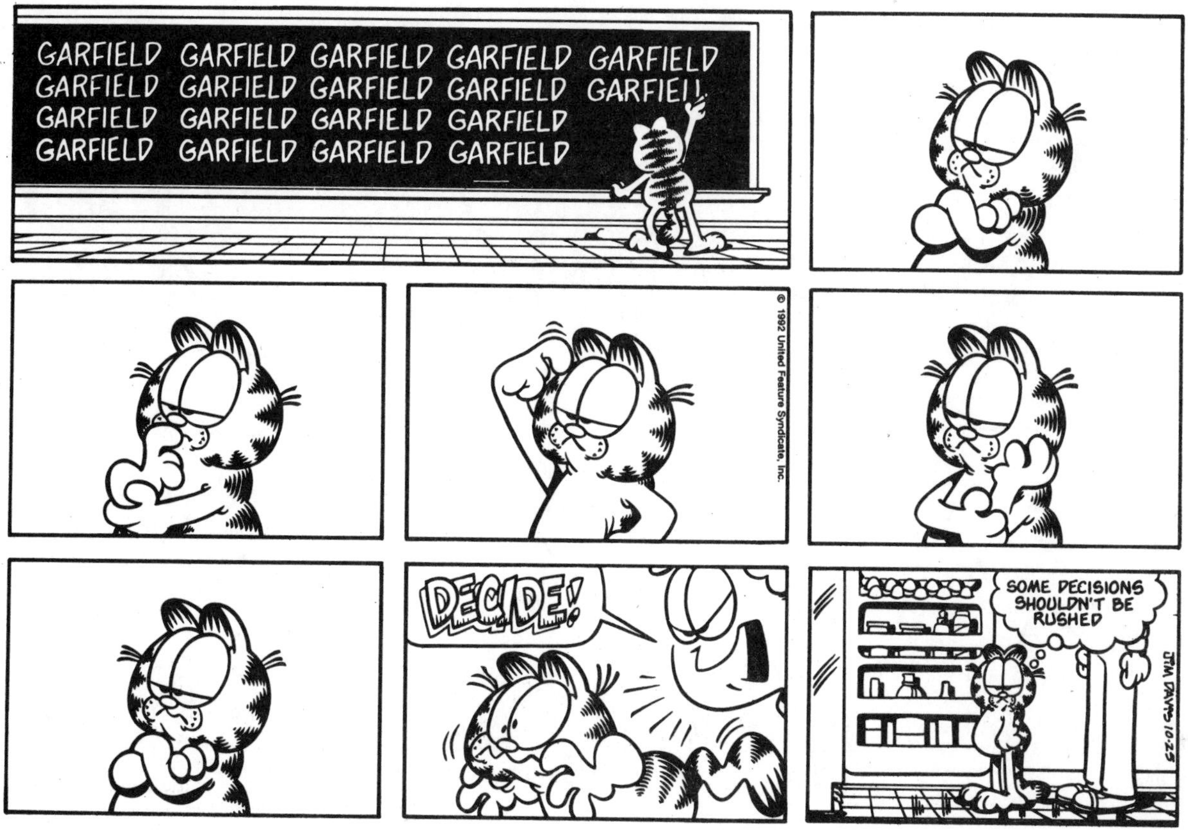
GARFIELD GARFIELD GARFIELD GARFIELD GARFIELD
GARFIELD GARFIELD GARFIELD GARFIELD GARFIEL
GARFIELD GARFIELD GARFIELD GARFIELD
GARFIELD GARFIELD GARFIELD GARFIELD
© 1992 United Feature Syndicate, Inc.
DECIDE!
SOME DECISIONS SHOULDN'T BE RUSHED
JIM DAVIS 10-25

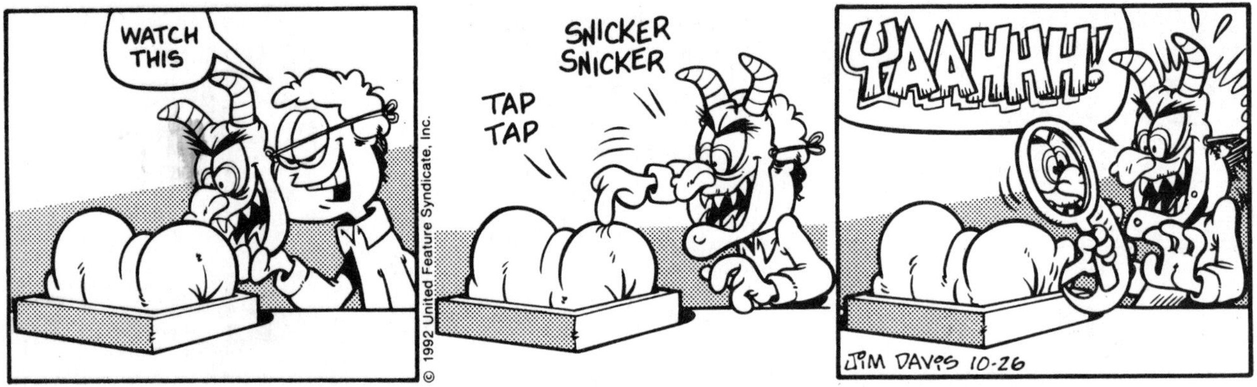
WATCH THIS
© 1992 United Feature Syndicate, Inc.
TAP TAP
SNICKER SNICKER
YAAHHH!
JIM DAVIS 10-26

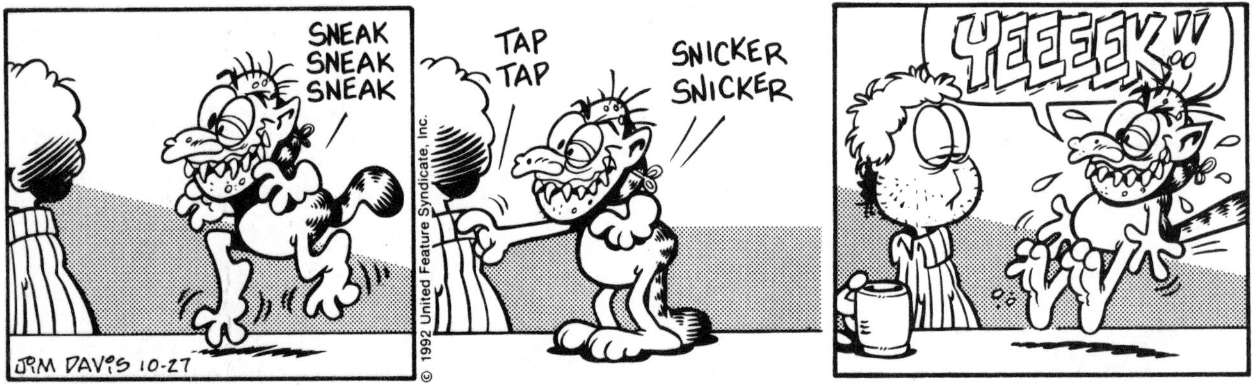
SNEAK SNEAK SNEAK
JIM DAVIS 10-27
© 1992 United Feature Syndicate, Inc.
TAP TAP
SNICKER SNICKER
YEEEEK!!

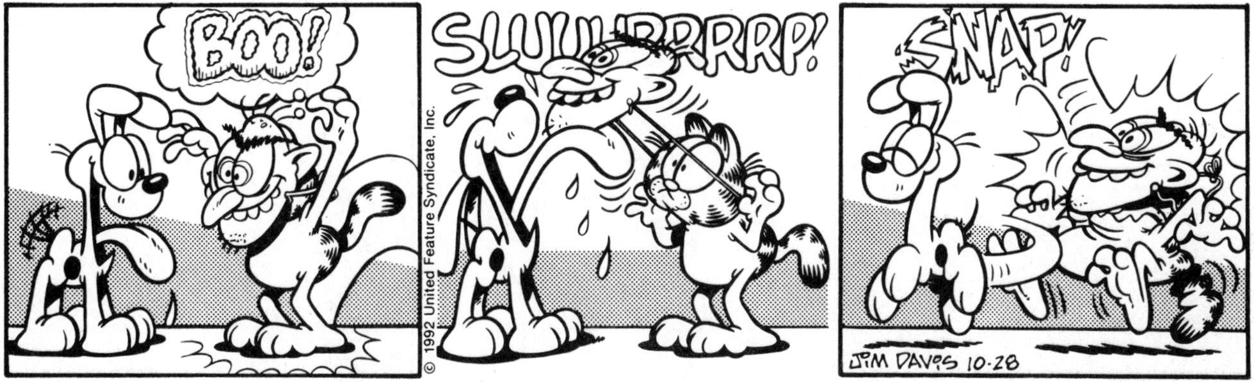
BOO!
SLUUURRRRP!
SNAP!
© 1992 United Feature Syndicate, Inc.
JIM DAVIS 10-28

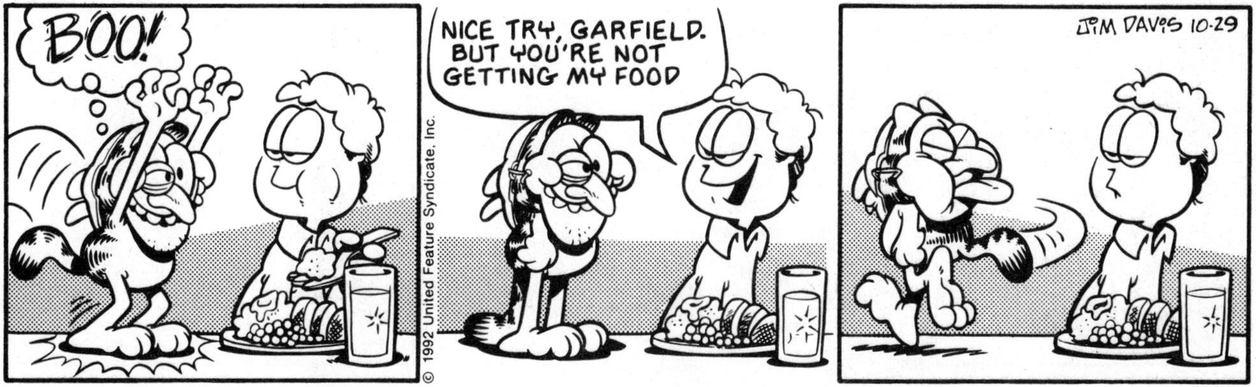
BOO!
NICE TRY, GARFIELD. BUT YOU'RE NOT GETTING MY FOOD
© 1992 United Feature Syndicate, Inc.
JIM DAVIS 10-29

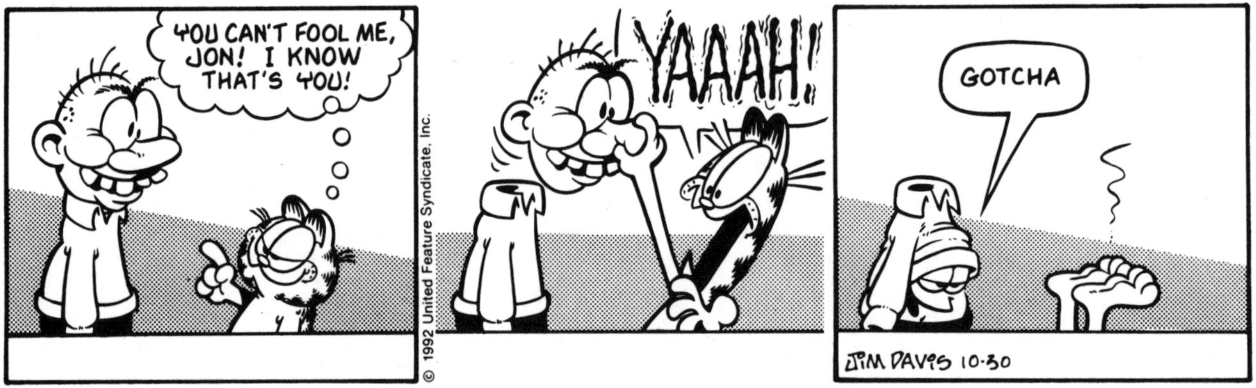
YOU CAN'T FOOL ME, JON! I KNOW THAT'S YOU!
YAAAH!
GOTCHA
© 1992 United Feature Syndicate, Inc.
JIM DAVIS 10-30

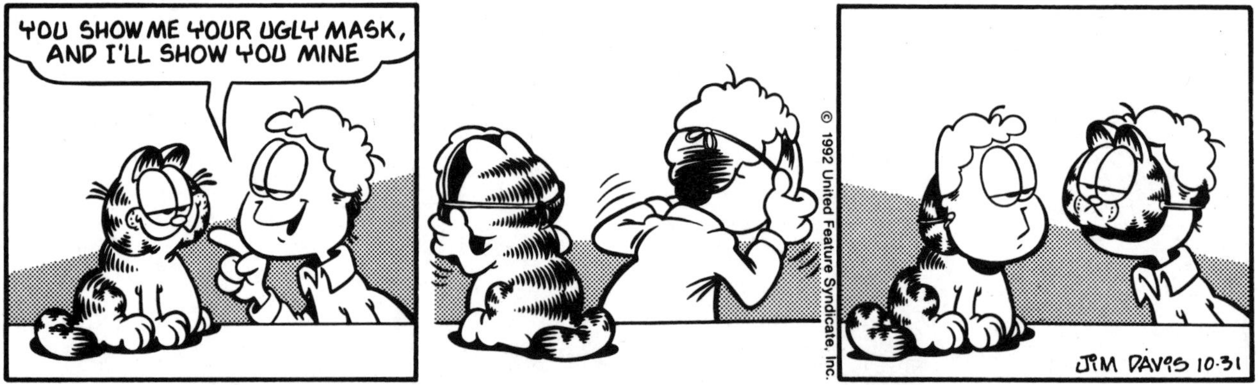
YOU SHOW ME YOUR UGLY MASK, AND I'LL SHOW YOU MINE
© 1992 United Feature Syndicate, Inc.
JIM DAVIS 10-31

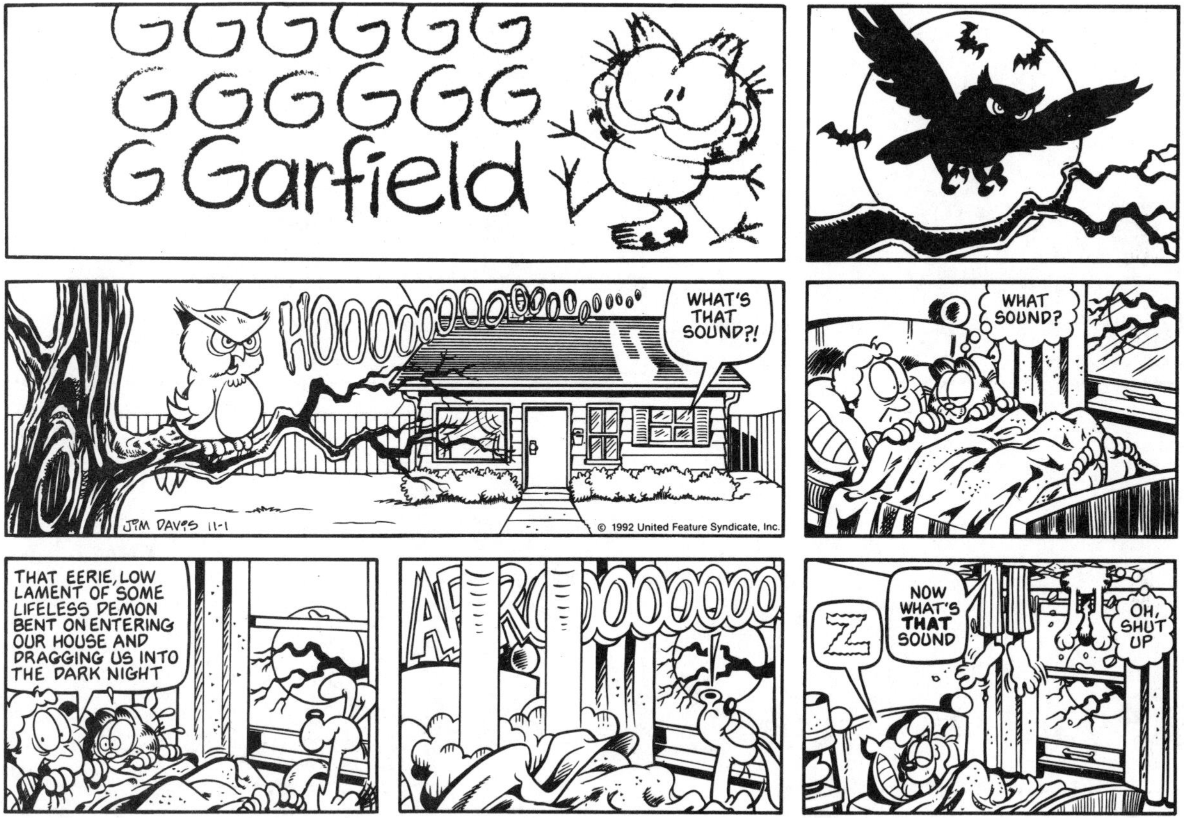

GGGGGG
GGGGGG
G Garfield
HOOOOOOOOOOOOOOOOOOO
WHAT'S THAT SOUND?!
JIM DAVIS 11-1
© 1992 United Feature Syndicate, Inc.
WHAT SOUND?
THAT EERIE, LOW LAMENT OF SOME LIFELESS DEMON BENT ON ENTERING OUR HOUSE AND DRAGGING US INTO THE DARK NIGHT
ARROOOOOOOOO
Z
NOW WHAT'S **THAT** SOUND
OH, SHUT UP

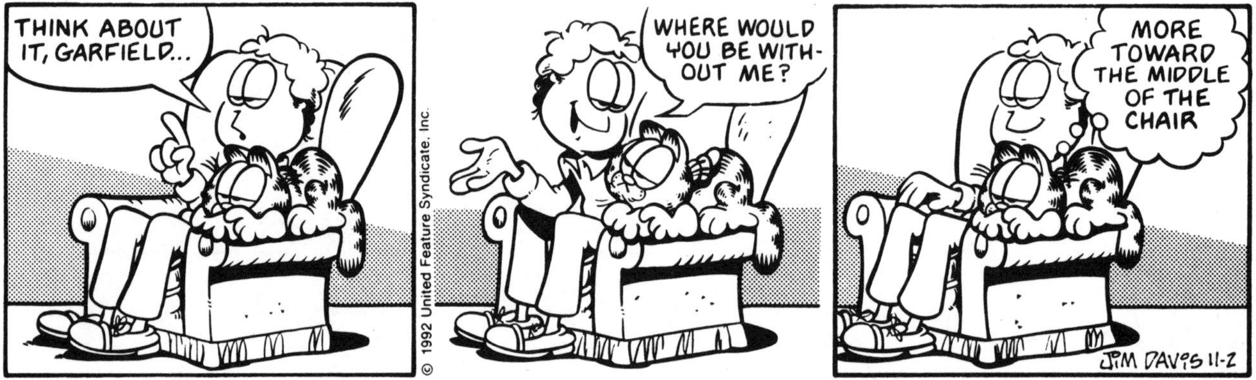
THINK ABOUT IT, GARFIELD...
WHERE WOULD YOU BE WITH-OUT ME?
MORE TOWARD THE MIDDLE OF THE CHAIR
© 1992 United Feature Syndicate, Inc.
JIM DAVIS 11-2

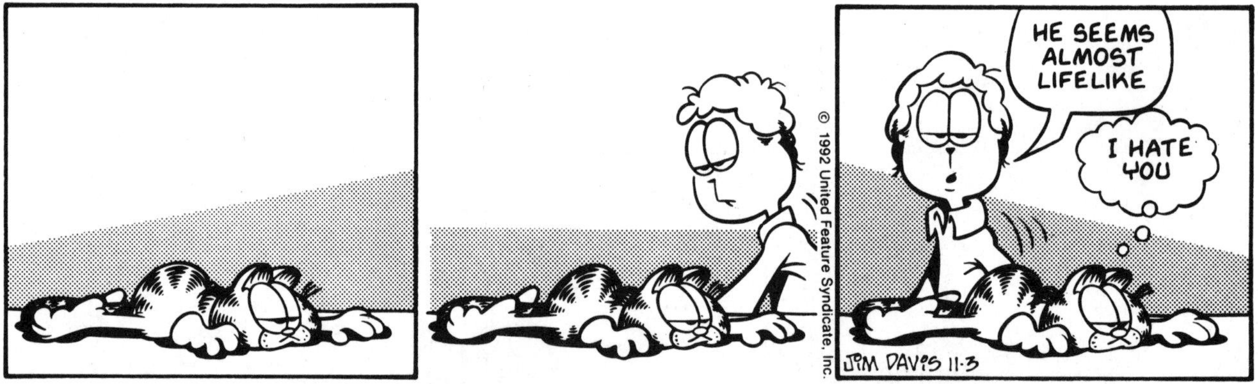
HE SEEMS ALMOST LIFELIKE
I HATE YOU
© 1992 United Feature Syndicate, Inc.
JIM DAVIS 11-3

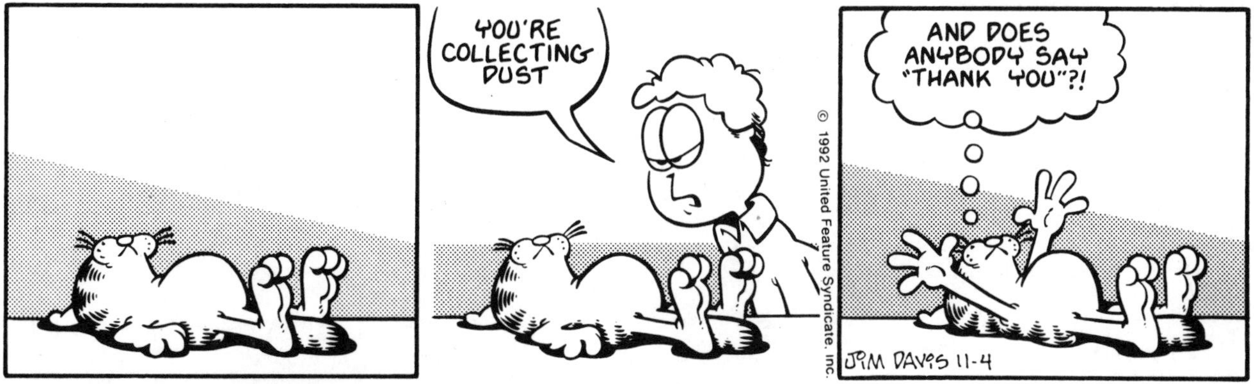
YOU'RE COLLECTING DUST
© 1992 United Feature Syndicate, Inc.
AND DOES ANYBODY SAY "THANK YOU"?!
JIM DAVIS 11-4

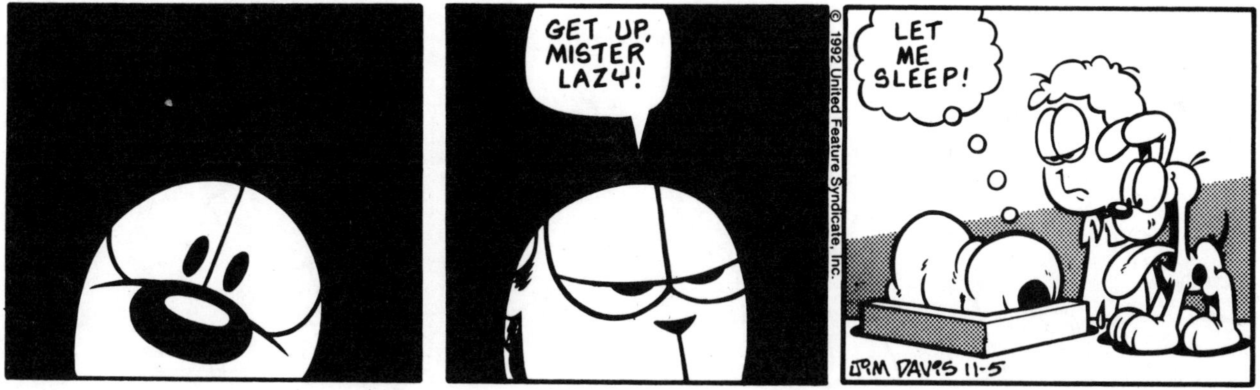
GET UP, MISTER LAZY!
© 1992 United Feature Syndicate, Inc.
LET ME SLEEP!
JIM DAVIS 11-5

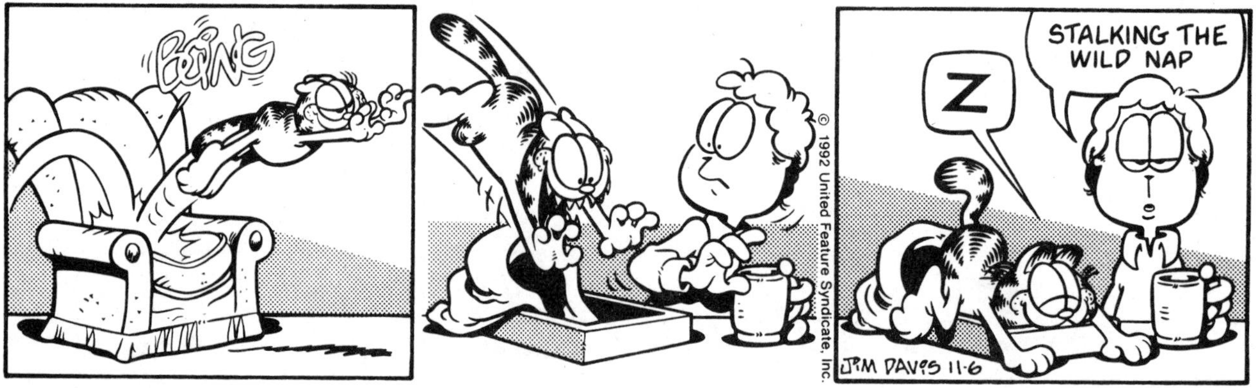
BOING
Z
STALKING THE WILD NAP
© 1992 United Feature Syndicate, Inc.
JIM DAVIS 11-6

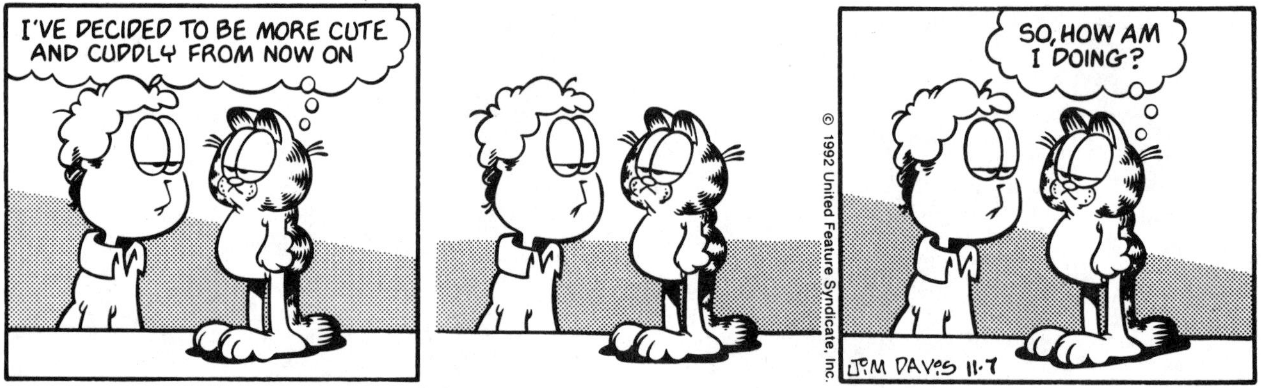
I'VE DECIDED TO BE MORE CUTE AND CUDDLY FROM NOW ON
SO, HOW AM I DOING?
© 1992 United Feature Syndicate, Inc.
JIM DAVIS 11-7

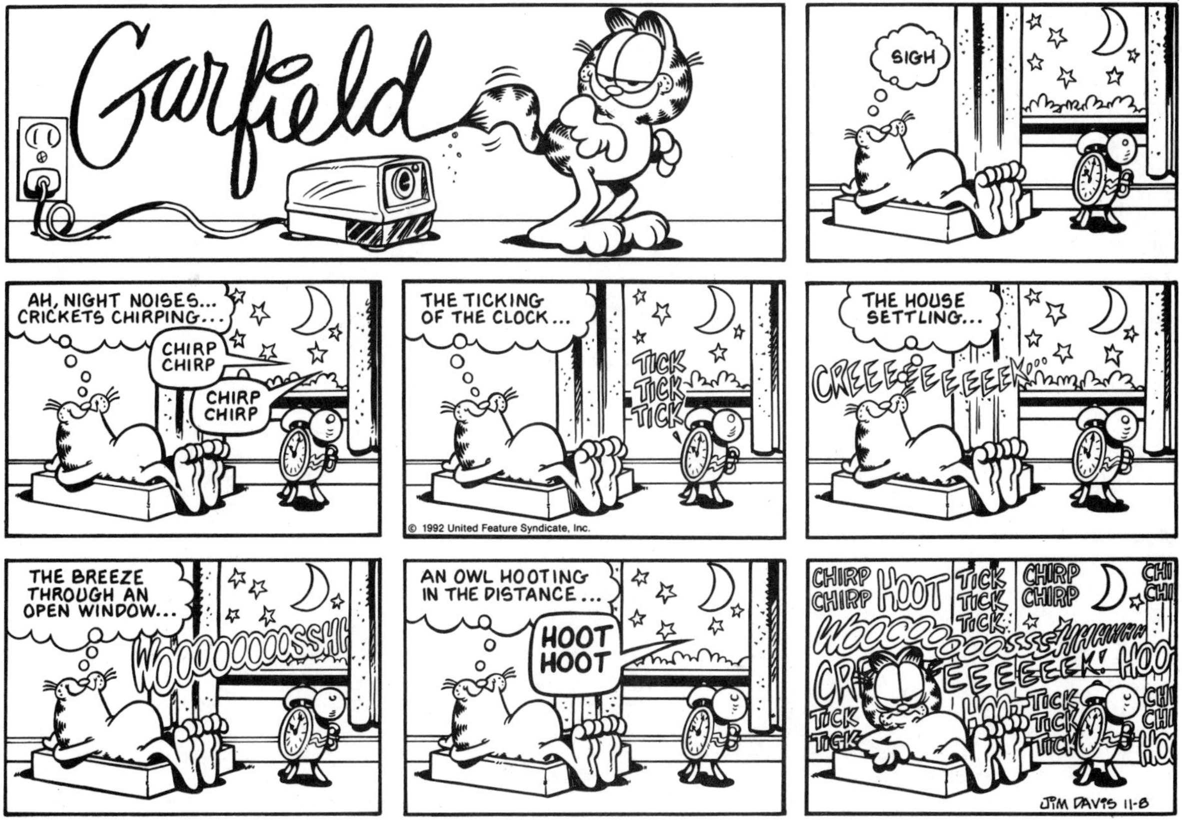
Garfield
SIGH
AH, NIGHT NOISES... CRICKETS CHIRPING...
CHIRP CHIRP
CHIRP CHIRP
THE TICKING OF THE CLOCK...
TICK TICK TICK
THE HOUSE SETTLING...
CREEEEEEEEEEEK...
THE BREEZE THROUGH AN OPEN WINDOW...
WOOOOOOOOOSSHH
AN OWL HOOTING IN THE DISTANCE...
HOOT HOOT
CHIRP CHIRP
HOOT
TICK TICK TICK
CHIRP CHIRP
EEEEEEEK!
JIM DAVIS 11-8

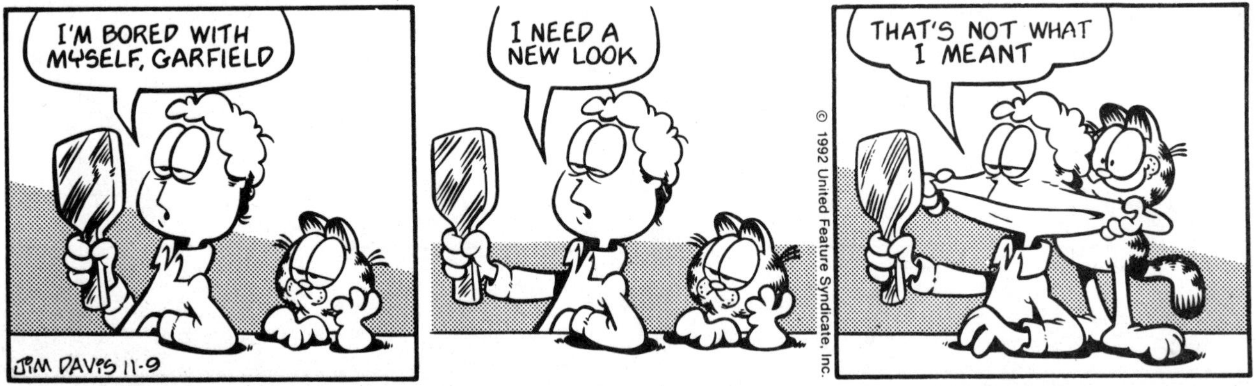
I'M BORED WITH MYSELF, GARFIELD
JIM DAVIS 11-9
I NEED A NEW LOOK
© 1992 United Feature Syndicate, Inc.
THAT'S NOT WHAT I MEANT

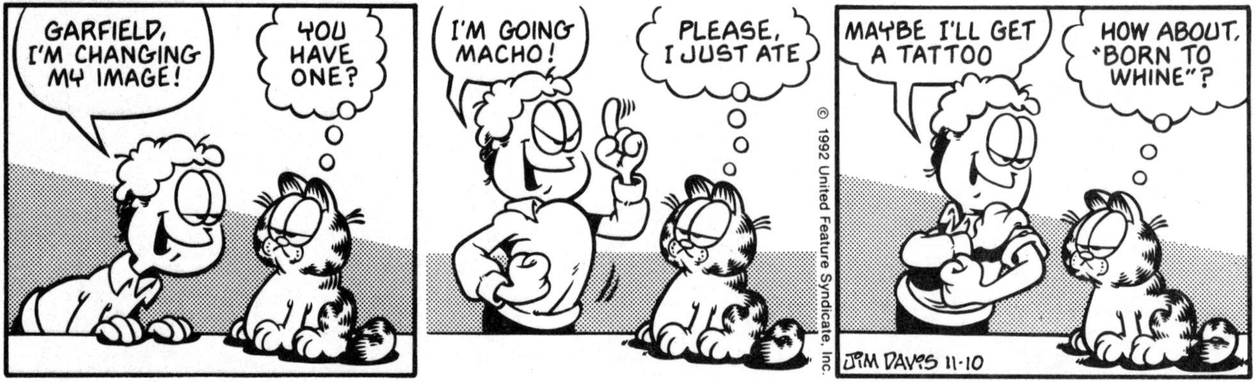
GARFIELD, I'M CHANGING MY IMAGE!
YOU HAVE ONE?
I'M GOING MACHO!
PLEASE, I JUST ATE
© 1992 United Feature Syndicate, Inc.
MAYBE I'LL GET A TATTOO
HOW ABOUT, "BORN TO WHINE"?
JIM DAVIS 11-10

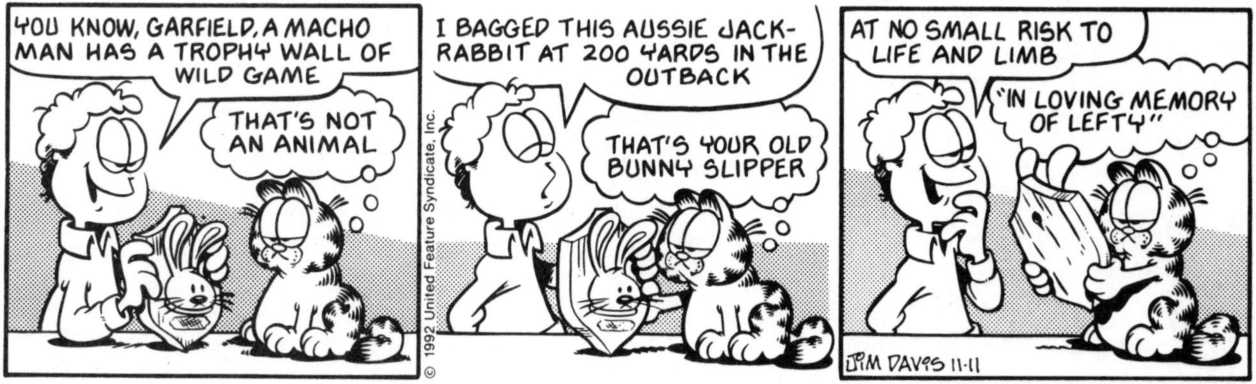
YOU KNOW, GARFIELD, A MACHO MAN HAS A TROPHY WALL OF WILD GAME
THAT'S NOT AN ANIMAL
© 1992 United Feature Syndicate, Inc.
I BAGGED THIS AUSSIE JACK-RABBIT AT 200 YARDS IN THE OUTBACK
THAT'S YOUR OLD BUNNY SLIPPER
AT NO SMALL RISK TO LIFE AND LIMB
"IN LOVING MEMORY OF LEFTY"
JIM DAVIS 11-11

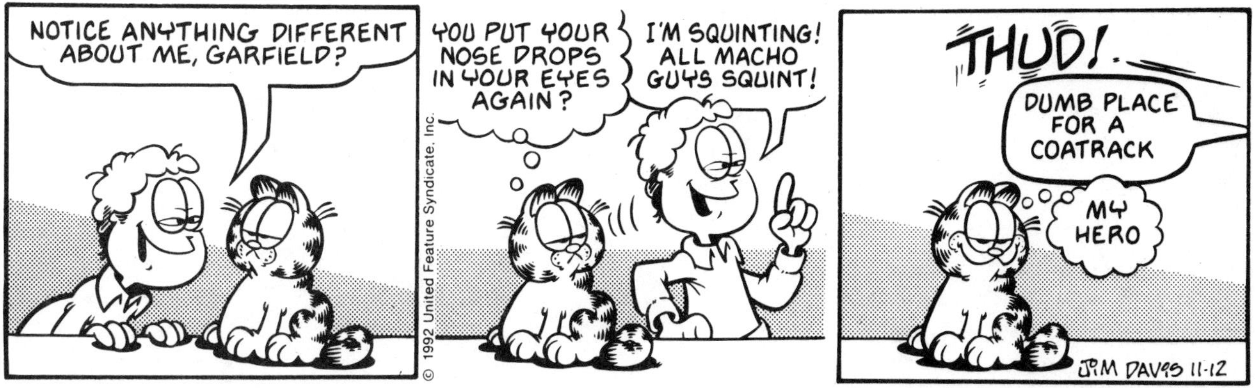
NOTICE ANYTHING DIFFERENT ABOUT ME, GARFIELD?
© 1992 United Feature Syndicate, Inc.
YOU PUT YOUR NOSE DROPS IN YOUR EYES AGAIN?
I'M SQUINTING! ALL MACHO GUYS SQUINT!
THUD!
DUMB PLACE FOR A COATRACK
MY HERO
JIM DAVIS 11-12

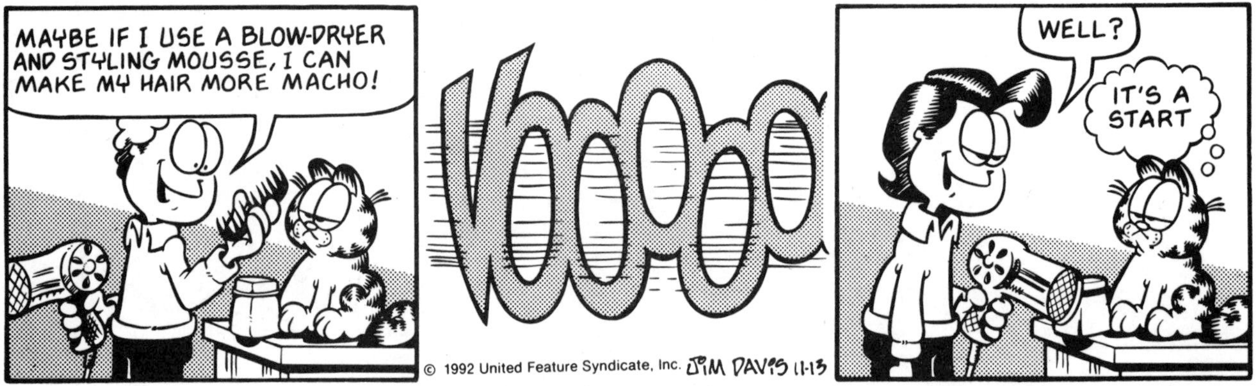
MAYBE IF I USE A BLOW-DRYER AND STYLING MOUSSE, I CAN MAKE MY HAIR MORE MACHO!
VOOOOOO
© 1992 United Feature Syndicate, Inc. JIM DAVIS 11-13
WELL?
IT'S A START

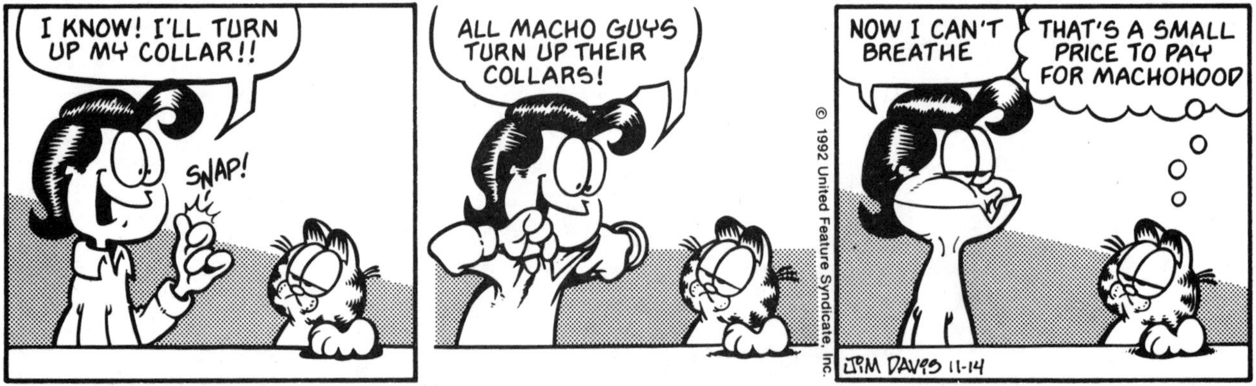
I KNOW! I'LL TURN UP MY COLLAR!!
SNAP!
ALL MACHO GUYS TURN UP THEIR COLLARS!
© 1992 United Feature Syndicate, Inc.
NOW I CAN'T BREATHE
THAT'S A SMALL PRICE TO PAY FOR MACHOHOOD
JIM DAVIS 11-14

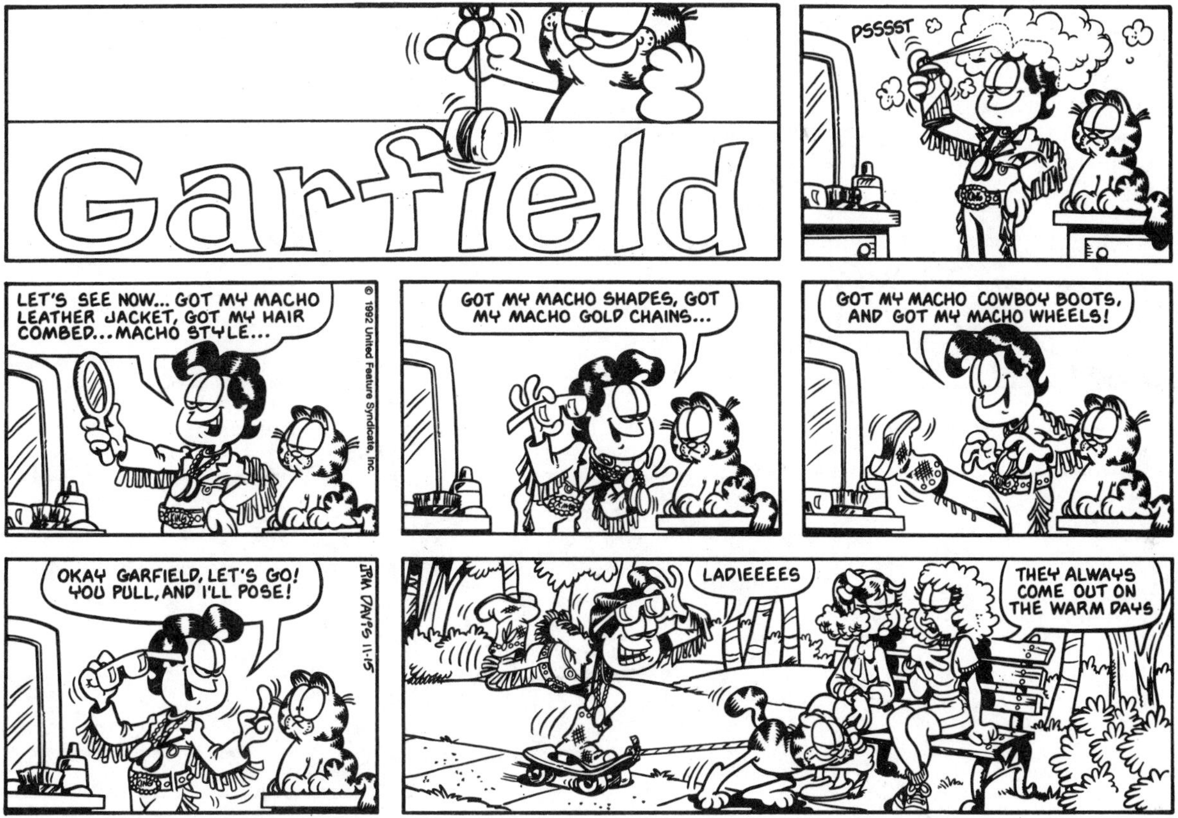
Garfield
PSSSST
LET'S SEE NOW... GOT MY MACHO LEATHER JACKET, GOT MY HAIR COMBED...MACHO STYLE...
© 1992 United Feature Syndicate, Inc.
GOT MY MACHO SHADES, GOT MY MACHO GOLD CHAINS...
GOT MY MACHO COWBOY BOOTS, AND GOT MY MACHO WHEELS!
OKAY GARFIELD, LET'S GO! YOU PULL, AND I'LL POSE!
JIM DAVIS 11-15
LADIEEEES
THEY ALWAYS COME OUT ON THE WARM DAYS

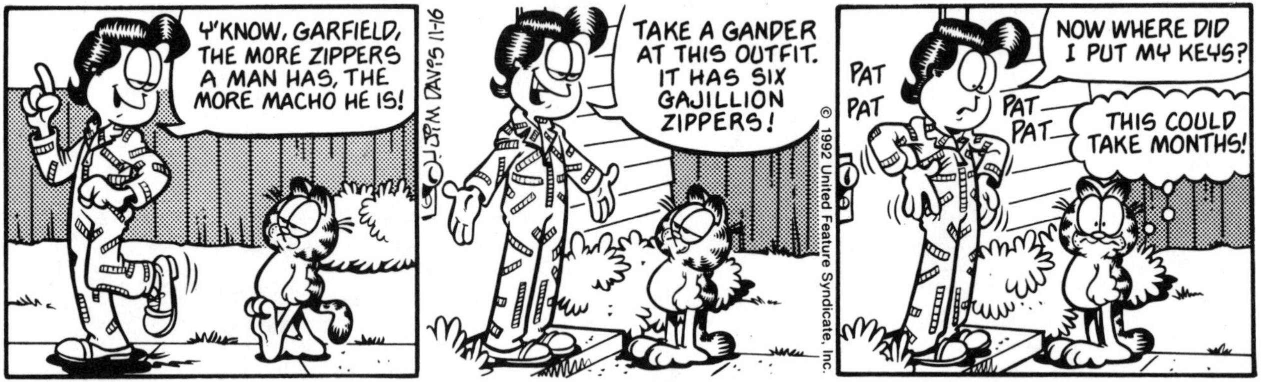

Y'KNOW, GARFIELD, THE MORE ZIPPERS A MAN HAS, THE MORE MACHO HE IS!
© JIM DAVIS 11-16
TAKE A GANDER AT THIS OUTFIT. IT HAS SIX GAJILLION ZIPPERS!
© 1992 United Feature Syndicate, Inc.
NOW WHERE DID I PUT MY KEYS?
PAT PAT
PAT PAT
THIS COULD TAKE MONTHS!


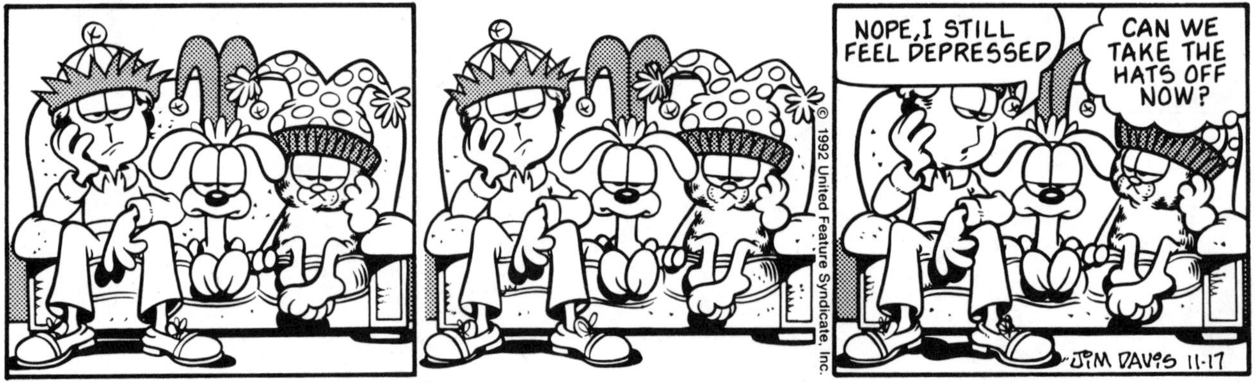

© 1992 United Feature Syndicate, Inc.
NOPE, I STILL FEEL DEPRESSED
CAN WE TAKE THE HATS OFF NOW?
JIM DAVIS 11-17

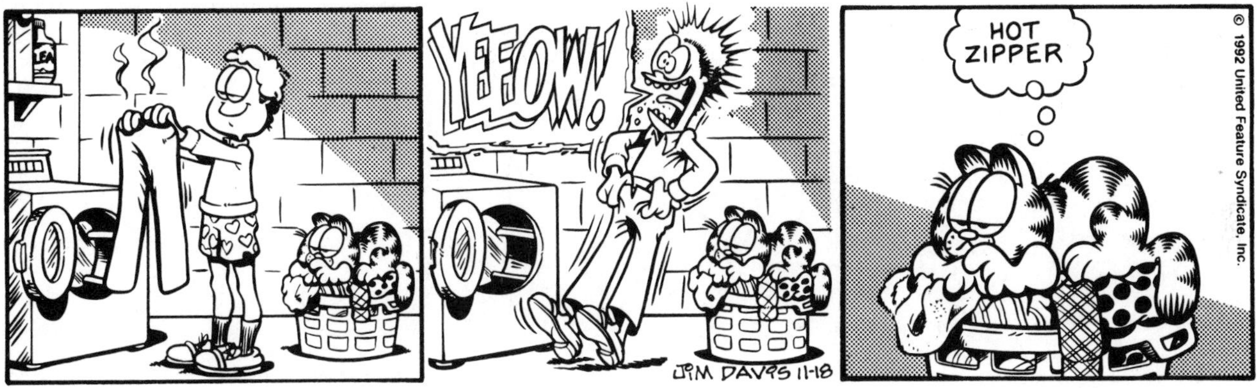
YEEOW!
HOT ZIPPER
JIM DAVIS 11-18


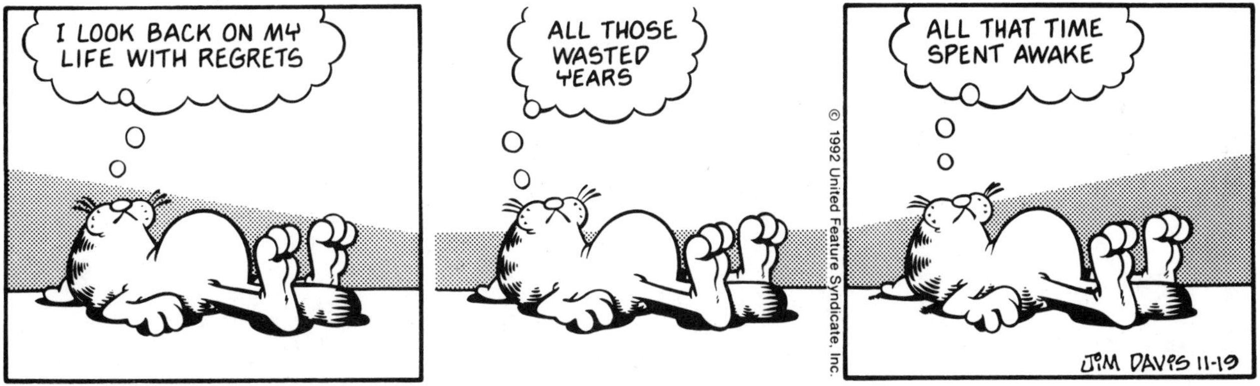
I LOOK BACK ON MY LIFE WITH REGRETS
ALL THOSE WASTED YEARS
ALL THAT TIME SPENT AWAKE
JIM DAVIS 11-19

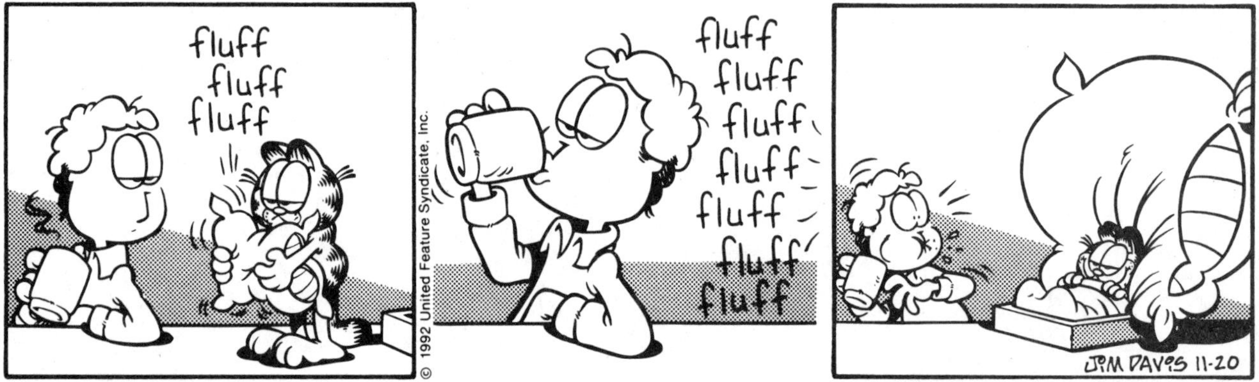
fluff
fluff
fluff
fluff
fluff
fluff
fluff
fluff
fluff
fluff
JIM DAVIS 11-20


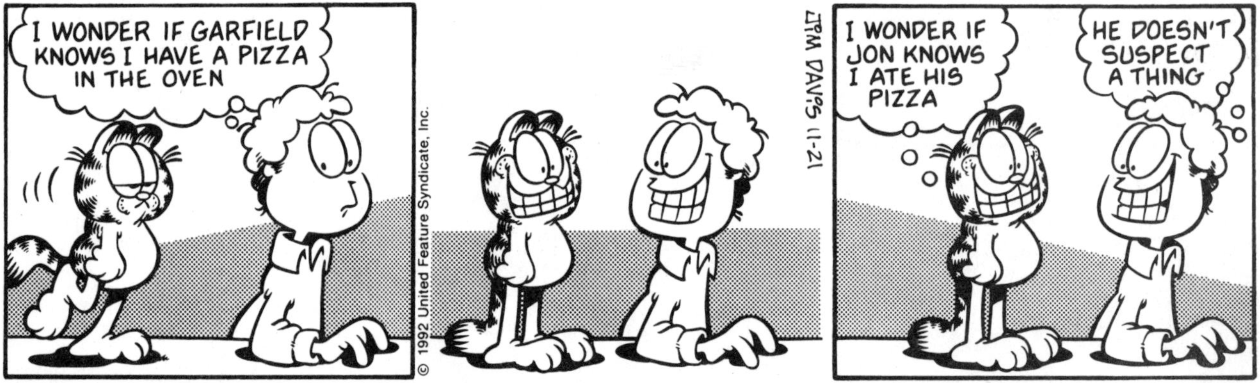
I WONDER IF GARFIELD KNOWS I HAVE A PIZZA IN THE OVEN
JIM DAVIS 11-21
I WONDER IF JON KNOWS I ATE HIS PIZZA
HE DOESN'T SUSPECT A THING

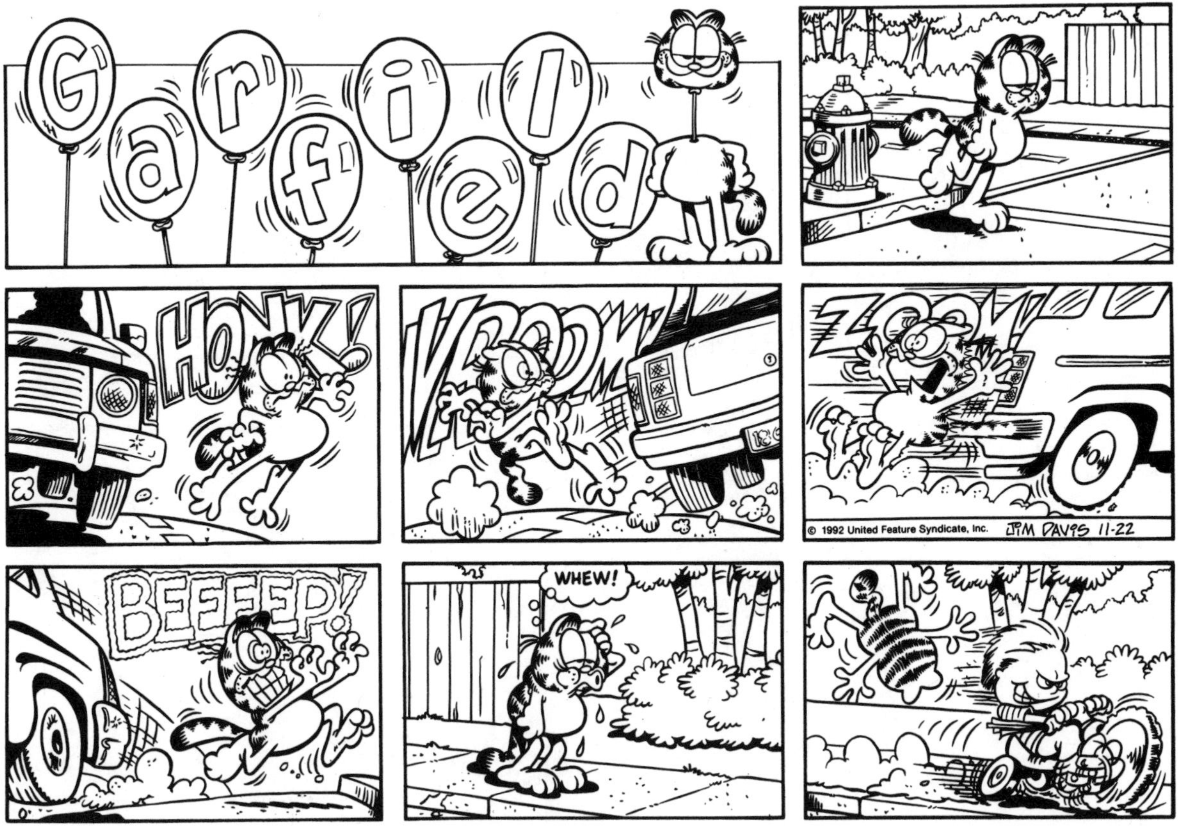
Garfield
HONK!
VROOOM!
ZOOM!
© 1992 United Feature Syndicate, Inc.
JIM DAVIS 11-22
BEEEEP!
WHEW!

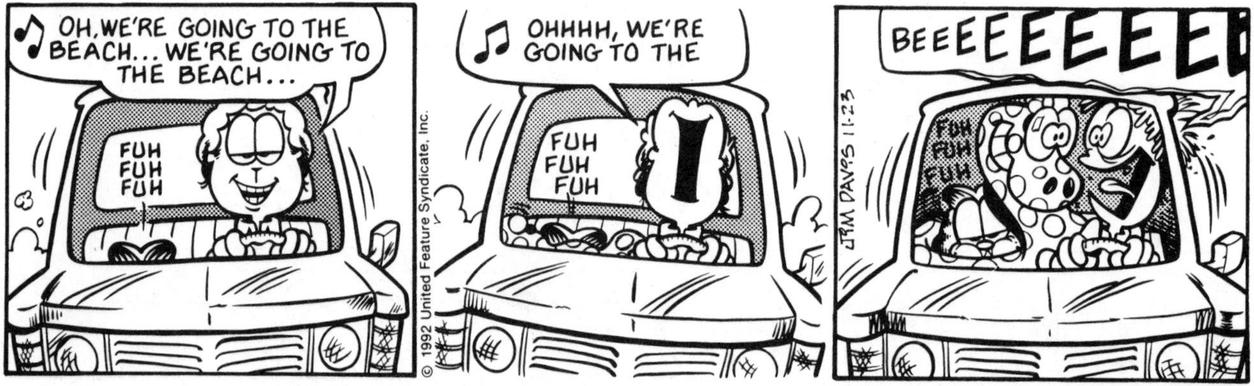
OH, WE'RE GOING TO THE BEACH... WE'RE GOING TO THE BEACH...
FUH FUH FUH
© 1992 United Feature Syndicate, Inc.
OHHHH, WE'RE GOING TO THE
FUH FUH FUH
BEEEEEEEEE
FUH FUH FUH
JIM DAVIS 11-23

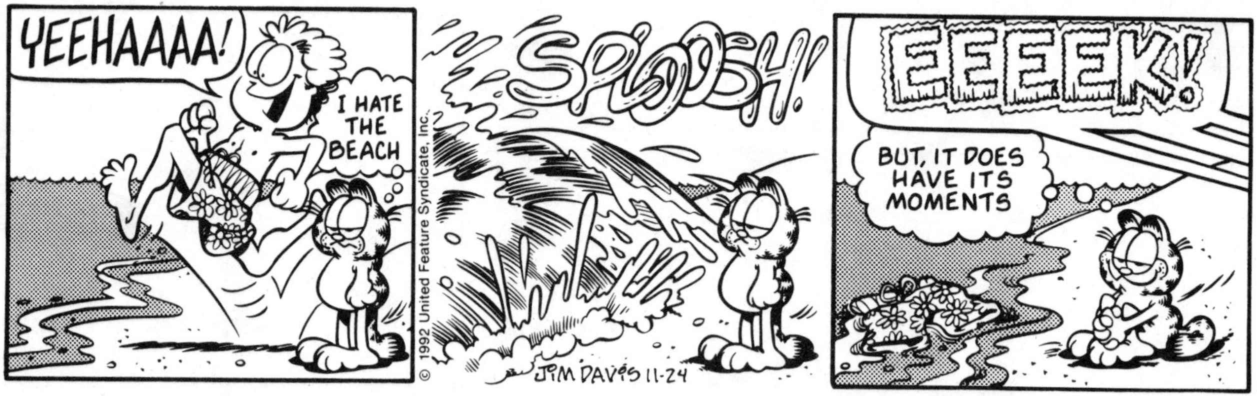
YEEHAAAA!
I HATE THE BEACH
© 1992 United Feature Syndicate, Inc.
SPLOOSH!
JIM DAVIS 11-24
EEEEK!
BUT, IT DOES HAVE ITS MOMENTS

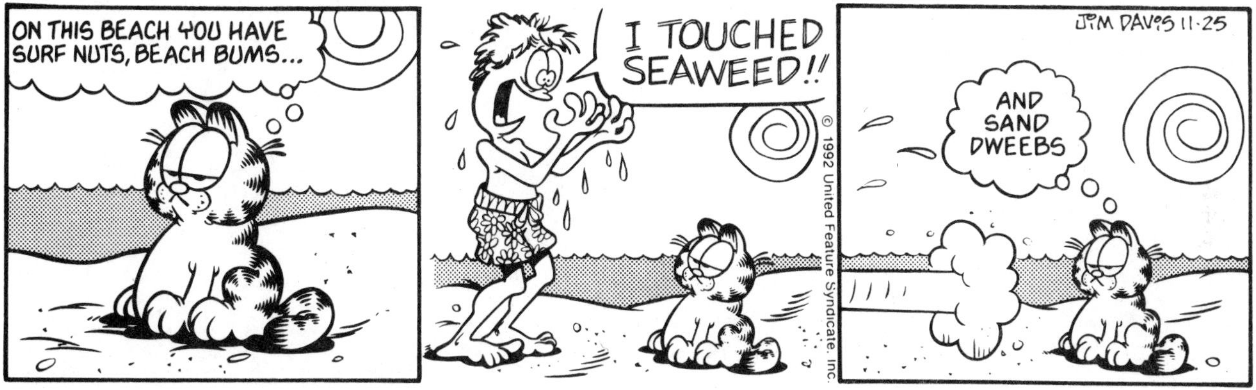
ON THIS BEACH YOU HAVE SURF NUTS, BEACH BUMS...
I TOUCHED SEAWEED!!
© 1992 United Feature Syndicate, Inc.
JIM DAVIS 11-25
AND SAND DWEEBS

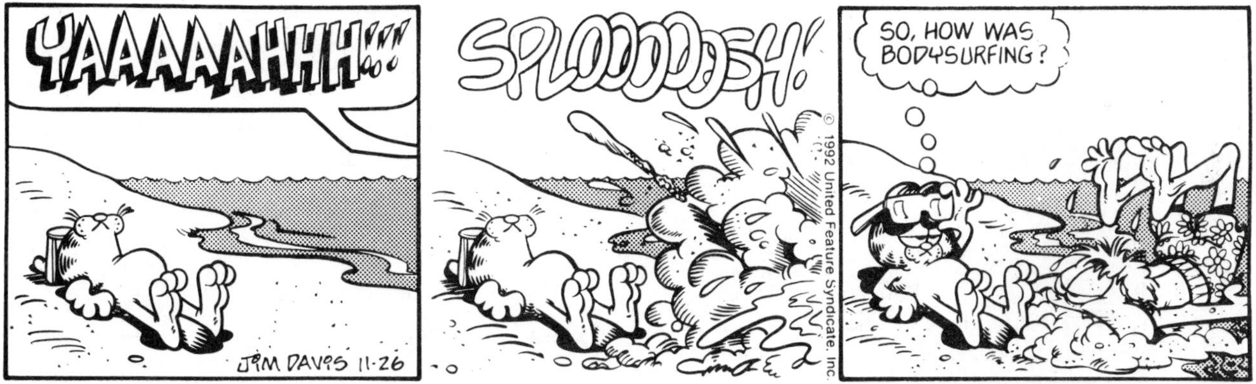
YAAAAAHHH!!!
JIM DAVIS 11-26
SPLOOOOOOSH!
© 1992 United Feature Syndicate, Inc.
SO, HOW WAS BODYSURFING?

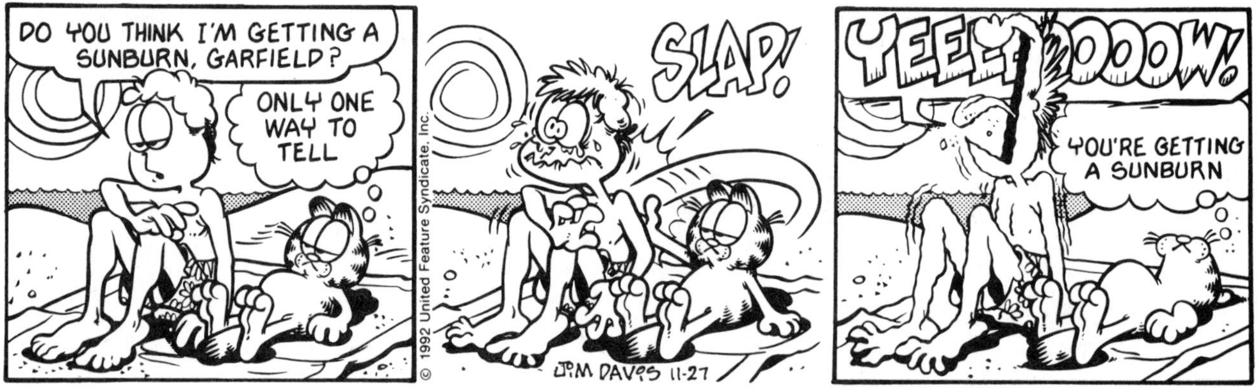
DO YOU THINK I'M GETTING A SUNBURN, GARFIELD?
ONLY ONE WAY TO TELL
SLAP!
YEEEOOOOW!
YOU'RE GETTING A SUNBURN
© 1992 United Feature Syndicate, Inc.
JIM DAVIS 11-27

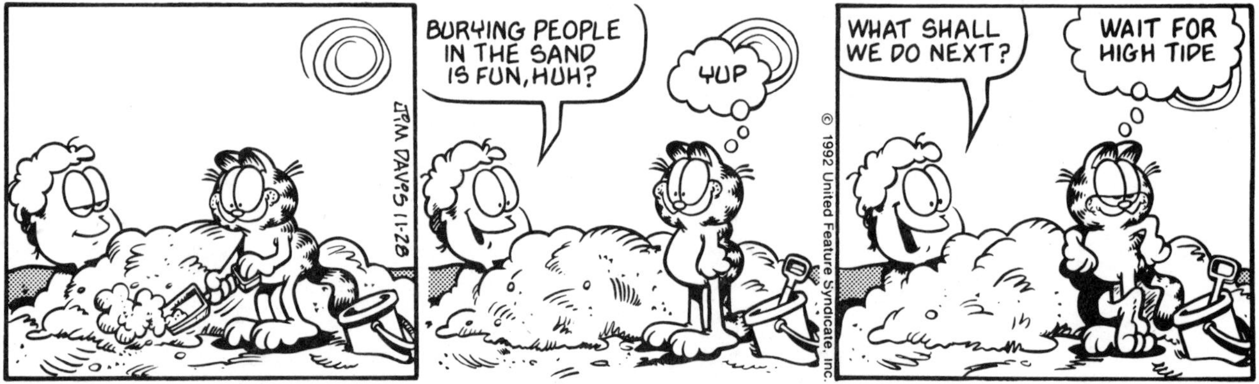
JIM DAVIS 11-28
BURYING PEOPLE IN THE SAND IS FUN, HUH?
YUP
WHAT SHALL WE DO NEXT?
WAIT FOR HIGH TIDE
© 1992 United Feature Syndicate, Inc.

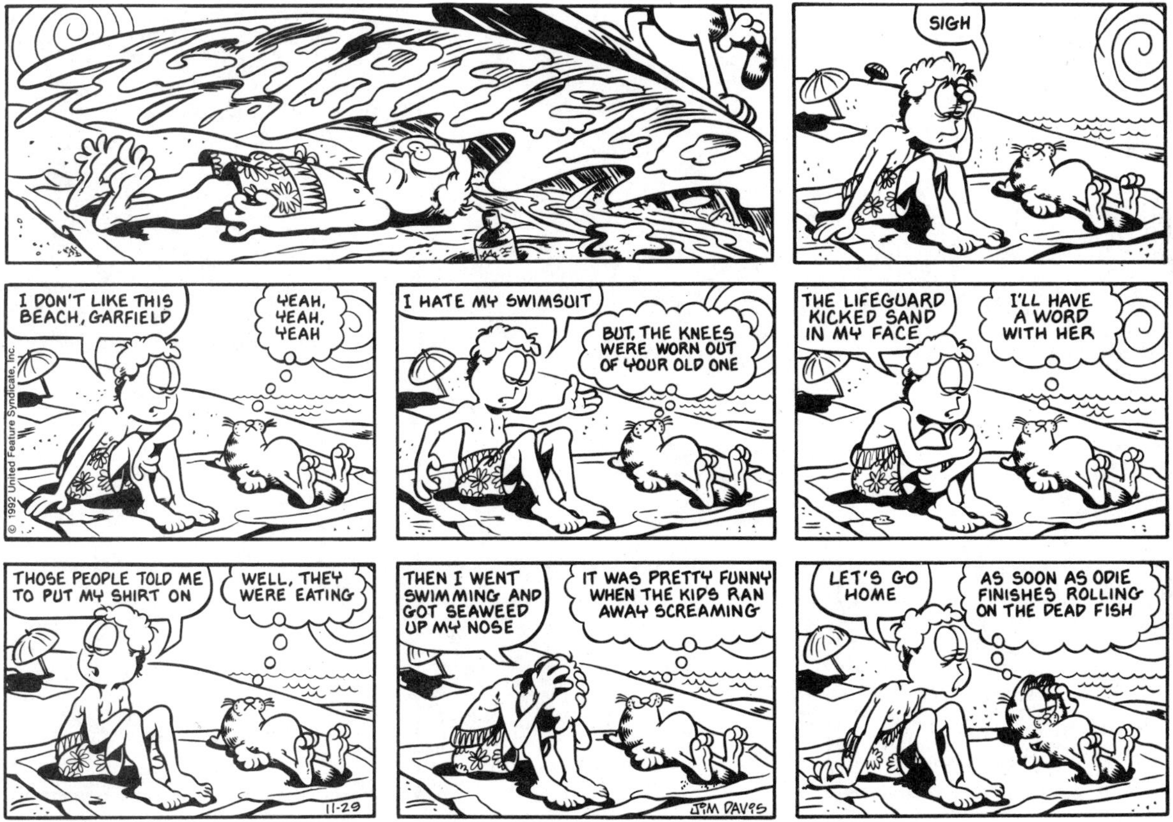
SIGH
I DON'T LIKE THIS BEACH, GARFIELD
YEAH, YEAH, YEAH
I HATE MY SWIMSUIT
BUT, THE KNEES WERE WORN OUT OF YOUR OLD ONE
THE LIFEGUARD KICKED SAND IN MY FACE
I'LL HAVE A WORD WITH HER
THOSE PEOPLE TOLD ME TO PUT MY SHIRT ON
WELL, THEY WERE EATING
THEN I WENT SWIMMING AND GOT SEAWEED UP MY NOSE
IT WAS PRETTY FUNNY WHEN THE KIDS RAN AWAY SCREAMING
LET'S GO HOME
AS SOON AS ODIE FINISHES ROLLING ON THE DEAD FISH
© 1992 United Feature Syndicate, Inc.
11-29
JIM DAVIS

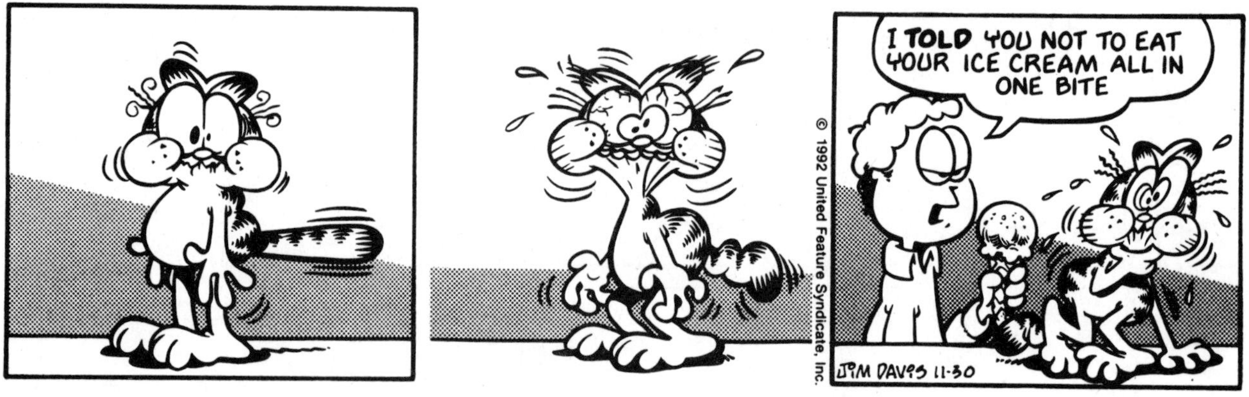
I TOLD YOU NOT TO EAT YOUR ICE CREAM ALL IN ONE BITE
© 1992 United Feature Syndicate, Inc.
JIM DAVIS 11-30

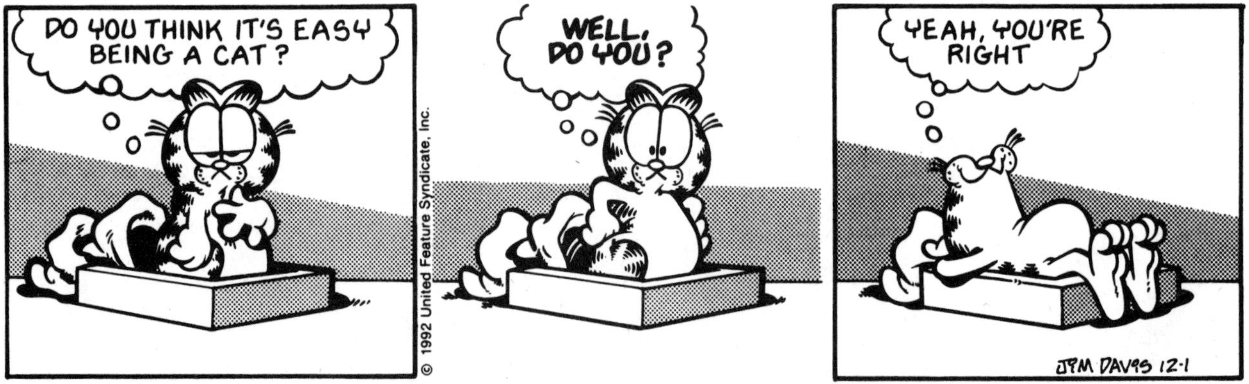
DO YOU THINK IT'S EASY BEING A CAT?
WELL, DO YOU?
YEAH, YOU'RE RIGHT
© 1992 United Feature Syndicate, Inc.
JIM DAVIS 12-1

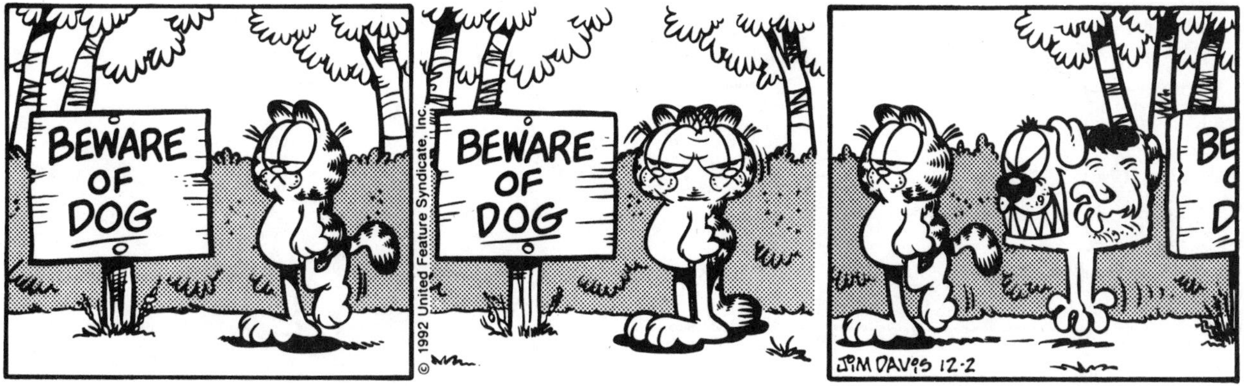
BEWARE OF DOG
BEWARE OF DOG
© 1992 United Feature Syndicate, Inc.
JIM DAVIS 12-2

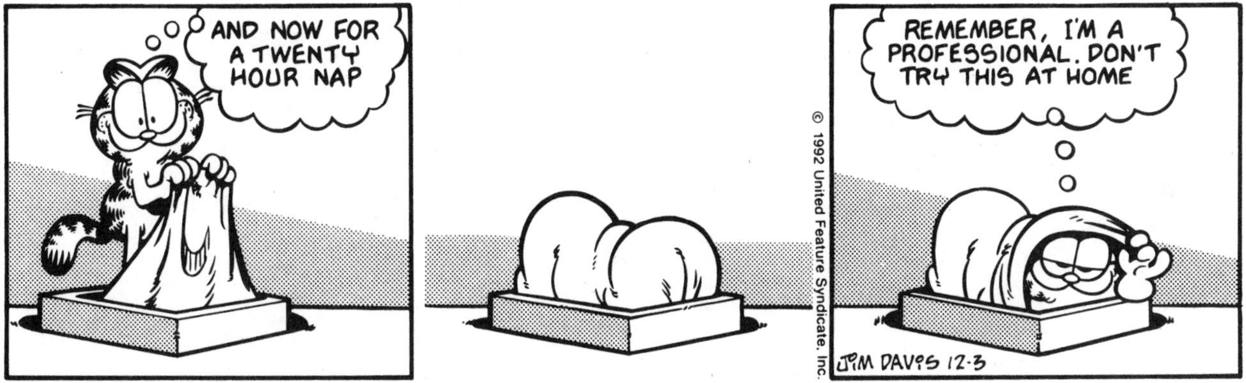
AND NOW FOR A TWENTY HOUR NAP
REMEMBER, I'M A PROFESSIONAL. DON'T TRY THIS AT HOME
© 1992 United Feature Syndicate, Inc.
JIM DAVIS 12-3

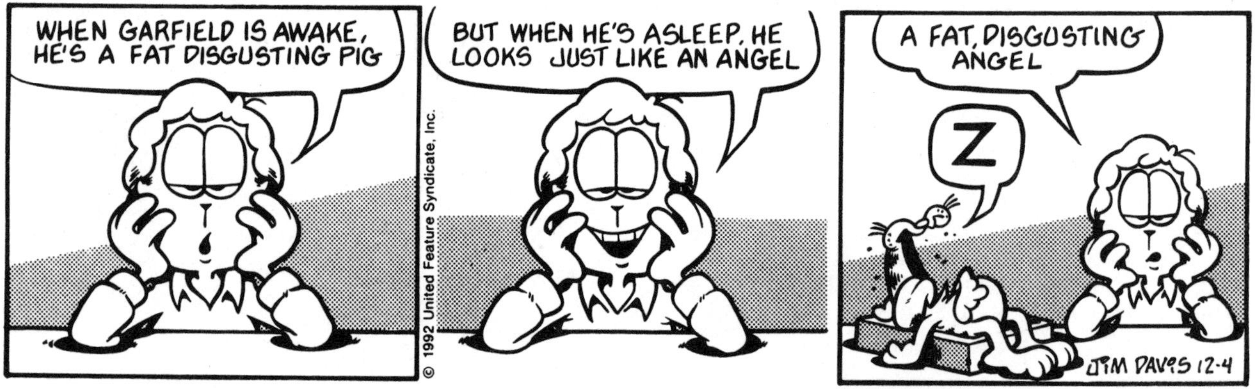

WHEN GARFIELD IS AWAKE, HE'S A FAT DISGUSTING PIG
BUT WHEN HE'S ASLEEP, HE LOOKS JUST LIKE AN ANGEL
Z
A FAT, DISGUSTING ANGEL
JIM DAVIS 12-4
© 1992 United Feature Syndicate, Inc.


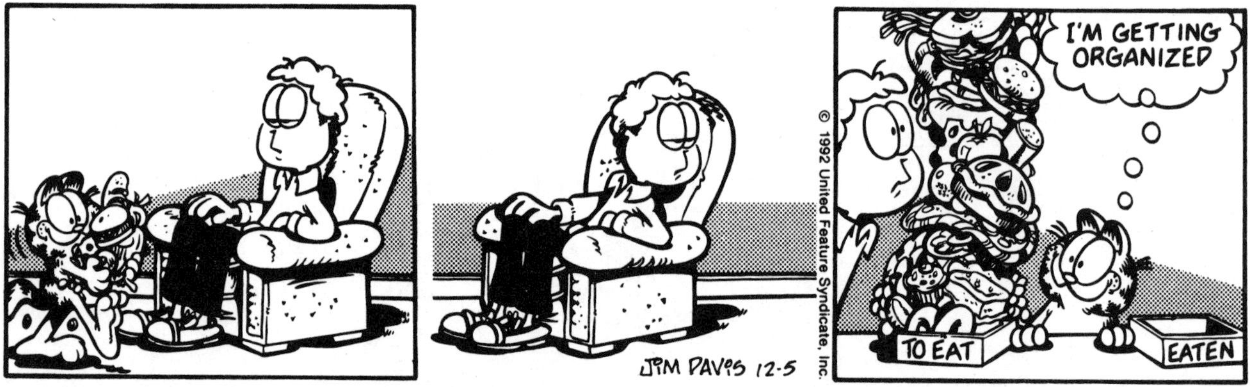

JIM DAVIS 12-5
© 1992 United Feature Syndicate, Inc.
I'M GETTING ORGANIZED
TO EAT
EATEN

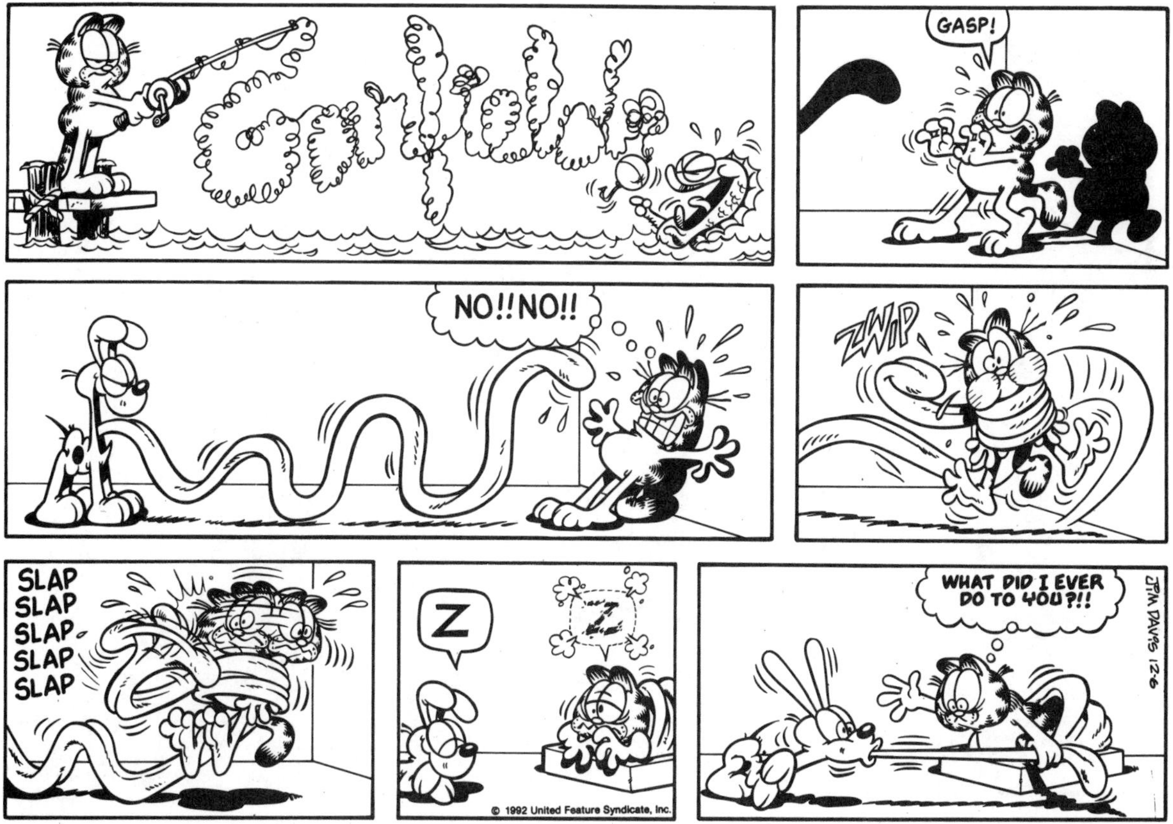
GARFIELD
GASP!
NO!! NO!!
ZWIP
SLAP
SLAP
SLAP
SLAP
SLAP
SLAP
Z
Z
WHAT DID I EVER DO TO YOU?!!
JPM DAVIS 12-6
© 1992 United Feature Syndicate, Inc.

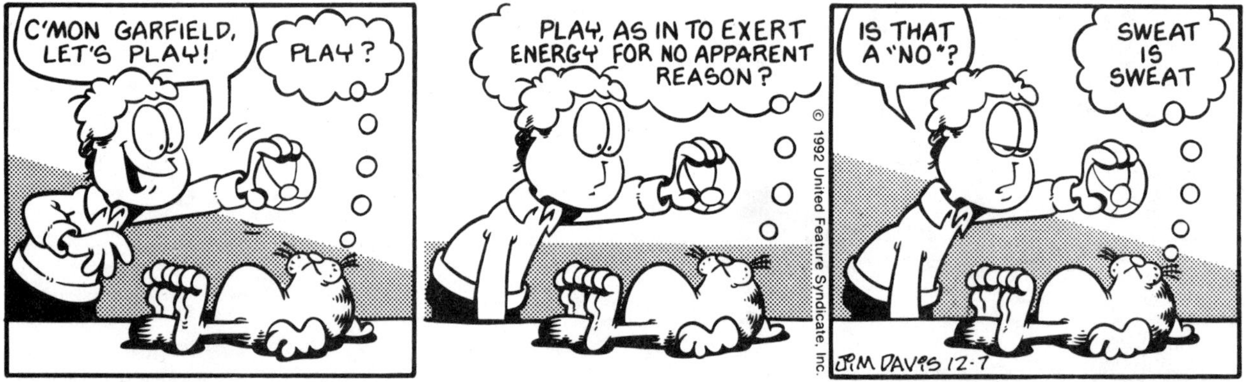
C'MON GARFIELD, LET'S PLAY!
PLAY?
PLAY, AS IN TO EXERT ENERGY FOR NO APPARENT REASON?
IS THAT A "NO"?
SWEAT IS SWEAT
© 1992 United Feature Syndicate, Inc.
JIM DAVIS 12-7

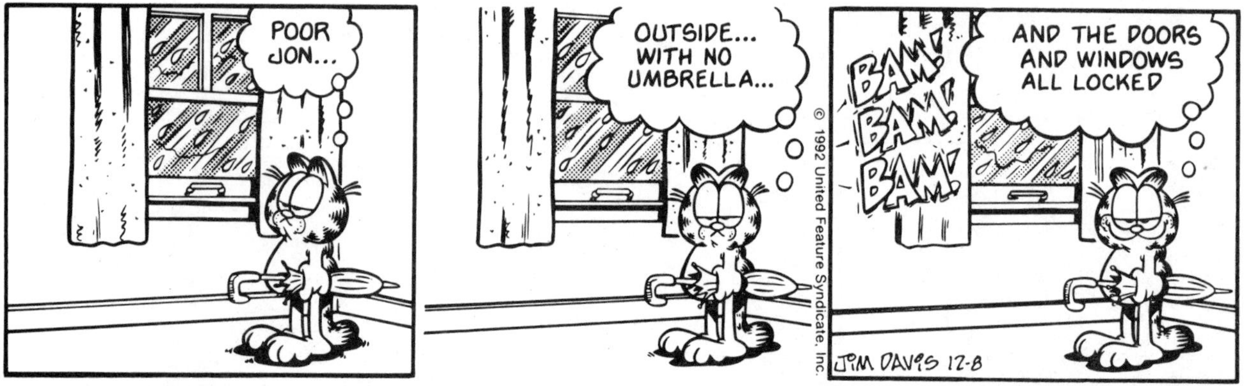
POOR JON...
OUTSIDE... WITH NO UMBRELLA...
BAM! BAM! BAM!
AND THE DOORS AND WINDOWS ALL LOCKED
© 1992 United Feature Syndicate, Inc.
JIM DAVIS 12-8

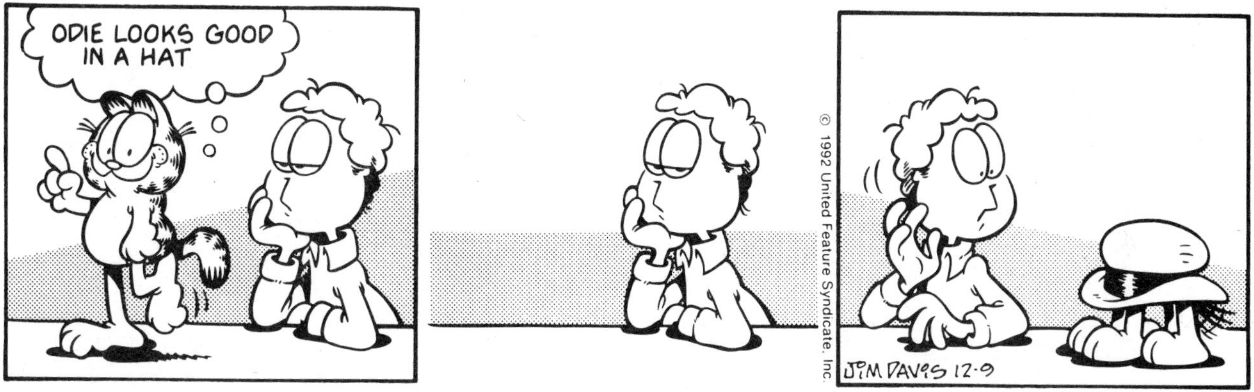
ODIE LOOKS GOOD IN A HAT
© 1992 United Feature Syndicate, Inc.
JIM DAVIS 12-9

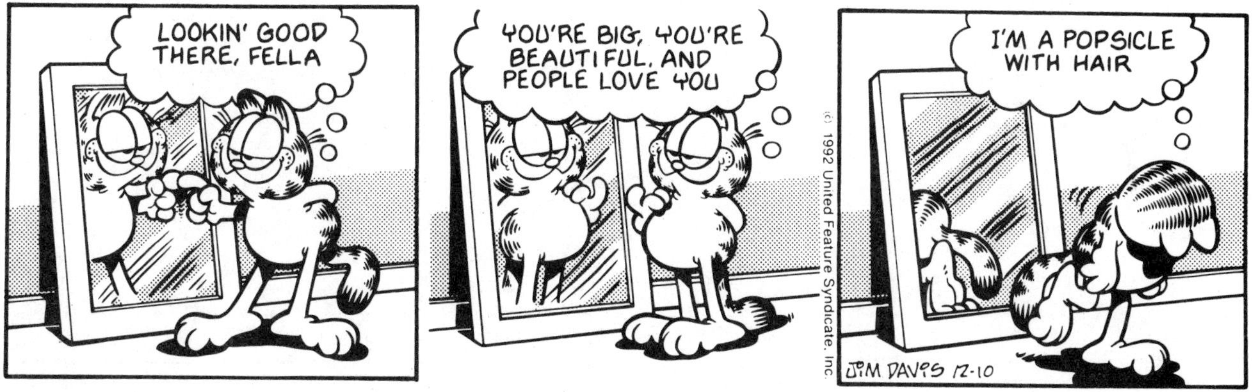
LOOKIN' GOOD THERE, FELLA
YOU'RE BIG, YOU'RE BEAUTIFUL, AND PEOPLE LOVE YOU
I'M A POPSICLE WITH HAIR
(c) 1992 United Feature Syndicate, Inc.
JIM DAVIS 12-10

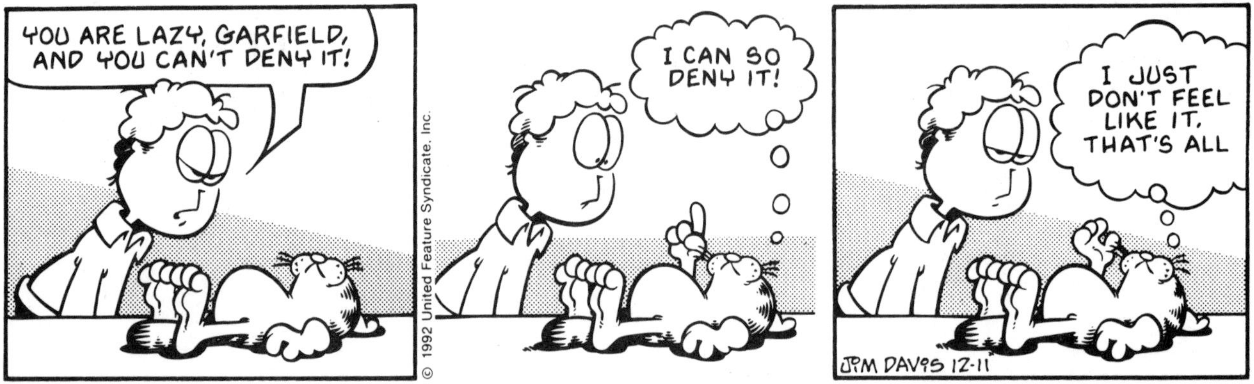
YOU ARE LAZY, GARFIELD, AND YOU CAN'T DENY IT!
I CAN SO DENY IT!
I JUST DON'T FEEL LIKE IT, THAT'S ALL
JIM DAVIS 12-11


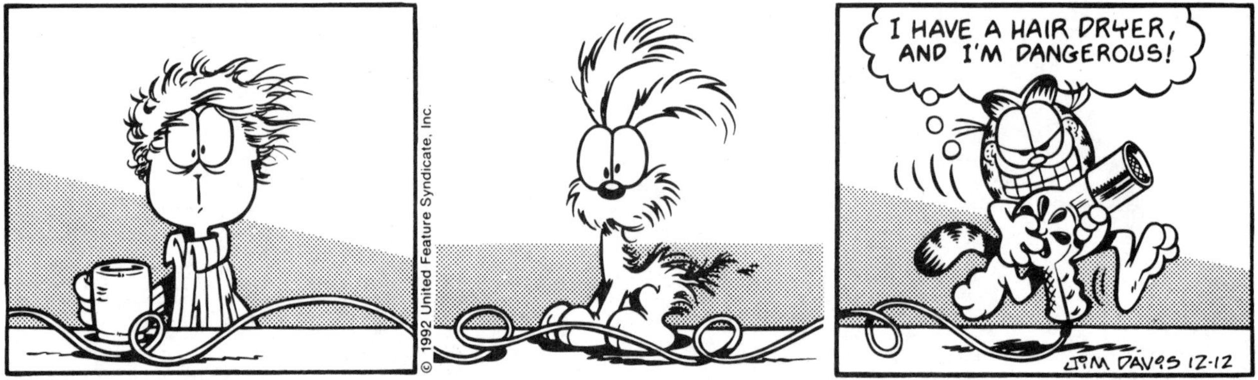
I HAVE A HAIR DRYER, AND I'M DANGEROUS!
JIM DAVIS 12-12

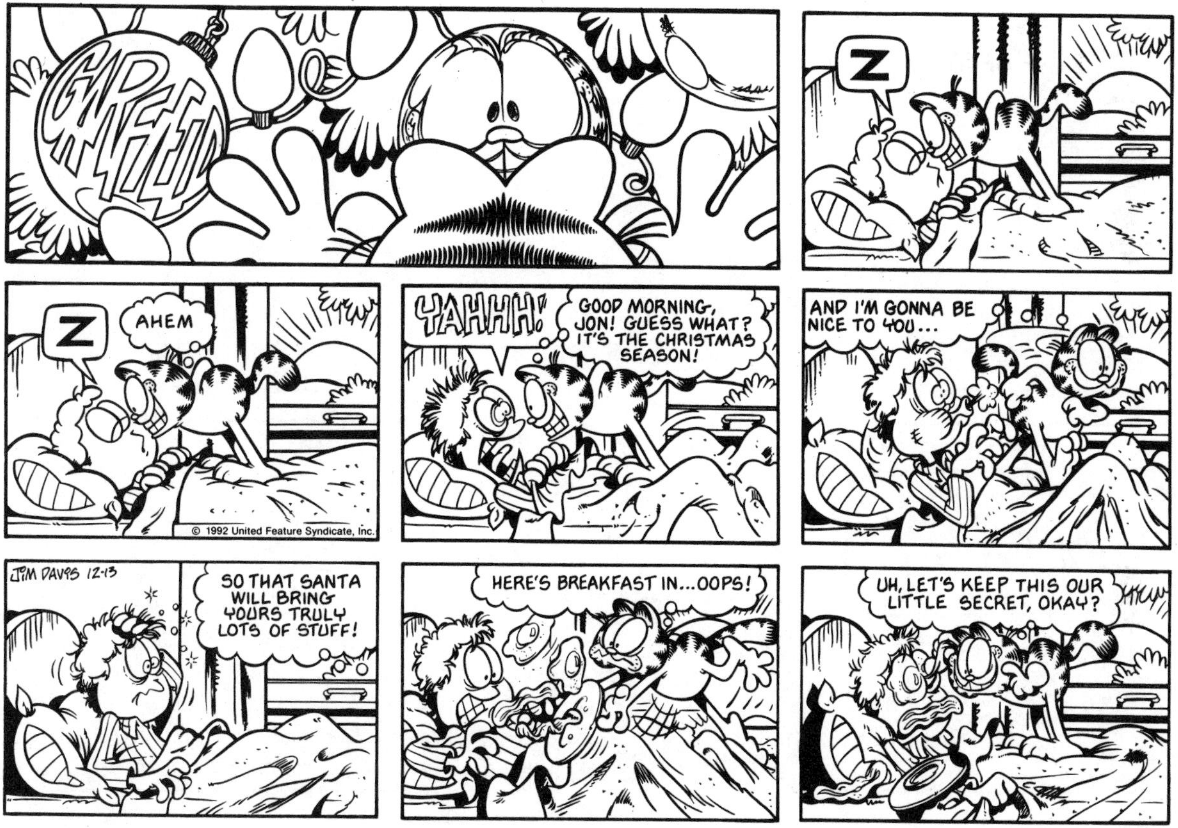
GARFIELD
Z
Z
AHEM
© 1992 United Feature Syndicate, Inc.
YAHHH!
GOOD MORNING, JON! GUESS WHAT? IT'S THE CHRISTMAS SEASON!
AND I'M GONNA BE NICE TO YOU...
JIM DAVIS 12-13
SO THAT SANTA WILL BRING YOURS TRULY LOTS OF STUFF!
HERE'S BREAKFAST IN...OOPS!
UH, LET'S KEEP THIS OUR LITTLE SECRET, OKAY?

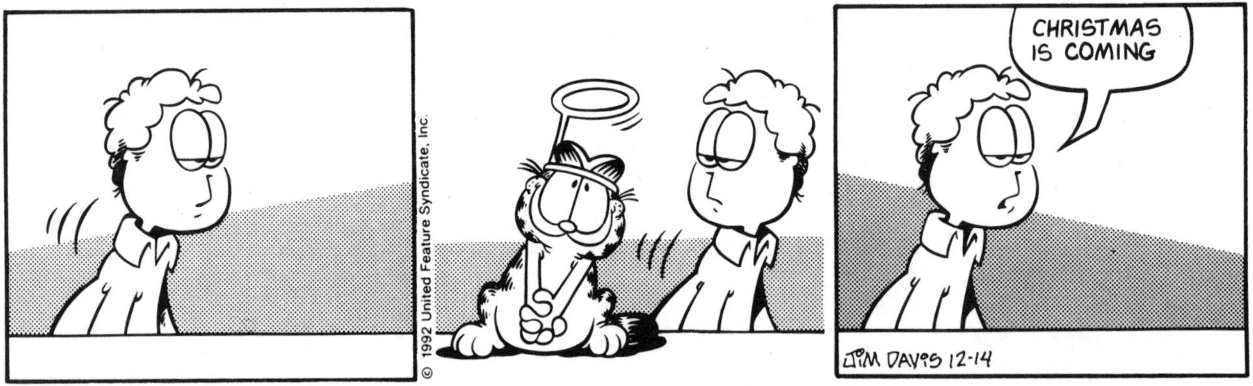
© 1992 United Feature Syndicate, Inc.
CHRISTMAS IS COMING
JIM DAVIS 12-14

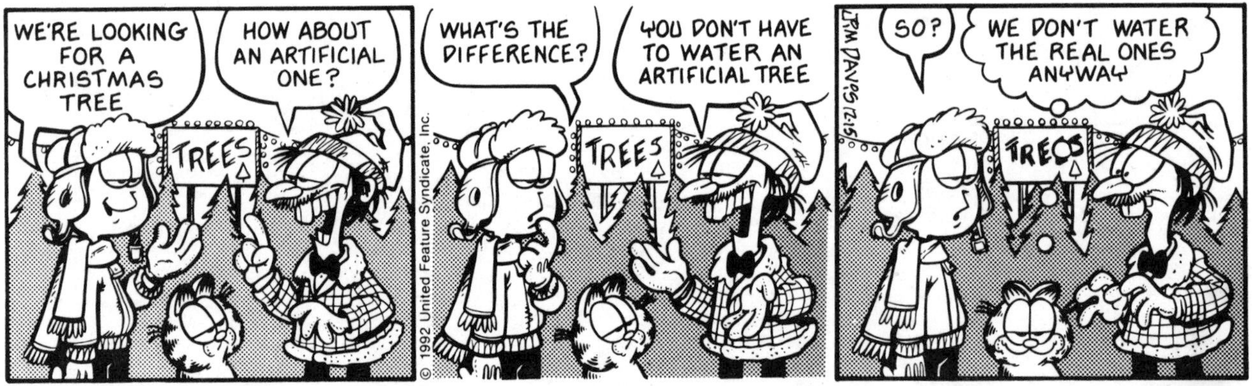
WE'RE LOOKING FOR A CHRISTMAS TREE
HOW ABOUT AN ARTIFICIAL ONE?
TREES
© 1992 United Feature Syndicate, Inc.
WHAT'S THE DIFFERENCE?
YOU DON'T HAVE TO WATER AN ARTIFICIAL TREE
TREES
JIM DAVIS 12-15
SO?
WE DON'T WATER THE REAL ONES ANYWAY

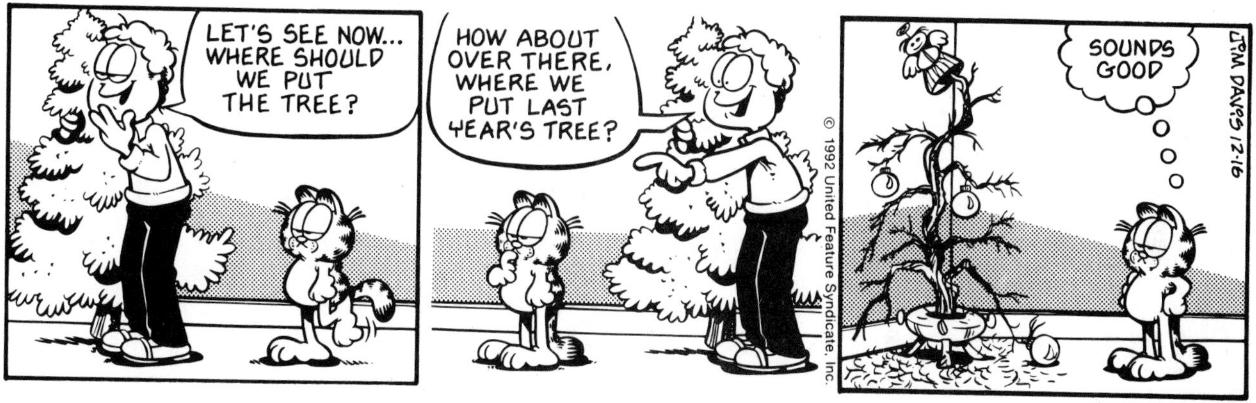
LET'S SEE NOW... WHERE SHOULD WE PUT THE TREE?
HOW ABOUT OVER THERE, WHERE WE PUT LAST YEAR'S TREE?
© 1992 United Feature Syndicate, Inc.
SOUNDS GOOD
JIM DAVIS 12-16

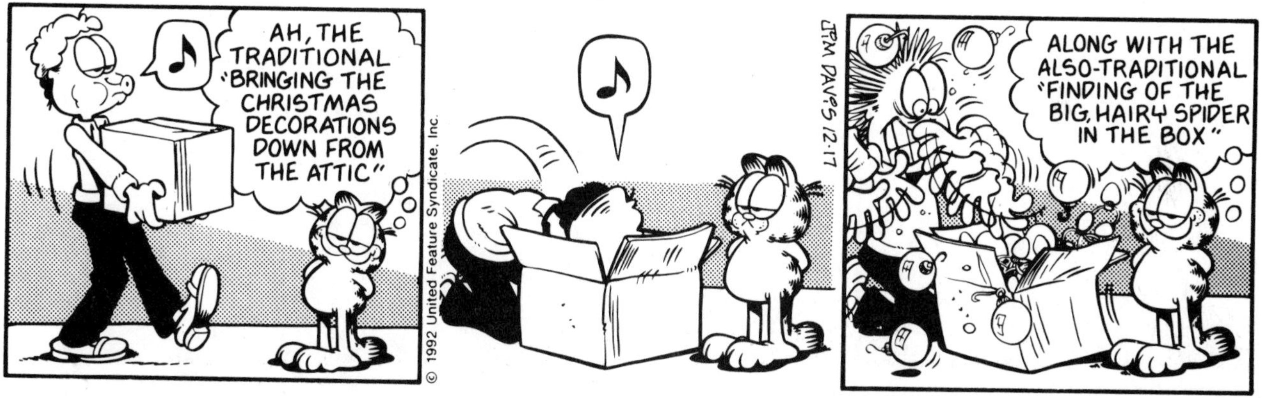
♪
AH, THE TRADITIONAL "BRINGING THE CHRISTMAS DECORATIONS DOWN FROM THE ATTIC"
© 1992 United Feature Syndicate, Inc.
♪
JIM DAVIS 12-17
ALONG WITH THE ALSO-TRADITIONAL "FINDING OF THE BIG, HAIRY SPIDER IN THE BOX"

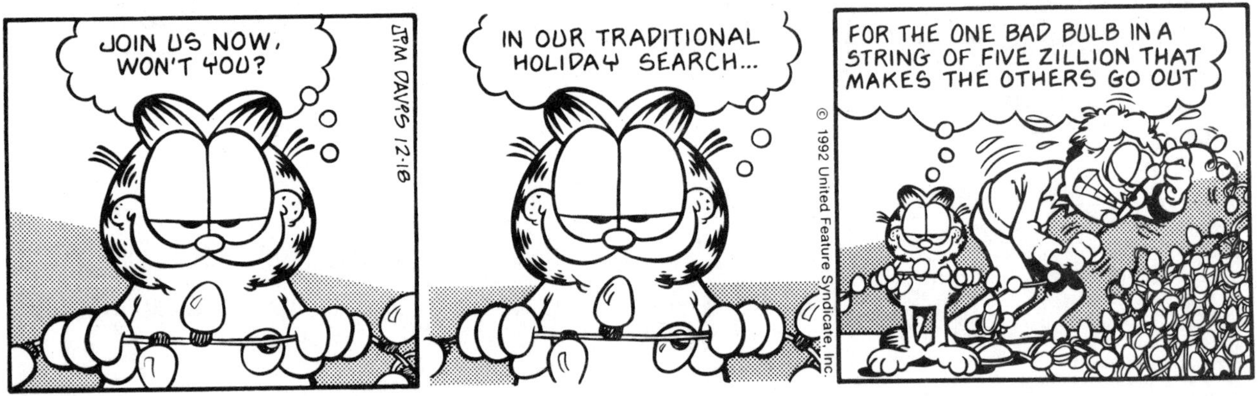
JOIN US NOW, WON'T YOU?
JIM DAVIS 12-18
IN OUR TRADITIONAL HOLIDAY SEARCH...
FOR THE ONE BAD BULB IN A STRING OF FIVE ZILLION THAT MAKES THE OTHERS GO OUT


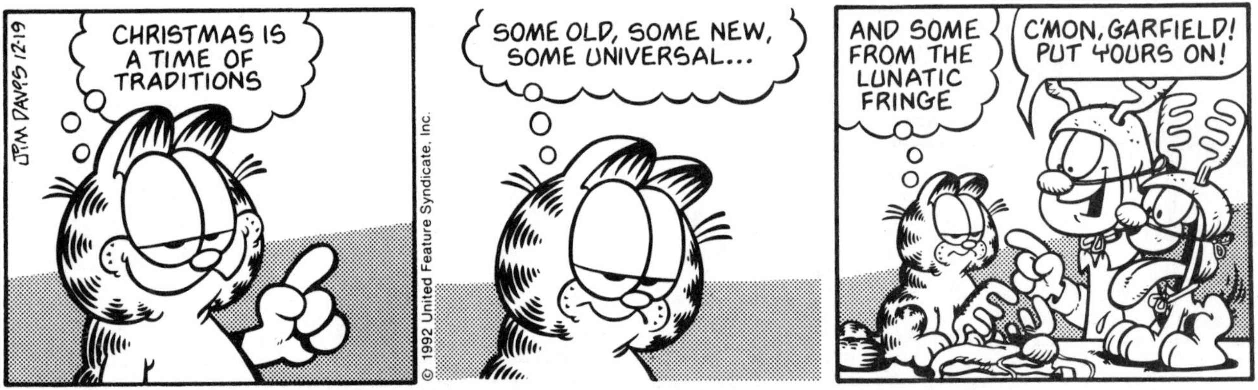
JIM DAVIS 12-19
CHRISTMAS IS A TIME OF TRADITIONS
SOME OLD, SOME NEW, SOME UNIVERSAL...
AND SOME FROM THE LUNATIC FRINGE
C'MON, GARFIELD! PUT YOURS ON!

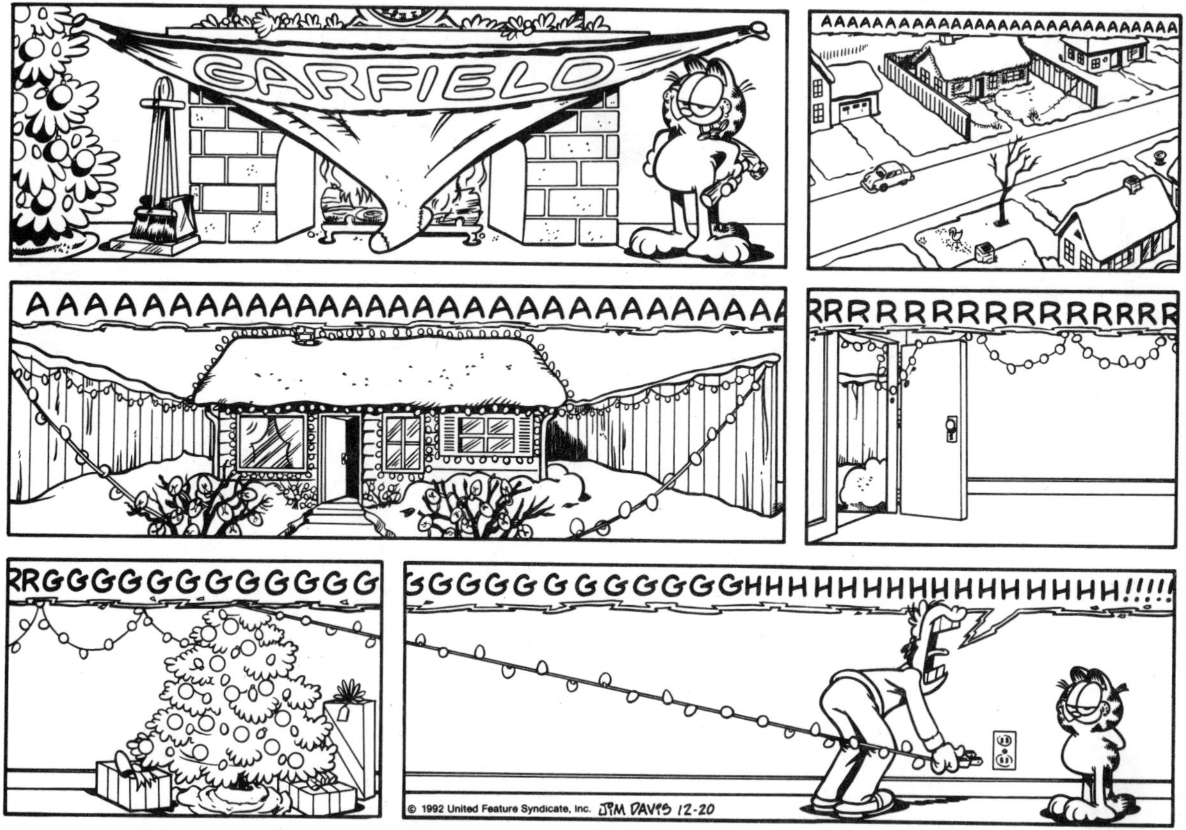
GARFIELD
AAAAAAAAAAAAAAAAAAAAAAAAAAA
AAAAAAAAAAAAAAAAAAAAAAAAAAAA
RRRRRRRRRRRRR
RRGGGGGGGGGGG
GGGGGGGGGGGHHHHHHHHHHHHHHHH!!!!!
© 1992 United Feature Syndicate, Inc. JIM DAVIS 12-20

# The Garfield Birthday Gallery

1978

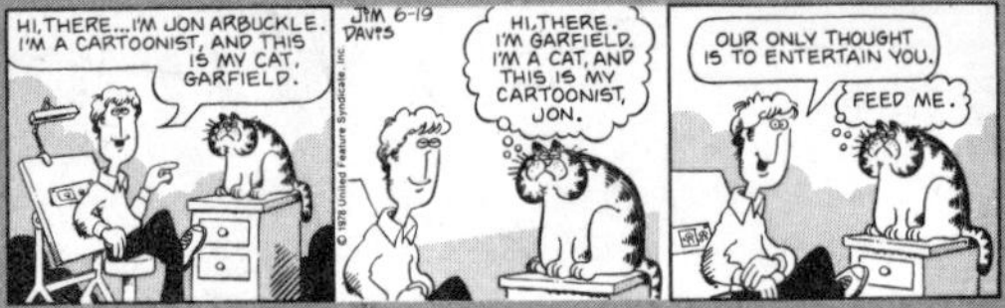
HI, THERE... I'M JON ARBUCKLE. I'M A CARTOONIST, AND THIS IS MY CAT, GARFIELD.
JIM DAVIS 6-19
HI, THERE. I'M GARFIELD. I'M A CAT, AND THIS IS MY CARTOONIST, JON.
OUR ONLY THOUGHT IS TO ENTERTAIN YOU.
FEED ME.

1979

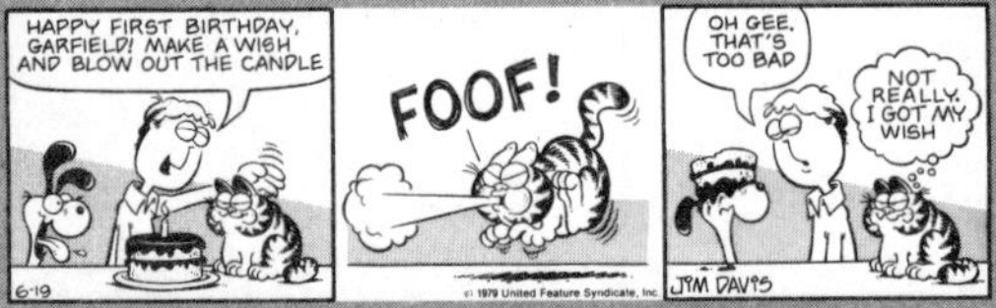
HAPPY FIRST BIRTHDAY, GARFIELD! MAKE A WISH AND BLOW OUT THE CANDLE
6-19
FOOF!
© 1979 United Feature Syndicate, Inc.
OH GEE. THAT'S TOO BAD
NOT REALLY. I GOT MY WISH
JIM DAVIS

1980

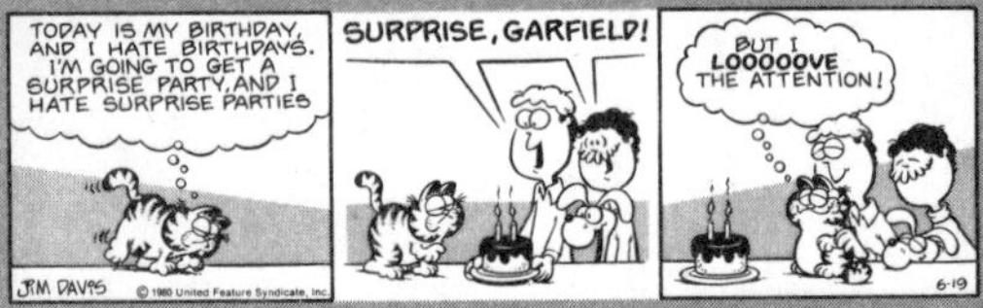
TODAY IS MY BIRTHDAY, AND I HATE BIRTHDAYS. I'M GOING TO GET A SURPRISE PARTY, AND I HATE SURPRISE PARTIES
JIM DAVIS
© 1980 United Feature Syndicate, Inc.
SURPRISE, GARFIELD!
BUT I LOOOOOVE THE ATTENTION!
6-19

1981

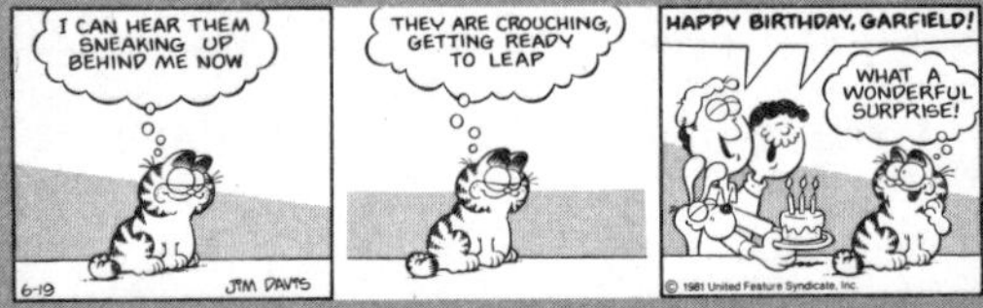
I CAN HEAR THEM SNEAKING UP BEHIND ME NOW
6-19
JIM DAVIS
THEY ARE CROUCHING, GETTING READY TO LEAP
HAPPY BIRTHDAY, GARFIELD!
WHAT A WONDERFUL SURPRISE!
© 1981 United Feature Syndicate, Inc.

1982

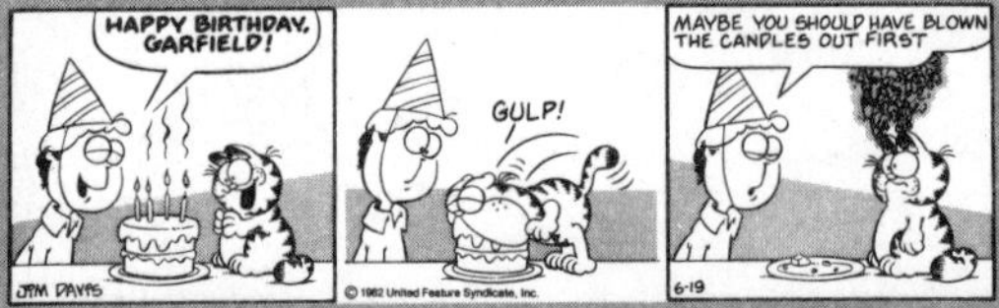
HAPPY BIRTHDAY, GARFIELD!
JIM DAVIS
GULP!
© 1982 United Feature Syndicate, Inc.
MAYBE YOU SHOULD HAVE BLOWN THE CANDLES OUT FIRST
6-19

1983

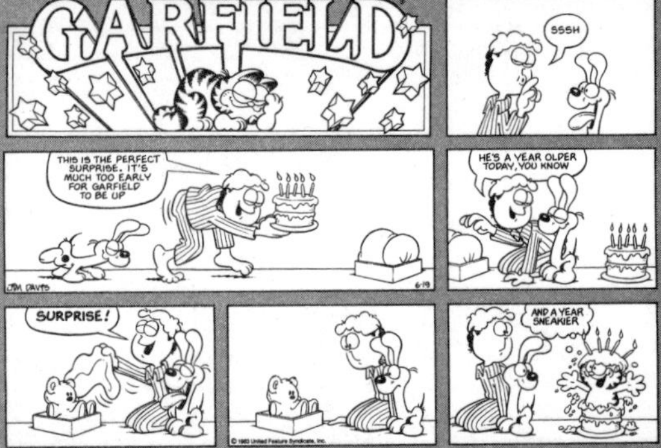
GARFIELD
SSSH
THIS IS THE PERFECT SURPRISE. IT'S MUCH TOO EARLY FOR GARFIELD TO BE UP
JIM DAVIS
6-19
HE'S A YEAR OLDER TODAY, YOU KNOW
SURPRISE!
© 1983 United Feature Syndicate, Inc.
AND A YEAR SNEAKIER

1984

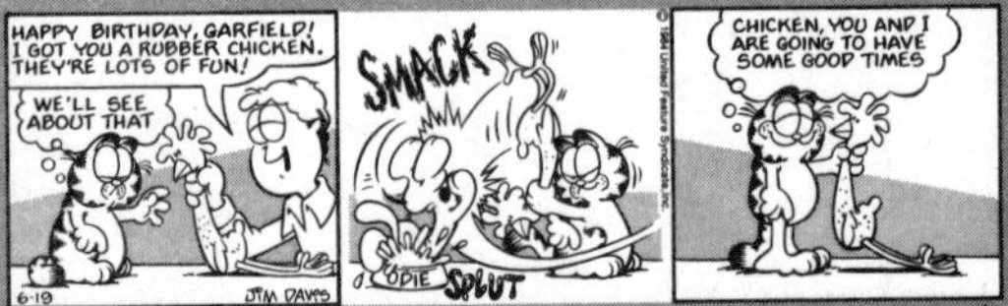
HAPPY BIRTHDAY, GARFIELD! I GOT YOU A RUBBER CHICKEN. THEY'RE LOTS OF FUN!
WE'LL SEE ABOUT THAT
6-19
JIM DAVIS
SMACK
ODIE
SPLUT
CHICKEN, YOU AND I ARE GOING TO HAVE SOME GOOD TIMES

1985

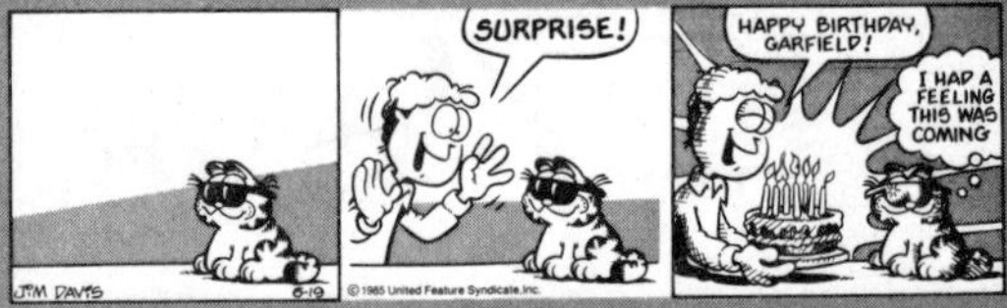
JIM DAVIS
6-19
SURPRISE!
© 1985 United Feature Syndicate, Inc.
HAPPY BIRTHDAY, GARFIELD!
I HAD A FEELING THIS WAS COMING

1986

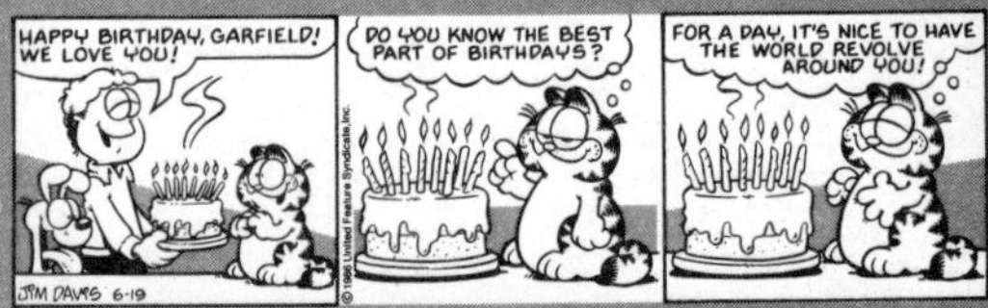
HAPPY BIRTHDAY, GARFIELD! WE LOVE YOU!
JIM DAVIS 6-19
DO YOU KNOW THE BEST PART OF BIRTHDAYS?
FOR A DAY, IT'S NICE TO HAVE THE WORLD REVOLVE AROUND YOU!

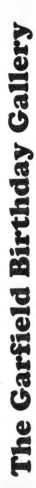

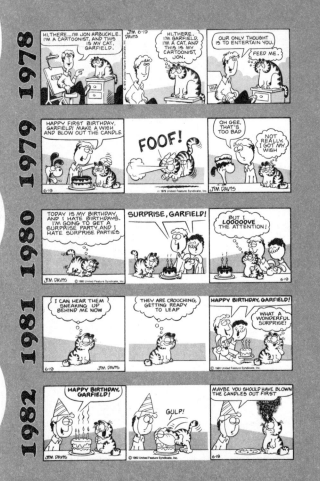

1987

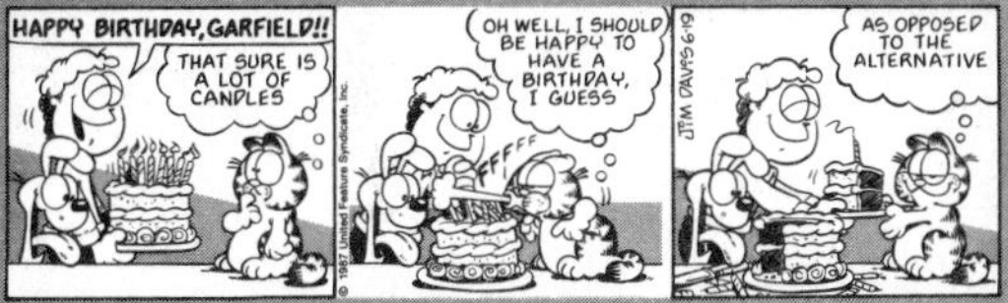
HAPPY BIRTHDAY, GARFIELD!!
THAT SURE IS A LOT OF CANDLES
OH WELL, I SHOULD BE HAPPY TO HAVE A BIRTHDAY, I GUESS
FFFFF
AS OPPOSED TO THE ALTERNATIVE
JIM DAVIS 6-19

1988

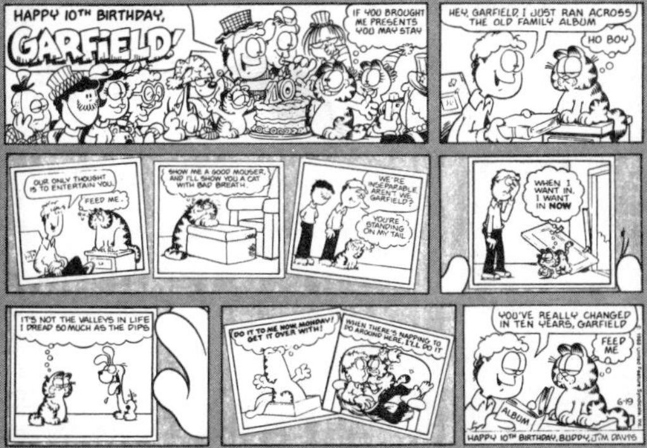
HAPPY 10TH BIRTHDAY,
GARFIELD!
IF YOU BROUGHT ME PRESENTS YOU MAY STAY
HEY, GARFIELD, I JUST RAN ACROSS THE OLD FAMILY ALBUM
HO BOY
OUR ONLY THOUGHT IS TO ENTERTAIN YOU.
FEED ME.
SHOW ME A GOOD MOUSER, AND I'LL SHOW YOU A CAT WITH BAD BREATH.
WE'RE INSEPARABLE AREN'T WE, GARFIELD?
YOU'RE STANDING ON MY TAIL
WHEN I WANT IN, I WANT IN NOW
IT'S NOT THE VALLEYS IN LIFE I DREAD SO MUCH AS THE DIPS
DO IT TO ME NOW MONDAY! GET IT OVER WITH!
WHEN THERE'S NAPPING TO DO AROUND HERE, I'LL DO IT
YOU'VE REALLY CHANGED IN TEN YEARS, GARFIELD
FEED ME
ALBUM
6-19
HAPPY 10TH BIRTHDAY, BUDDY, JIM DAVIS

1989

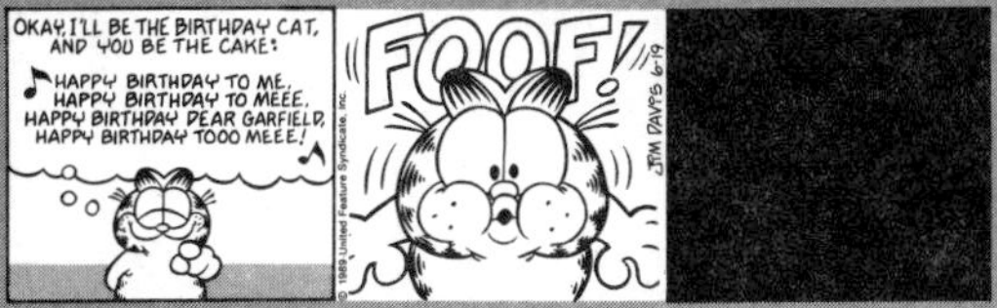
OKAY, I'LL BE THE BIRTHDAY CAT, AND YOU BE THE CAKE:
HAPPY BIRTHDAY TO ME,
HAPPY BIRTHDAY TO MEEE,
HAPPY BIRTHDAY DEAR GARFIELD,
HAPPY BIRTHDAY TOOO MEEE!
FOOF!
JIM DAVIS 6-19

1990

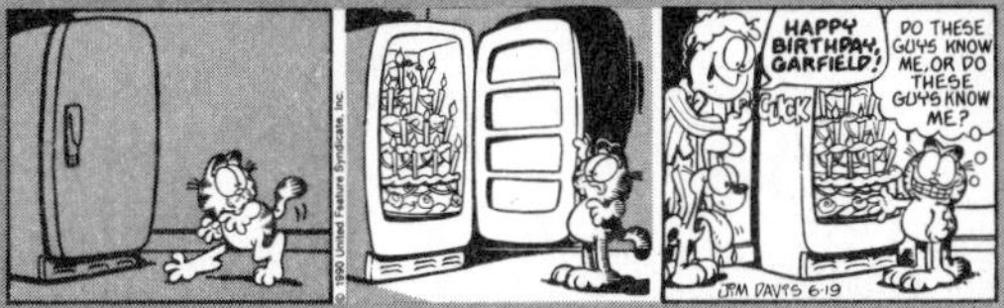
HAPPY BIRTHDAY, GARFIELD!
CLICK
DO THESE GUYS KNOW ME, OR DO THESE GUYS KNOW ME?
JIM DAVIS 6-19

1991

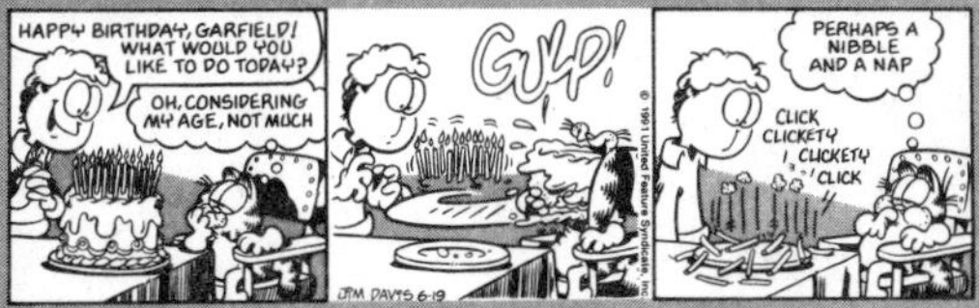
HAPPY BIRTHDAY, GARFIELD! WHAT WOULD YOU LIKE TO DO TODAY?
OH, CONSIDERING MY AGE, NOT MUCH
GULP!
JIM DAVIS 6-19
PERHAPS A NIBBLE AND A NAP
CLICK CLICKETY CLICKETY CLICK

1992

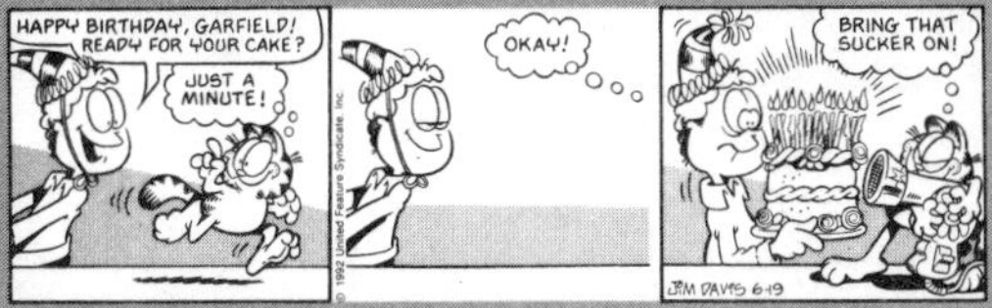
HAPPY BIRTHDAY, GARFIELD! READY FOR YOUR CAKE?
JUST A MINUTE!
OKAY!
BRING THAT SUCKER ON!
JIM DAVIS 6-19

1993

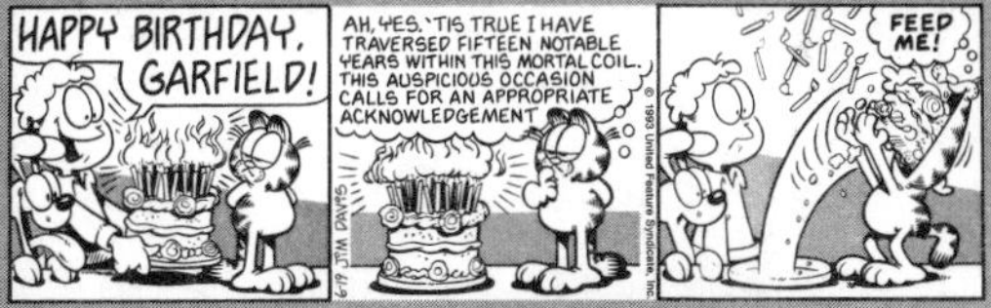
HAPPY BIRTHDAY, GARFIELD!
AH, YES. 'TIS TRUE I HAVE TRAVERSED FIFTEEN NOTABLE YEARS WITHIN THIS MORTAL COIL. THIS AUSPICIOUS OCCASION CALLS FOR AN APPROPRIATE ACKNOWLEDGEMENT
6-19 JIM DAVIS
FEED ME!

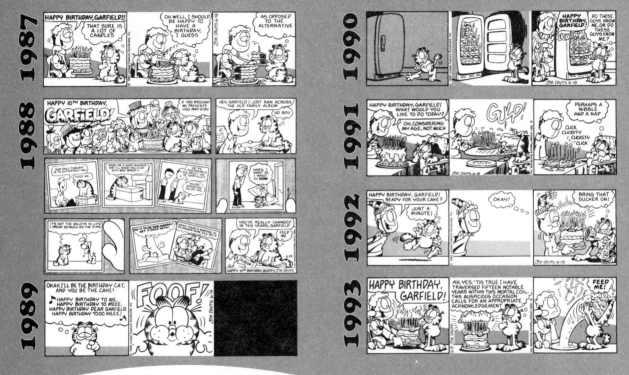

Feast your eyes on the Garfield Birthday Gallery. The famished feline has been perfecting the art of eating for fifteen years now. That's a bellyful of laughs and lasagna. And rest assured that the Picasso of cats will continue to color your world with fun for many years to come.

**15 CELEBRATING Fabulous Years!**
**1978·1993**

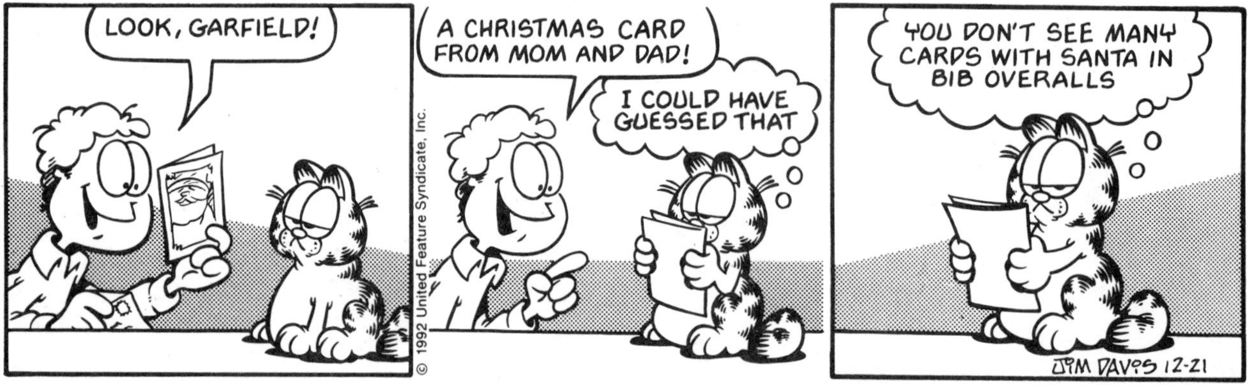
LOOK, GARFIELD!
A CHRISTMAS CARD FROM MOM AND DAD!
I COULD HAVE GUESSED THAT
YOU DON'T SEE MANY CARDS WITH SANTA IN BIB OVERALLS
© 1992 United Feature Syndicate, Inc.
JIM DAVIS 12-21

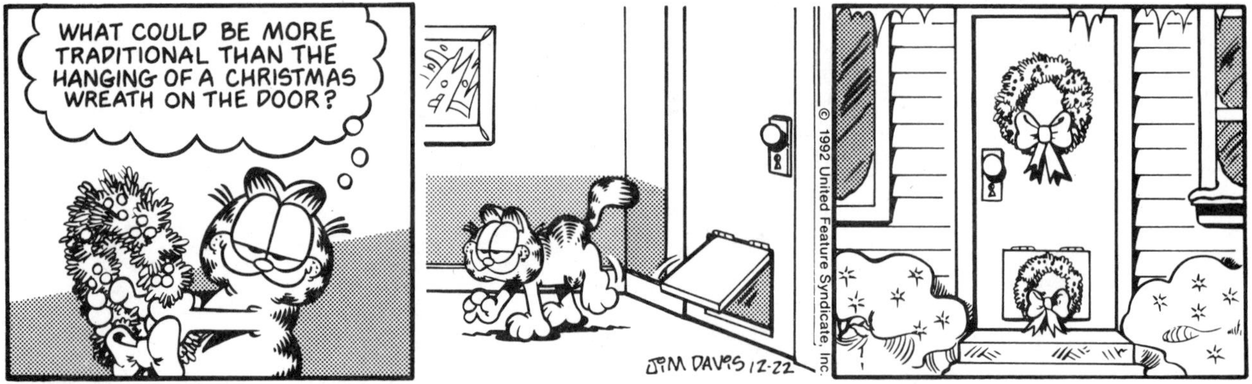
WHAT COULD BE MORE TRADITIONAL THAN THE HANGING OF A CHRISTMAS WREATH ON THE DOOR?
© 1992 United Feature Syndicate, Inc.
JIM DAVIS 12-22

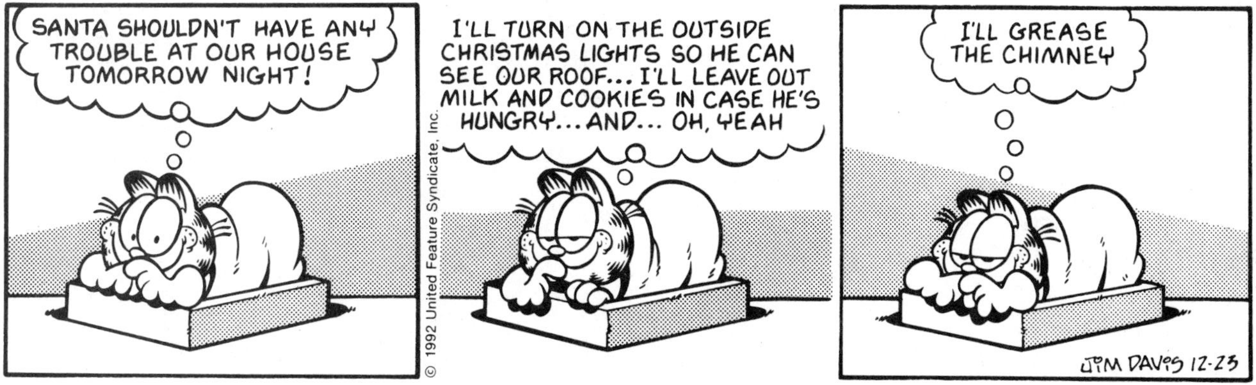
SANTA SHOULDN'T HAVE ANY TROUBLE AT OUR HOUSE TOMORROW NIGHT!
I'LL TURN ON THE OUTSIDE CHRISTMAS LIGHTS SO HE CAN SEE OUR ROOF... I'LL LEAVE OUT MILK AND COOKIES IN CASE HE'S HUNGRY... AND... OH, YEAH
I'LL GREASE THE CHIMNEY
JIM DAVIS 12-23
© 1992 United Feature Syndicate, Inc.

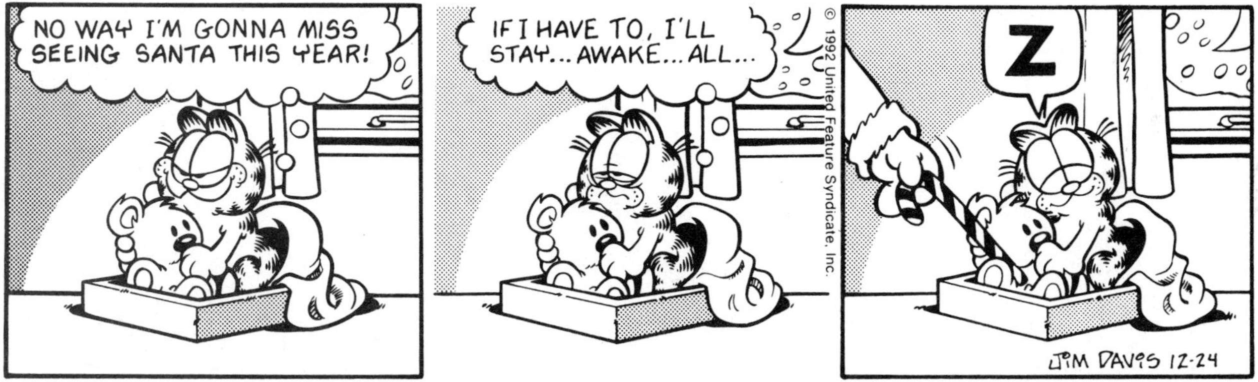
NO WAY I'M GONNA MISS SEEING SANTA THIS YEAR!
IF I HAVE TO, I'LL STAY... AWAKE... ALL...
Z
JIM DAVIS 12-24
© 1992 United Feature Syndicate, Inc.

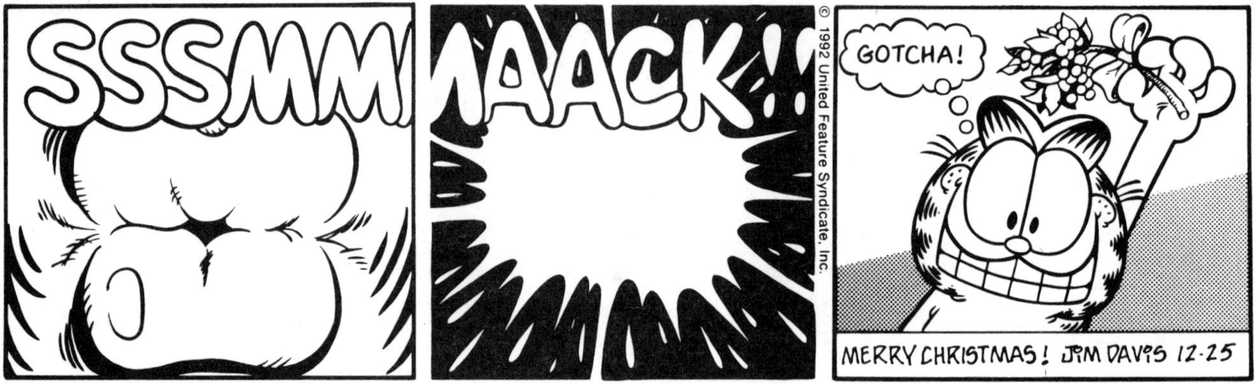
SSSMMMAACK!!
© 1992 United Feature Syndicate, Inc.
GOTCHA!
MERRY CHRISTMAS! JIM DAVIS 12-25

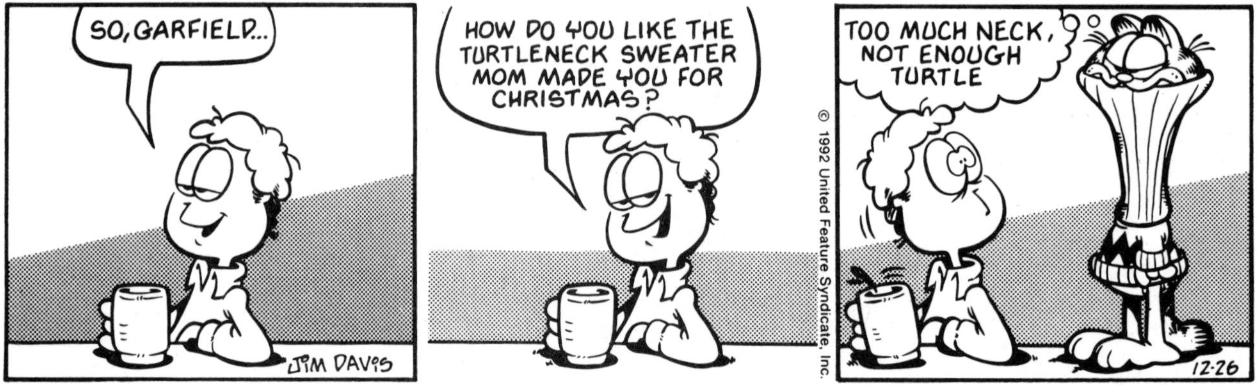
SO, GARFIELD...
JIM DAVIS
HOW DO YOU LIKE THE TURTLENECK SWEATER MOM MADE YOU FOR CHRISTMAS?
© 1992 United Feature Syndicate, Inc.
TOO MUCH NECK, NOT ENOUGH TURTLE
12-26

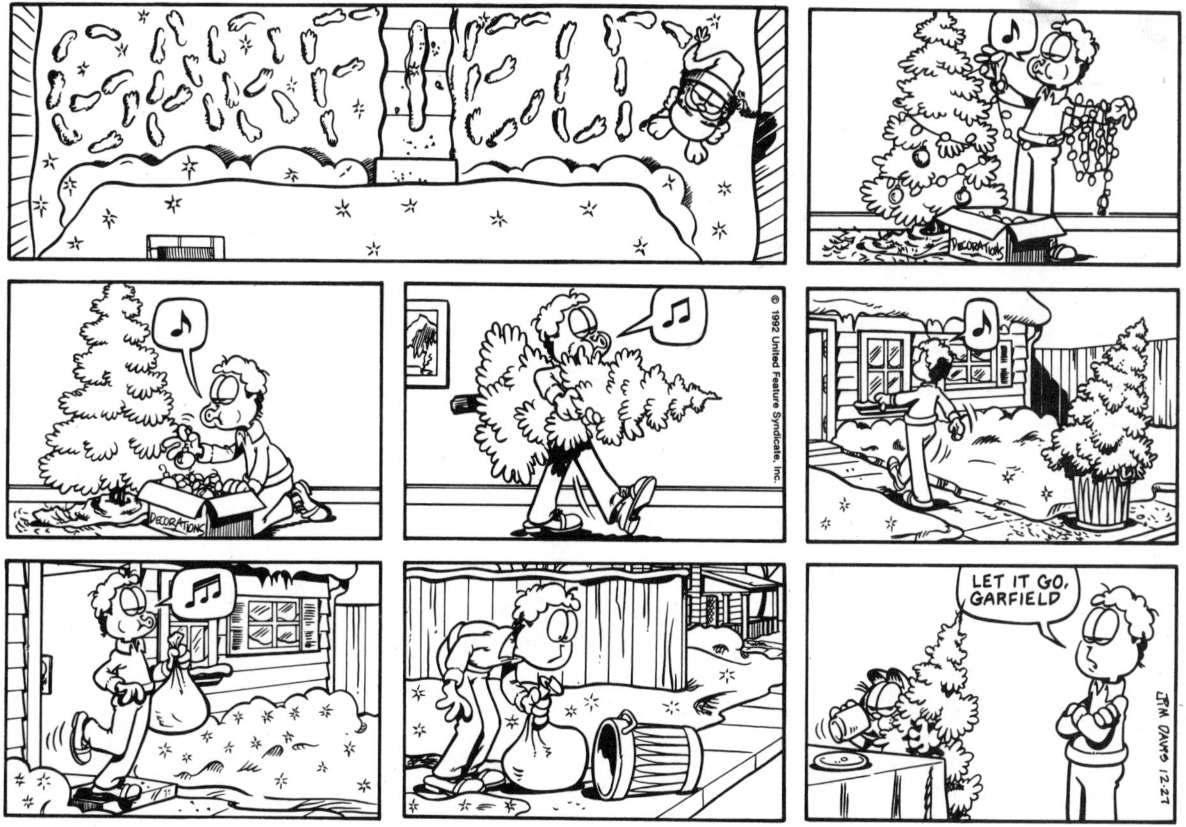
GARFIELD
DECORATIONS
DECORATIONS
© 1992 United Feature Syndicate, Inc.
LET IT GO, GARFIELD
JIM DAVIS 12-27

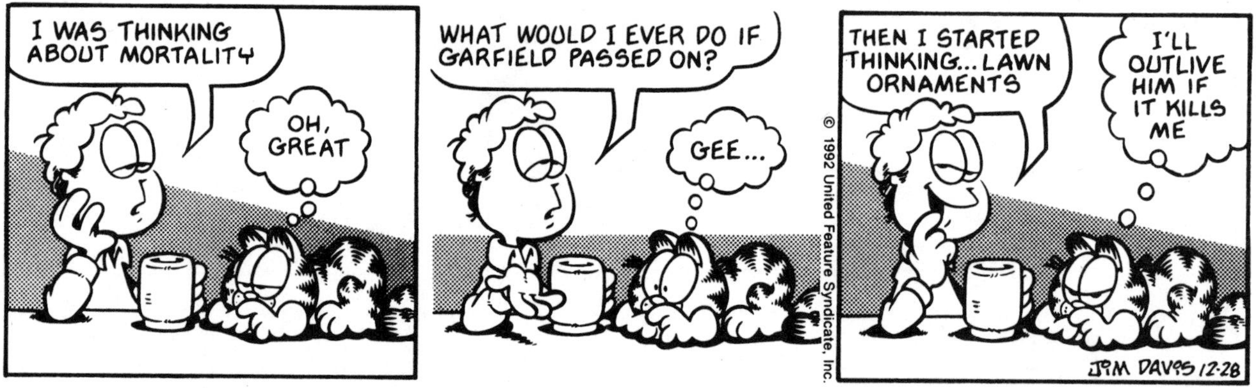
I WAS THINKING ABOUT MORTALITY
OH, GREAT
WHAT WOULD I EVER DO IF GARFIELD PASSED ON?
GEE...
THEN I STARTED THINKING... LAWN ORNAMENTS
I'LL OUTLIVE HIM IF IT KILLS ME
JIM DAVIS 12-28



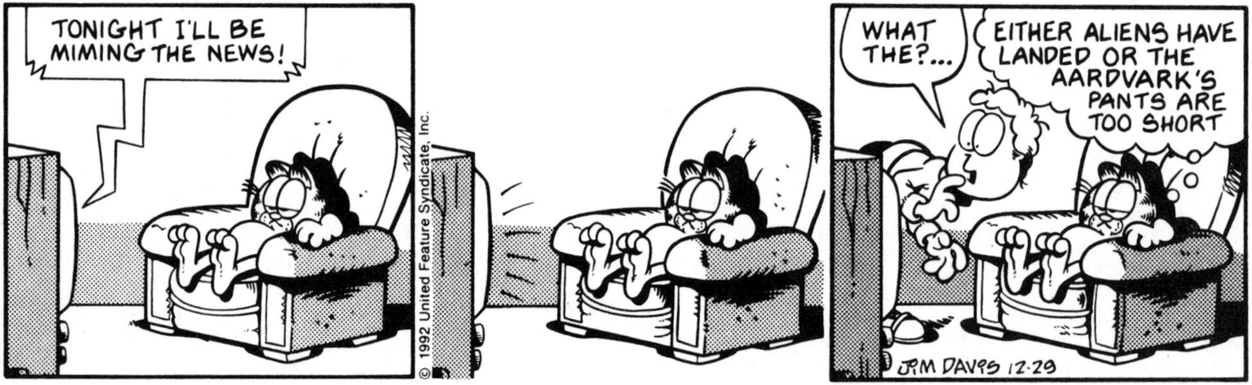
TONIGHT I'LL BE MIMING THE NEWS!
WHAT THE?...
EITHER ALIENS HAVE LANDED OR THE AARDVARK'S PANTS ARE TOO SHORT
JIM DAVIS 12-29

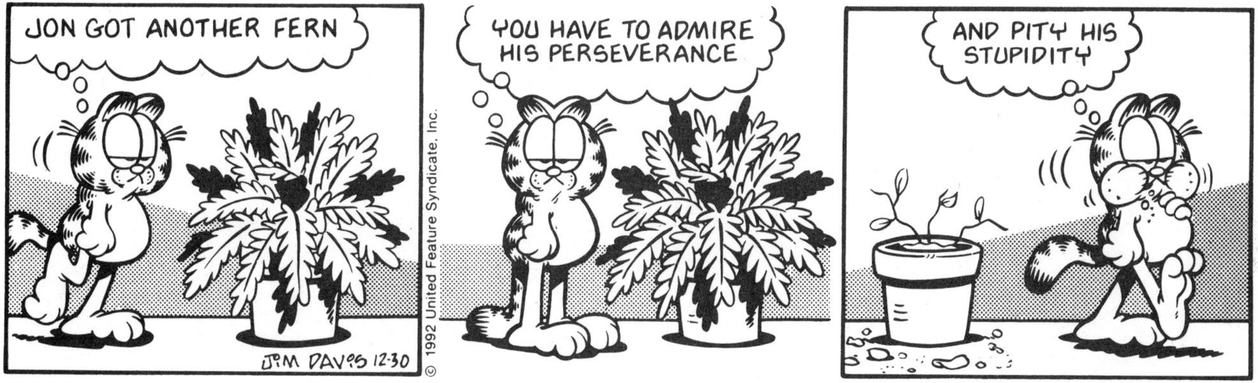
JON GOT ANOTHER FERN
YOU HAVE TO ADMIRE HIS PERSEVERANCE
AND PITY HIS STUPIDITY
JIM DAVIS 12-30
© 1992 United Feature Syndicate, Inc.

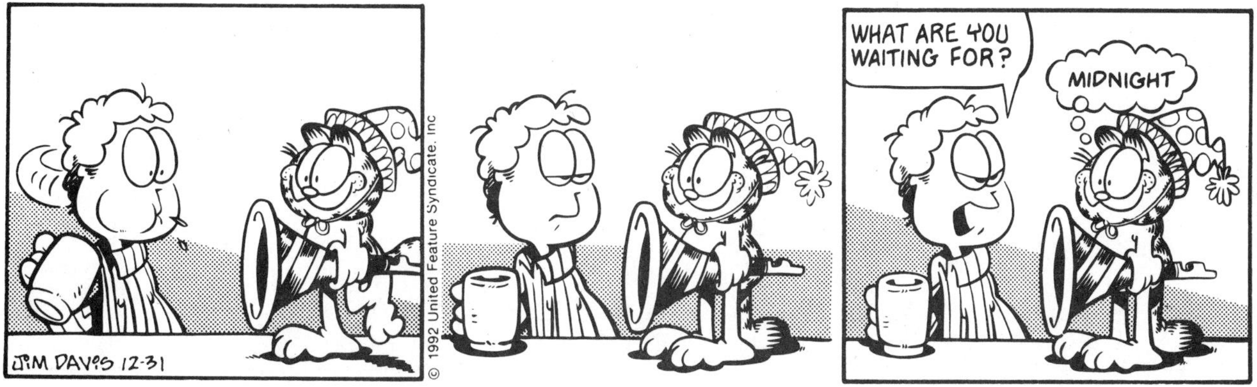
JIM DAVIS 12-31
© 1992 United Feature Syndicate, Inc.
WHAT ARE YOU WAITING FOR?
MIDNIGHT

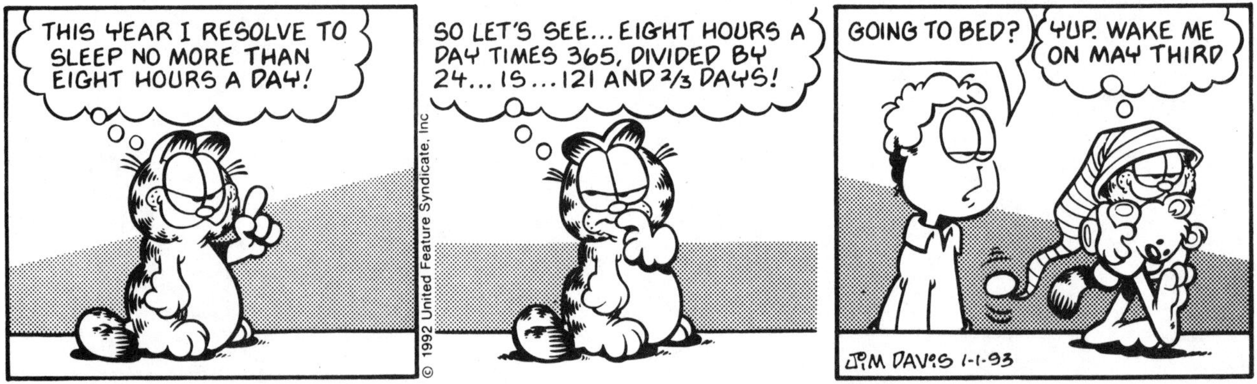
THIS YEAR I RESOLVE TO SLEEP NO MORE THAN EIGHT HOURS A DAY!
© 1992 United Feature Syndicate, Inc
SO LET'S SEE... EIGHT HOURS A DAY TIMES 365, DIVIDED BY 24... IS... 121 AND 2/3 DAYS!
GOING TO BED?
YUP. WAKE ME ON MAY THIRD
JIM DAVIS 1-1-93

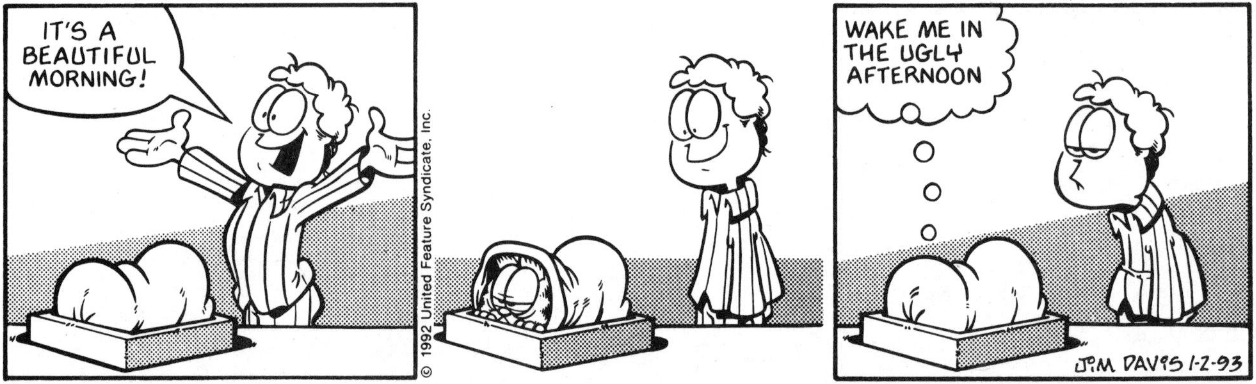
IT'S A BEAUTIFUL MORNING!
© 1992 United Feature Syndicate, Inc.
WAKE ME IN THE UGLY AFTERNOON
JIM DAVIS 1-2-93

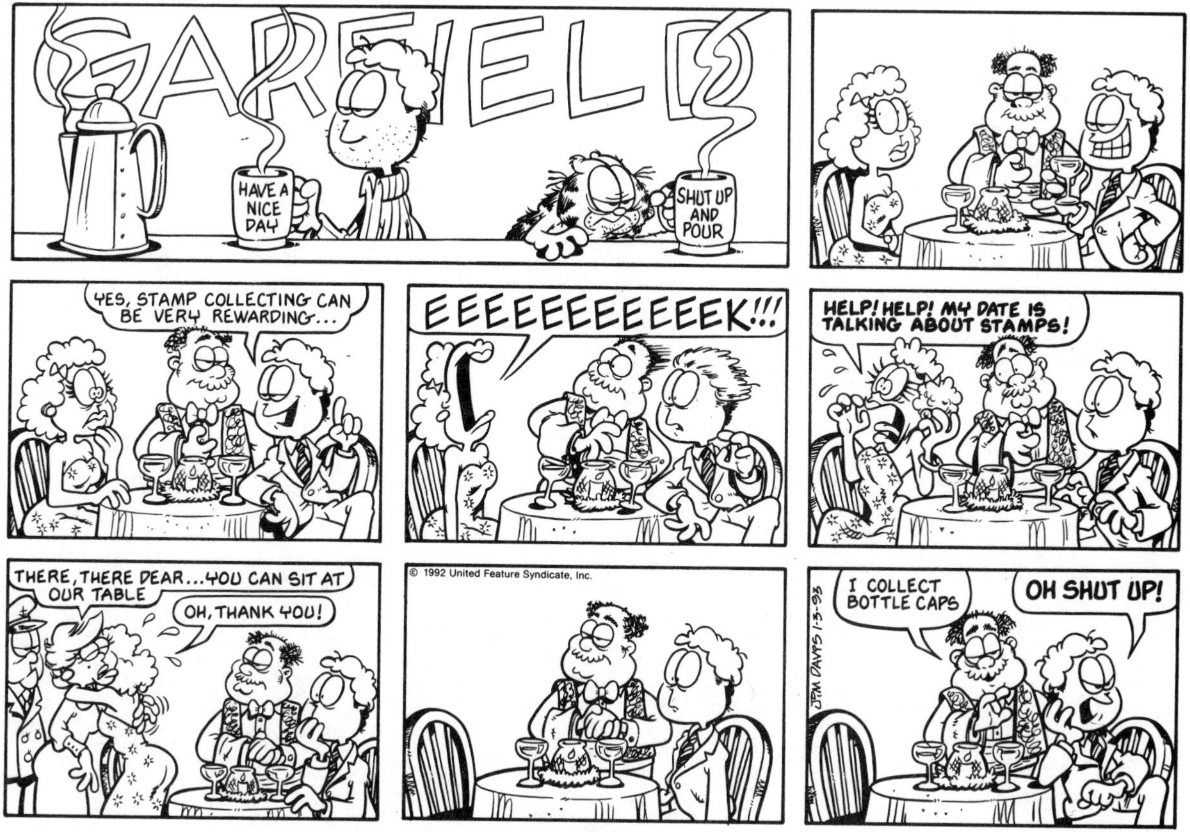
GARFIELD
HAVE A NICE DAY
SHUT UP AND POUR
YES, STAMP COLLECTING CAN BE VERY REWARDING...
EEEEEEEEEEEEK!!!
HELP! HELP! MY DATE IS TALKING ABOUT STAMPS!
THERE, THERE DEAR...YOU CAN SIT AT OUR TABLE
OH, THANK YOU!
© 1992 United Feature Syndicate, Inc.
JPM DAVIS 1-3-93
I COLLECT BOTTLE CAPS
OH SHUT UP!

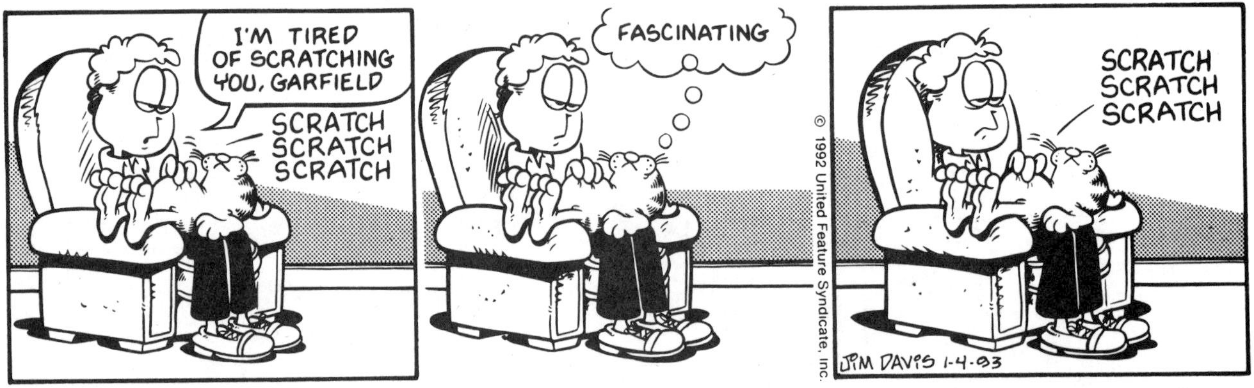
I'M TIRED OF SCRATCHING YOU, GARFIELD
SCRATCH SCRATCH SCRATCH
FASCINATING
© 1992 United Feature Syndicate, Inc.
SCRATCH SCRATCH SCRATCH
JIM DAVIS 1-4-93

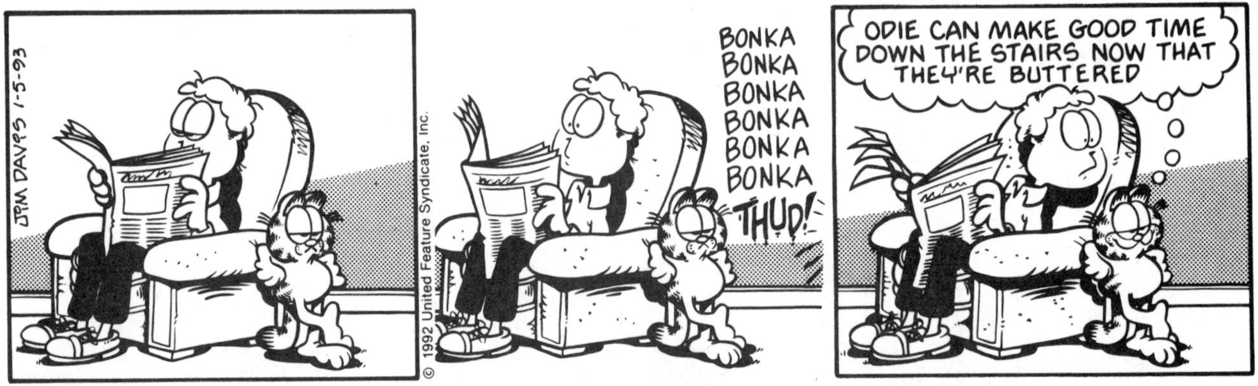
JIM DAVIS 1-5-93
© 1992 United Feature Syndicate, Inc.
BONKA BONKA BONKA BONKA BONKA BONKA BONKA
THUD!
ODIE CAN MAKE GOOD TIME DOWN THE STAIRS NOW THAT THEY'RE BUTTERED

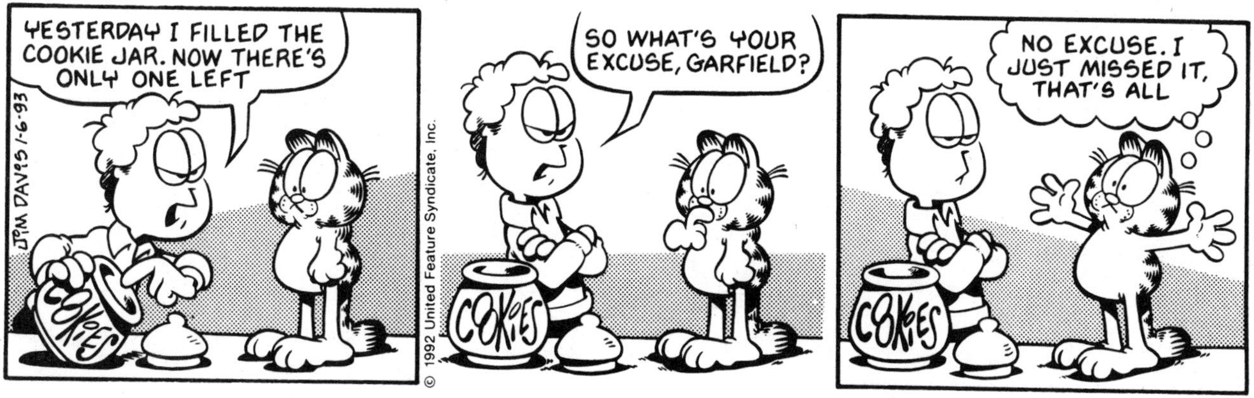
YESTERDAY I FILLED THE COOKIE JAR. NOW THERE'S ONLY ONE LEFT
JIM DAVIS 1-6-93
COOKIES
SO WHAT'S YOUR EXCUSE, GARFIELD?
COOKIES
NO EXCUSE. I JUST MISSED IT, THAT'S ALL
COOKIES


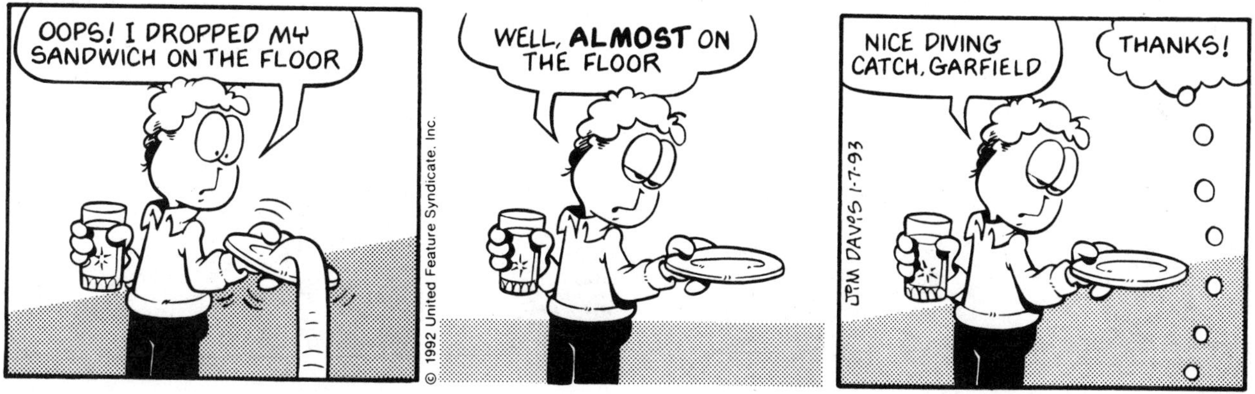
OOPS! I DROPPED MY SANDWICH ON THE FLOOR
WELL, **ALMOST** ON THE FLOOR
NICE DIVING CATCH, GARFIELD
THANKS!
JIM DAVIS 1-7-93

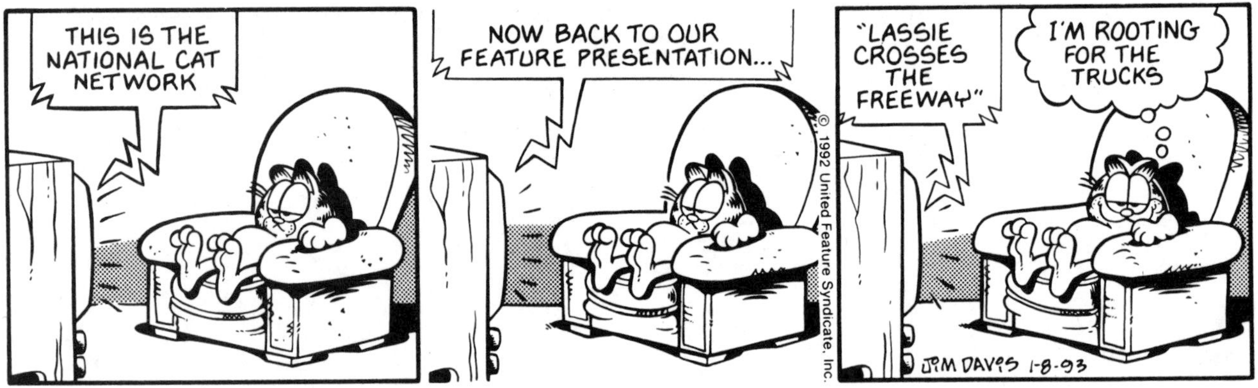
THIS IS THE NATIONAL CAT NETWORK
NOW BACK TO OUR FEATURE PRESENTATION...
"LASSIE CROSSES THE FREEWAY"
I'M ROOTING FOR THE TRUCKS
© 1992 United Feature Syndicate, Inc.
JIM DAVIS 1-8-93

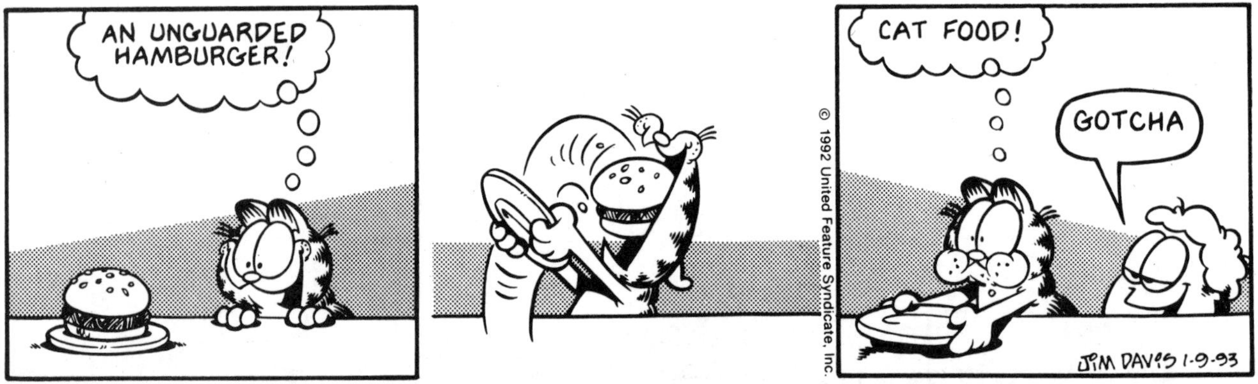
AN UNGUARDED HAMBURGER!
CAT FOOD!
GOTCHA
© 1992 United Feature Syndicate, Inc.
JIM DAVIS 1-9-93

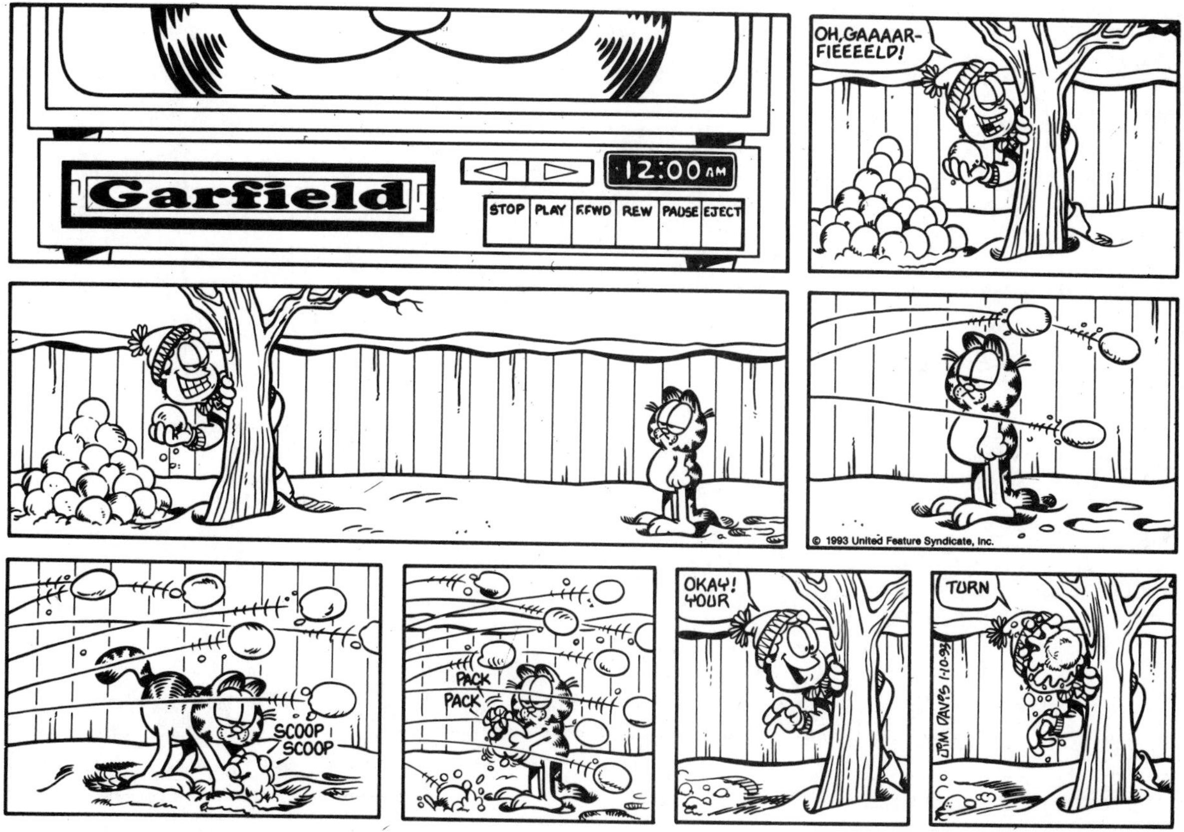
Garfield
12:00 AM
STOP
PLAY
F.FWD
REW
PAUSE
EJECT
OH, GAAAAR-FIEEEELD!
© 1993 United Feature Syndicate, Inc.
SCOOP SCOOP
PACK PACK
OKAY! YOUR
TURN
JIM DAVIS 1-10-93

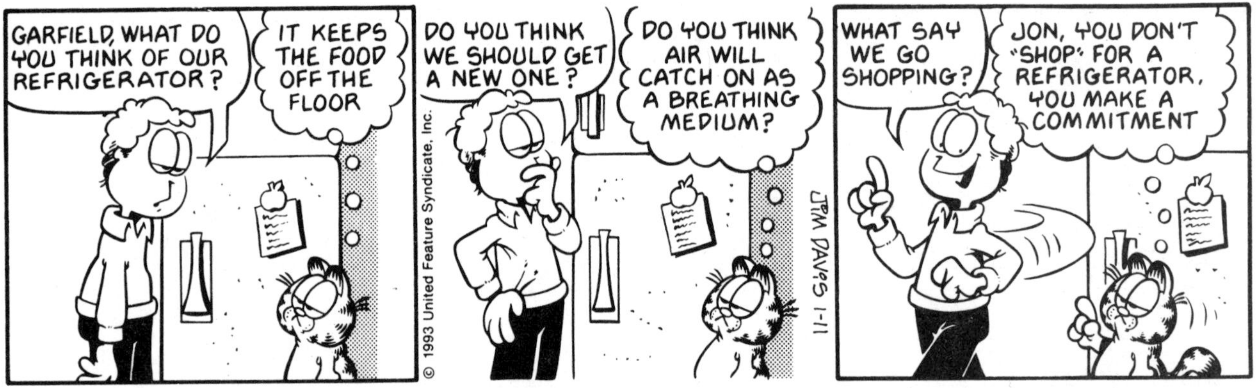
GARFIELD, WHAT DO YOU THINK OF OUR REFRIGERATOR?
IT KEEPS THE FOOD OFF THE FLOOR
DO YOU THINK WE SHOULD GET A NEW ONE?
DO YOU THINK AIR WILL CATCH ON AS A BREATHING MEDIUM?
WHAT SAY WE GO SHOPPING?
JON, YOU DON'T "SHOP" FOR A REFRIGERATOR, YOU MAKE A COMMITMENT
© 1993 United Feature Syndicate, Inc.
JIM DAVIS 1-11

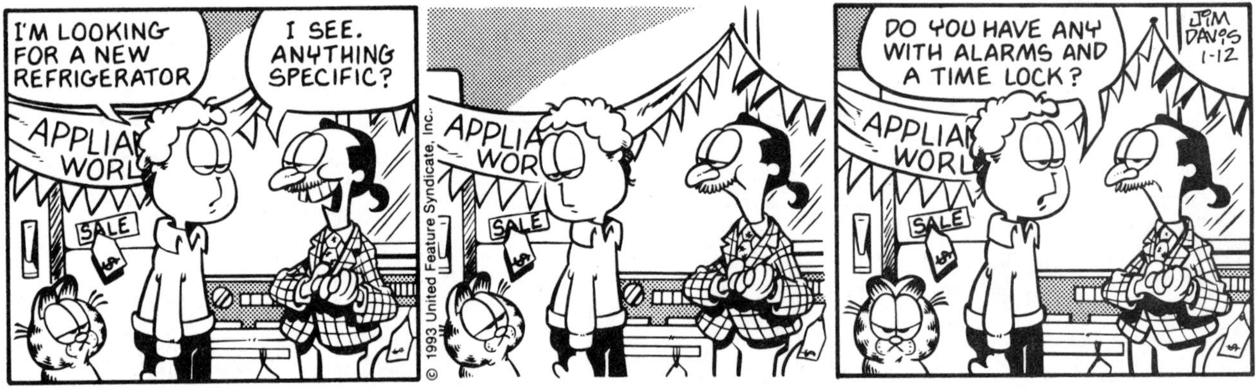
I'M LOOKING FOR A NEW REFRIGERATOR
I SEE. ANYTHING SPECIFIC?
APPLIA WORL
SALE
DO YOU HAVE ANY WITH ALARMS AND A TIME LOCK?
© 1993 United Feature Syndicate, Inc.
JIM DAVIS 1-12

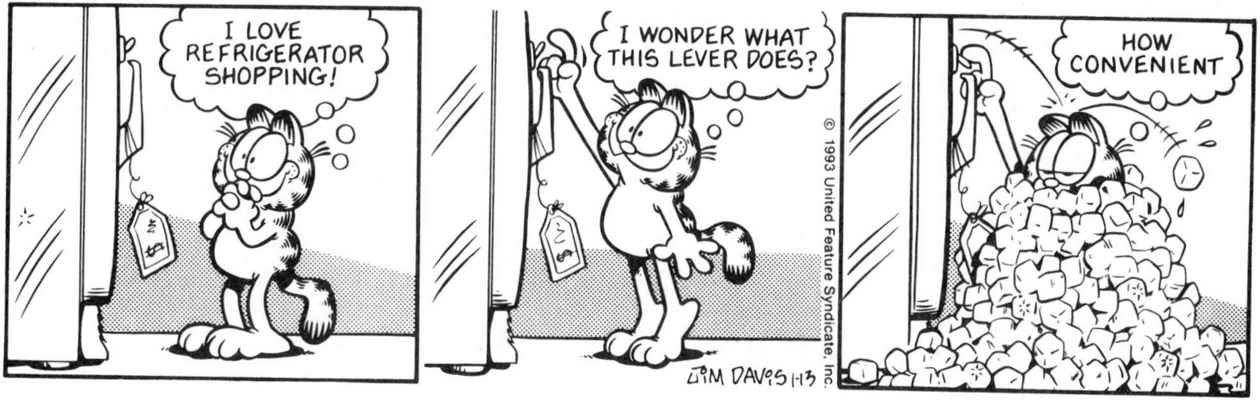
I LOVE REFRIGERATOR SHOPPING!
I WONDER WHAT THIS LEVER DOES?
HOW CONVENIENT
JIM DAVIS 1-13
© 1993 United Feature Syndicate, Inc.

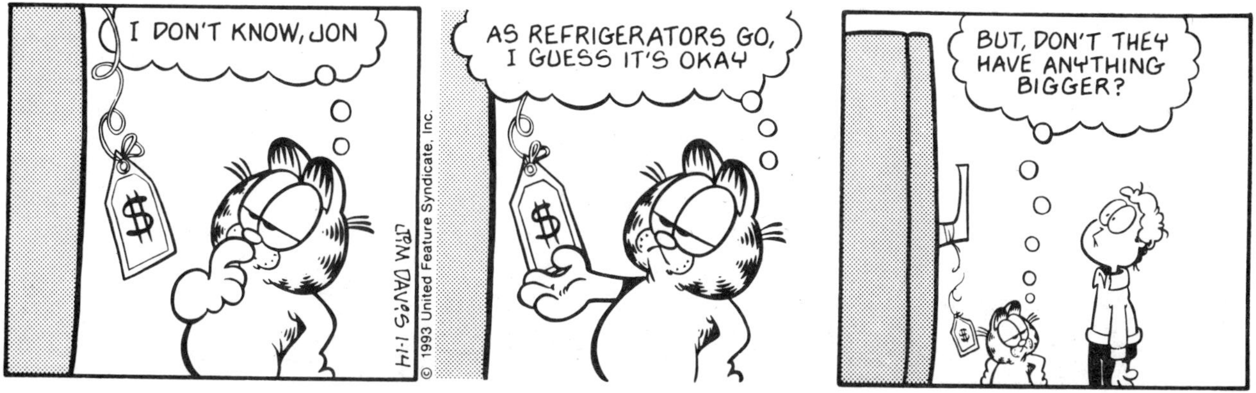
I DON'T KNOW, JON
AS REFRIGERATORS GO, I GUESS IT'S OKAY
BUT, DON'T THEY HAVE ANYTHING BIGGER?
JIM DAVIS 1-14
© 1993 United Feature Syndicate, Inc.

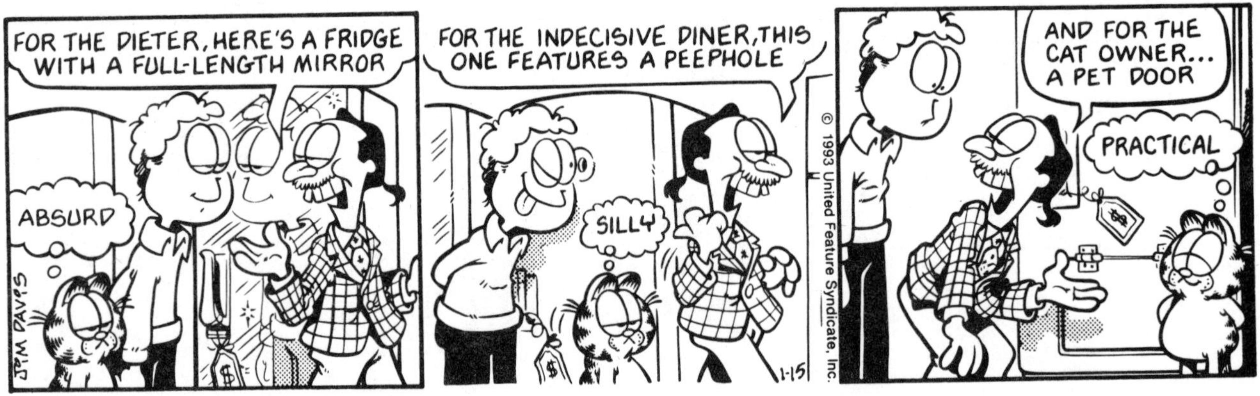
FOR THE DIETER, HERE'S A FRIDGE WITH A FULL-LENGTH MIRROR
ABSURD
JIM DAVIS
FOR THE INDECISIVE DINER, THIS ONE FEATURES A PEEPHOLE
SILLY
1-15
© 1993 United Feature Syndicate, Inc.
AND FOR THE CAT OWNER... A PET DOOR
PRACTICAL

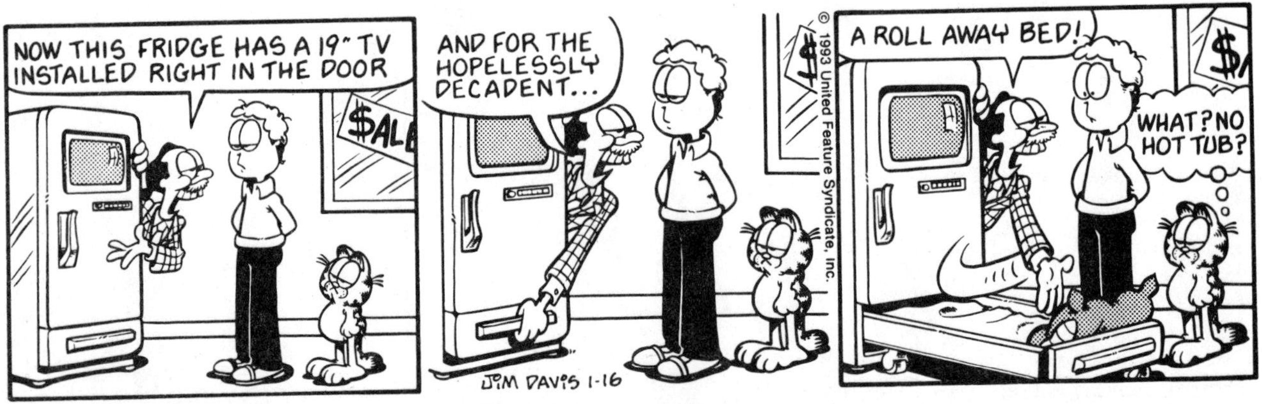
NOW THIS FRIDGE HAS A 19" TV INSTALLED RIGHT IN THE DOOR
$ALE
AND FOR THE HOPELESSLY DECADENT...
JIM DAVIS 1-16
© 1993 United Feature Syndicate, Inc.
A ROLL AWAY BED!
WHAT? NO HOT TUB?

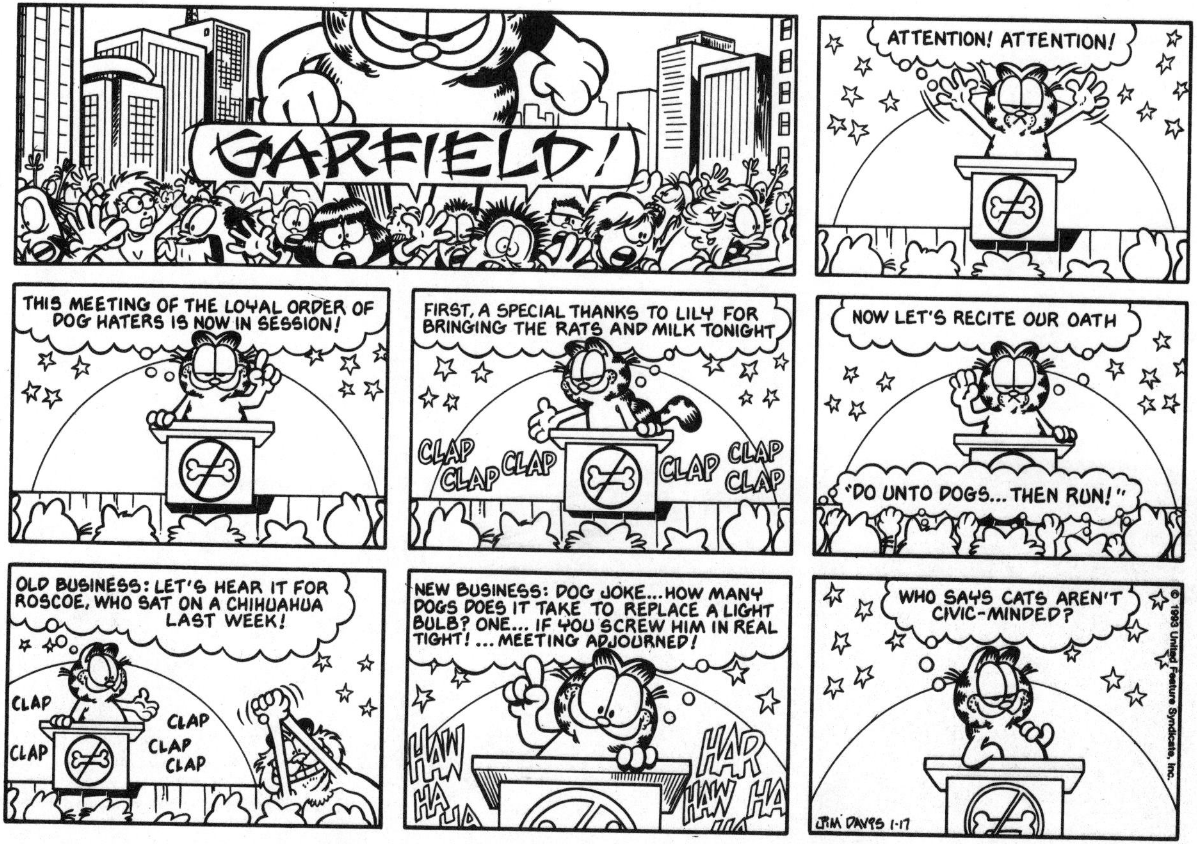
GARFIELD!
ATTENTION! ATTENTION!
THIS MEETING OF THE LOYAL ORDER OF DOG HATERS IS NOW IN SESSION!
FIRST, A SPECIAL THANKS TO LILY FOR BRINGING THE RATS AND MILK TONIGHT
CLAP CLAP CLAP CLAP CLAP CLAP
NOW LET'S RECITE OUR OATH
"DO UNTO DOGS... THEN RUN!"
OLD BUSINESS: LET'S HEAR IT FOR ROSCOE, WHO SAT ON A CHIHUAHUA LAST WEEK!
CLAP CLAP CLAP CLAP CLAP
NEW BUSINESS: DOG JOKE... HOW MANY DOGS DOES IT TAKE TO REPLACE A LIGHT BULB? ONE... IF YOU SCREW HIM IN REAL TIGHT! ... MEETING ADJOURNED!
HAW HA HAR HAW HA
WHO SAYS CATS AREN'T CIVIC-MINDED?
© 1993 United Feature Syndicate, Inc.
JIM DAVIS 1-17

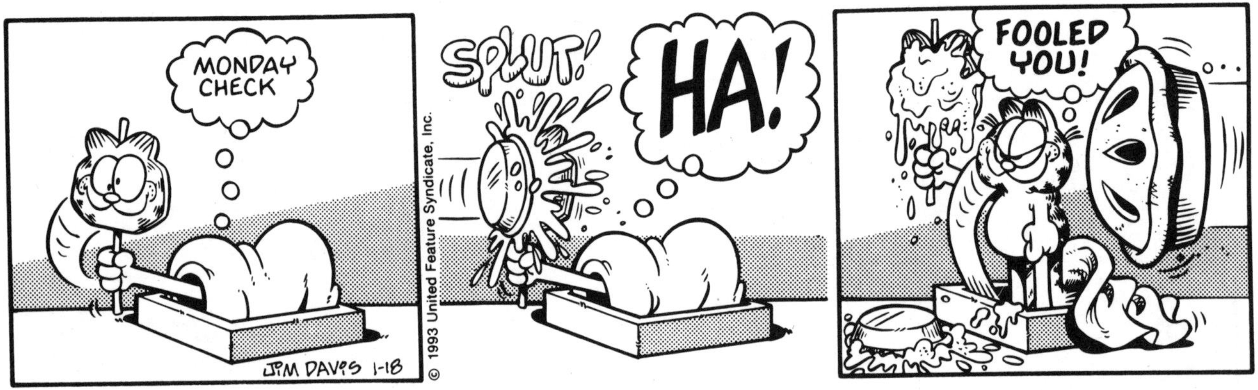
MONDAY CHECK
SPLUT!
HA!
FOOLED YOU!
O...
JIM DAVIS 1-18


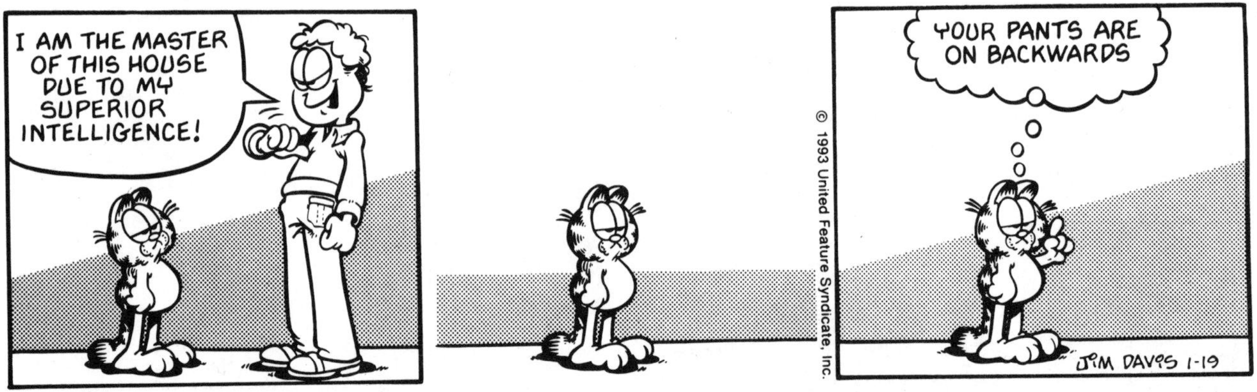
I AM THE MASTER OF THIS HOUSE DUE TO MY SUPERIOR INTELLIGENCE!
YOUR PANTS ARE ON BACKWARDS
JIM DAVIS 1-19

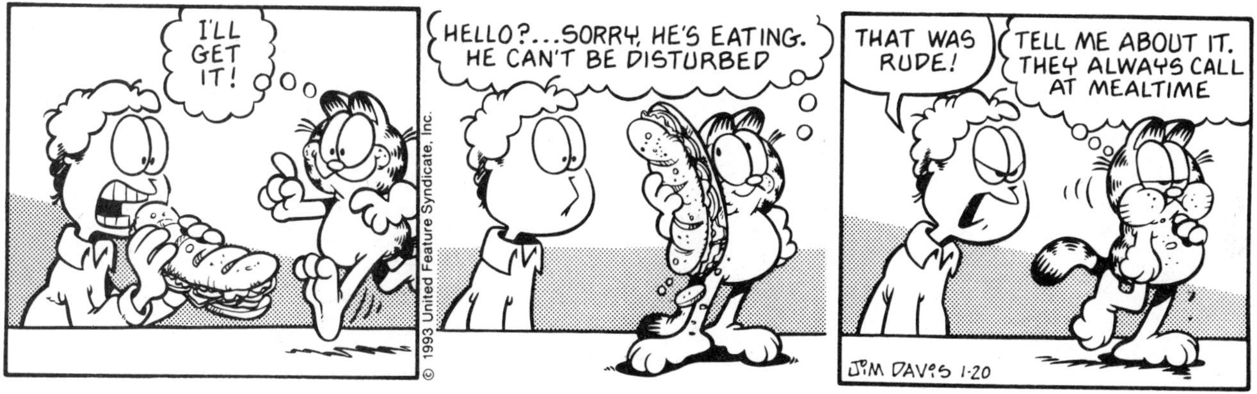
I'LL GET IT!
HELLO?...SORRY, HE'S EATING. HE CAN'T BE DISTURBED
THAT WAS RUDE!
TELL ME ABOUT IT. THEY ALWAYS CALL AT MEALTIME
JIM DAVIS 1-20


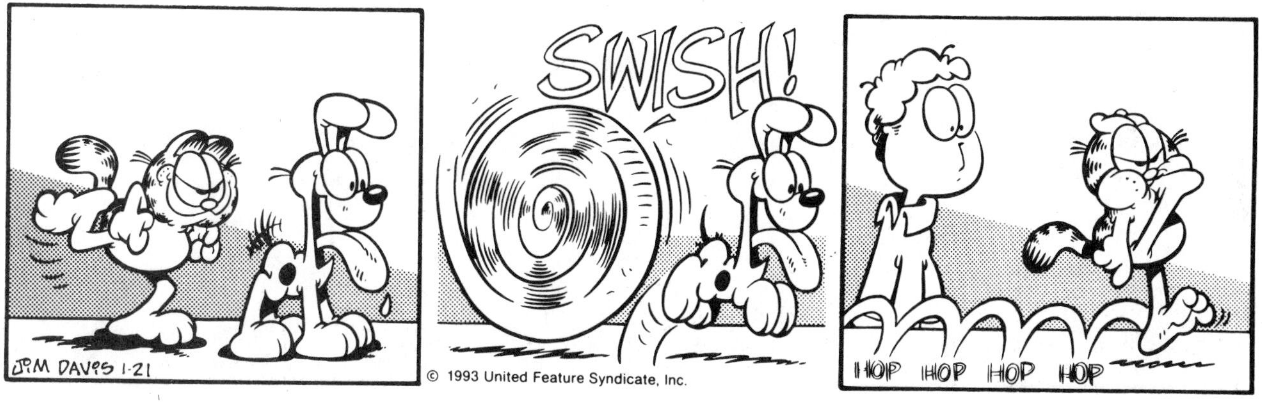
JIM DAVIS 1-21
SWISH!
HOP HOP HOP HOP

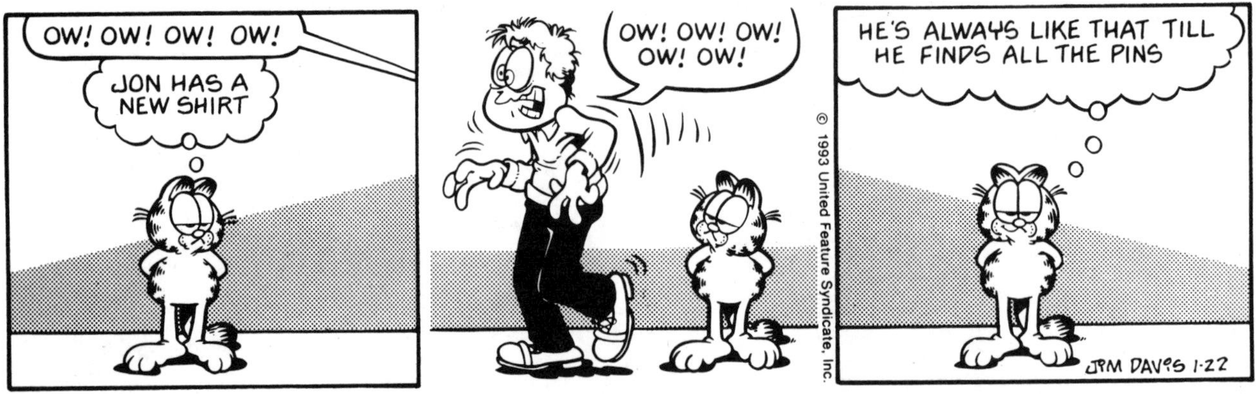
OW! OW! OW! OW!
JON HAS A NEW SHIRT
OW! OW! OW! OW! OW!
© 1993 United Feature Syndicate, Inc.
HE'S ALWAYS LIKE THAT TILL HE FINDS ALL THE PINS
JIM DAVIS 1-22

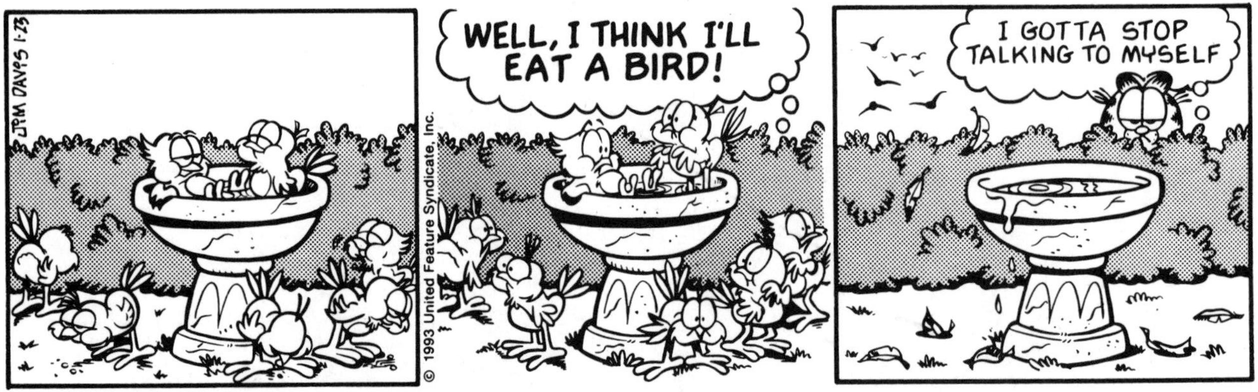
JIM DAVIS 1-23
© 1993 United Feature Syndicate, Inc.
WELL, I THINK I'LL EAT A BIRD!
I GOTTA STOP TALKING TO MYSELF

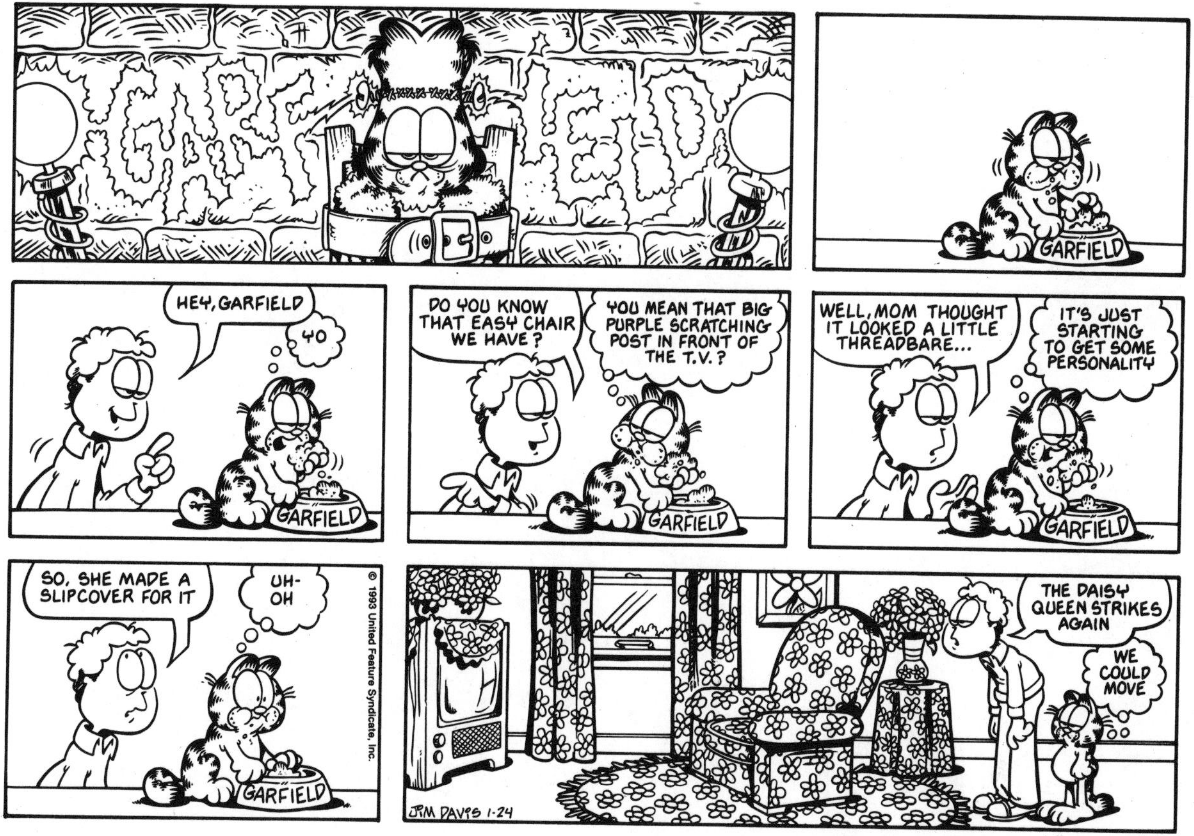
GARFIELD
HEY, GARFIELD
YO
DO YOU KNOW THAT EASY CHAIR WE HAVE?
YOU MEAN THAT BIG PURPLE SCRATCHING POST IN FRONT OF THE T.V.?
WELL, MOM THOUGHT IT LOOKED A LITTLE THREADBARE...
IT'S JUST STARTING TO GET SOME PERSONALITY
SO, SHE MADE A SLIPCOVER FOR IT
UH-OH
© 1993 United Feature Syndicate, Inc.
THE DAISY QUEEN STRIKES AGAIN
WE COULD MOVE
JIM DAVIS 1-24

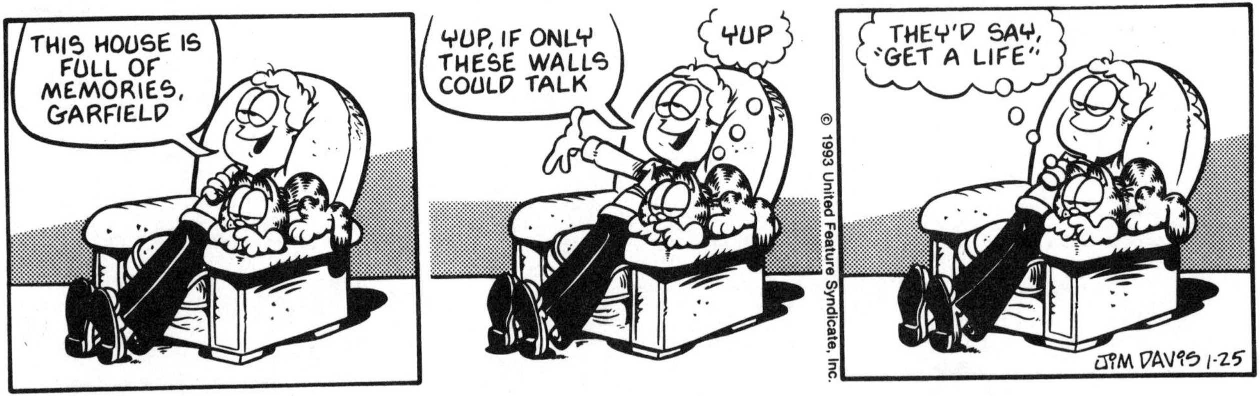
THIS HOUSE IS FULL OF MEMORIES, GARFIELD
YUP, IF ONLY THESE WALLS COULD TALK
YUP
THEY'D SAY, "GET A LIFE"
JIM DAVIS 1-25


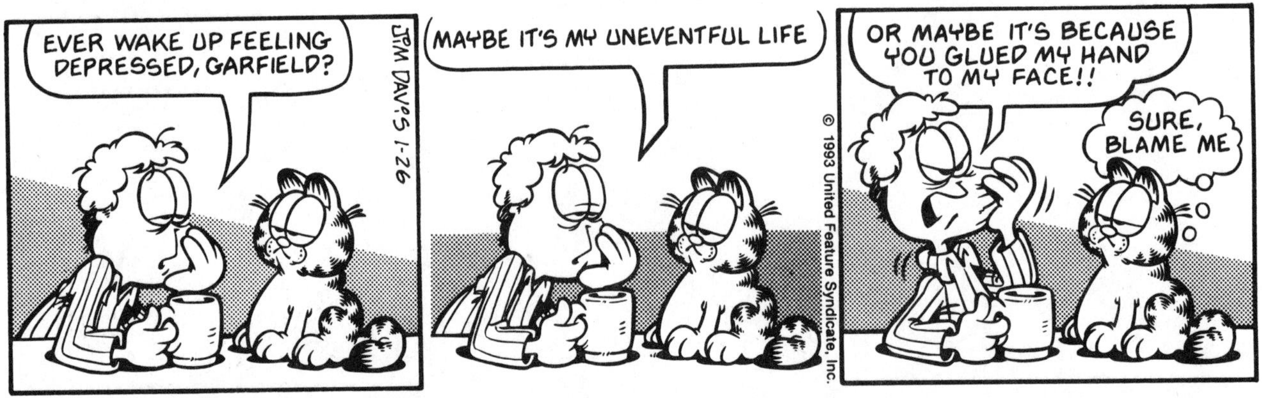
EVER WAKE UP FEELING DEPRESSED, GARFIELD?
JIM DAVIS 1-26
MAYBE IT'S MY UNEVENTFUL LIFE
OR MAYBE IT'S BECAUSE YOU GLUED MY HAND TO MY FACE!!
SURE, BLAME ME

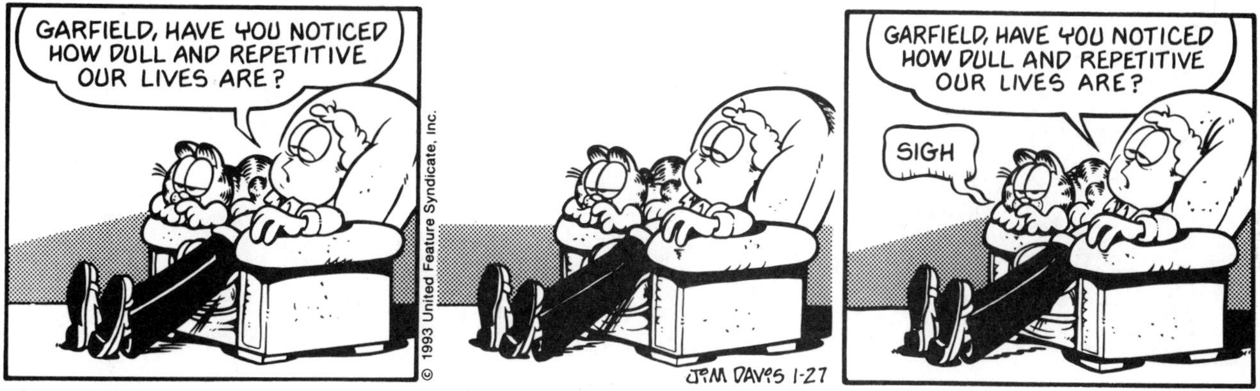
GARFIELD, HAVE YOU NOTICED HOW DULL AND REPETITIVE OUR LIVES ARE?
GARFIELD, HAVE YOU NOTICED HOW DULL AND REPETITIVE OUR LIVES ARE?
SIGH
JIM DAVIS 1-27
© 1993 United Feature Syndicate, Inc.

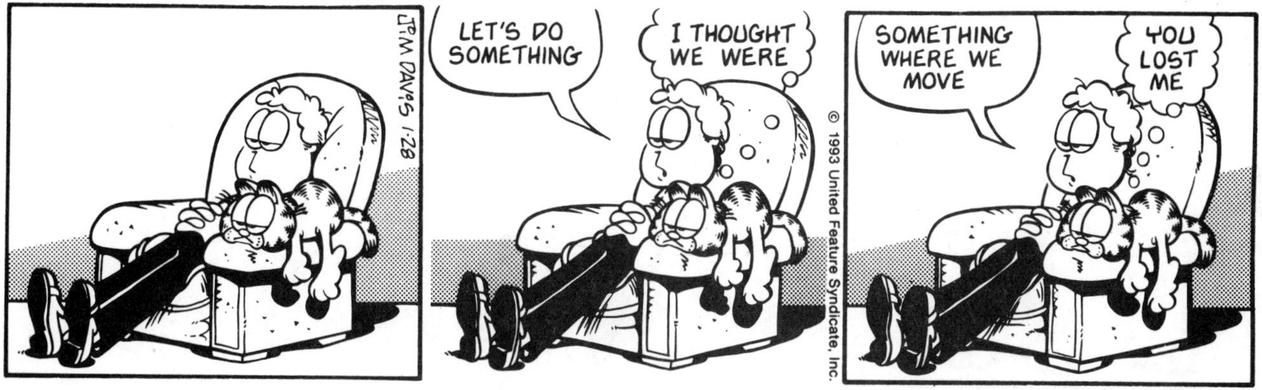
JIM DAVIS 1-28
LET'S DO SOMETHING
I THOUGHT WE WERE
SOMETHING WHERE WE MOVE
YOU LOST ME
© 1993 United Feature Syndicate, Inc.

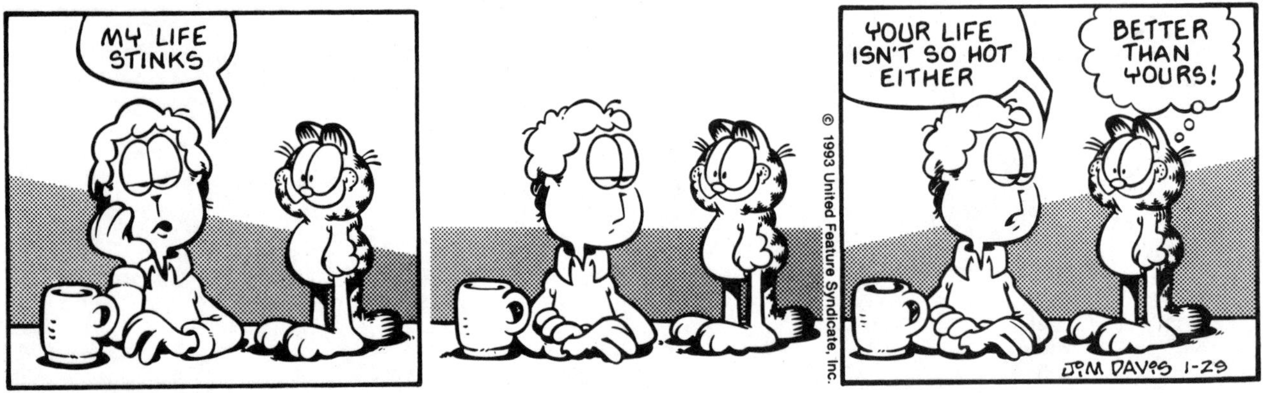
MY LIFE STINKS
YOUR LIFE ISN'T SO HOT EITHER
BETTER THAN YOURS!
JIM DAVIS 1-29
© 1993 United Feature Syndicate, Inc.

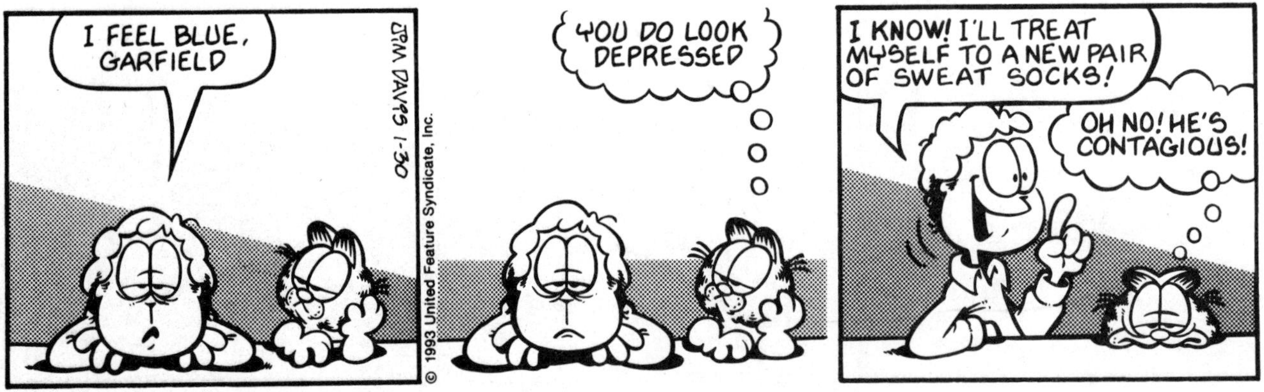
I FEEL BLUE, GARFIELD
YOU DO LOOK DEPRESSED
I KNOW! I'LL TREAT MYSELF TO A NEW PAIR OF SWEAT SOCKS!
OH NO! HE'S CONTAGIOUS!
JIM DAVIS 1-30
© 1993 United Feature Syndicate, Inc.

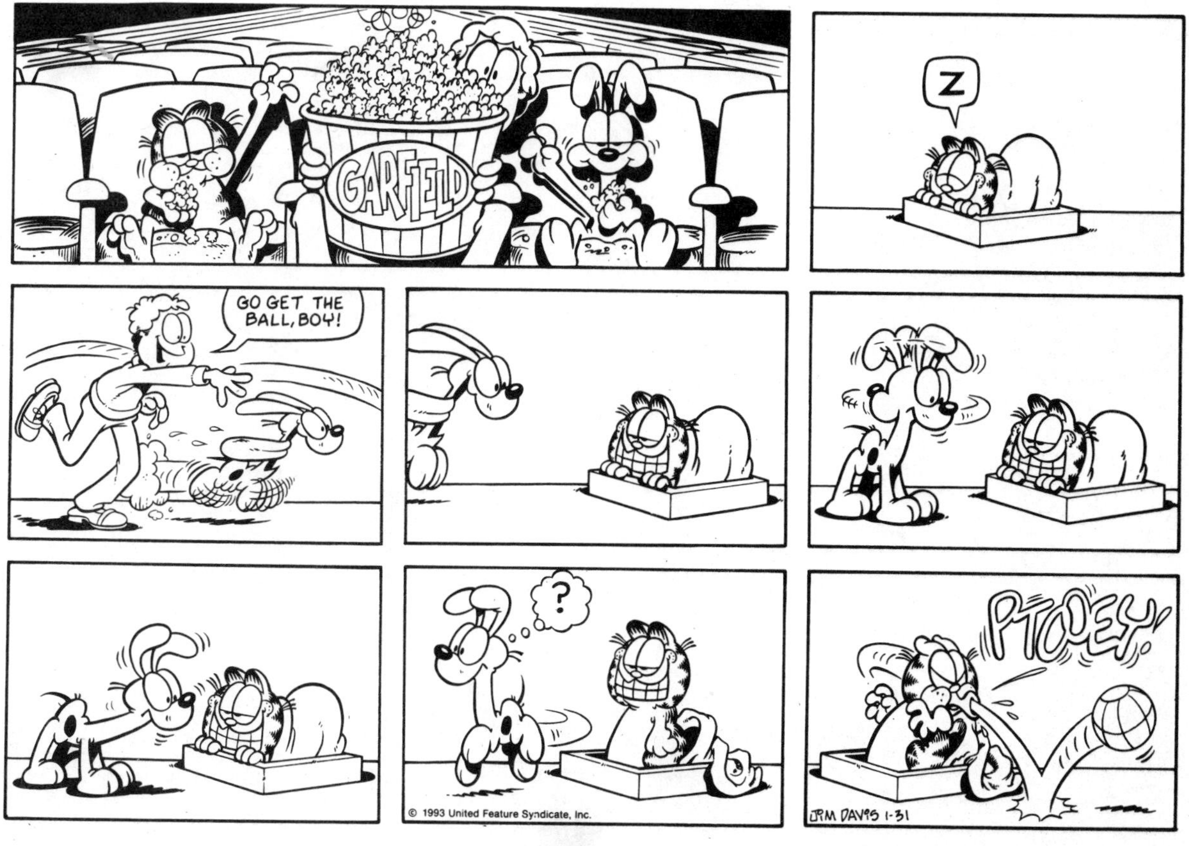
GARFIELD
Z
GO GET THE BALL, BOY!
?
PTOOEY!
© 1993 United Feature Syndicate, Inc.
JIM DAVIS 1-31

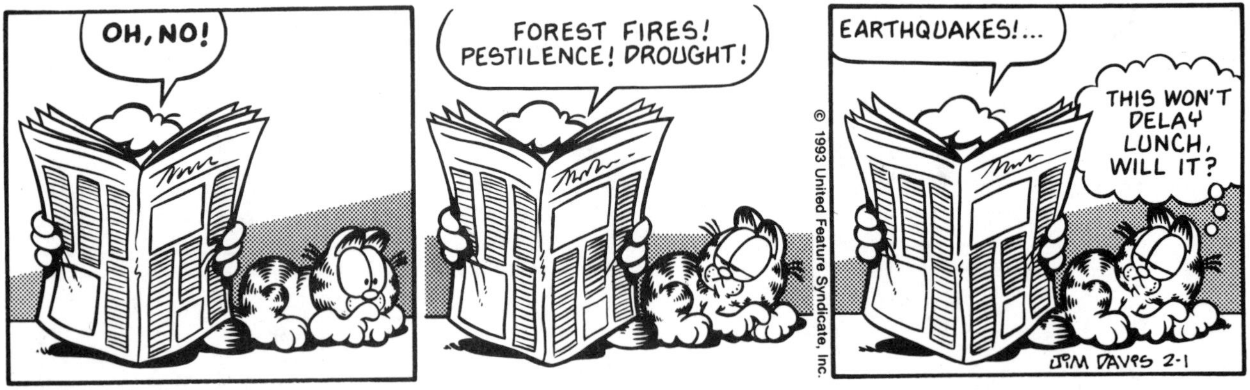
OH, NO!
FOREST FIRES! PESTILENCE! DROUGHT!
EARTHQUAKES!...
THIS WON'T DELAY LUNCH, WILL IT?
JIM DAVIS 2-1
© 1993 United Feature Syndicate, Inc.

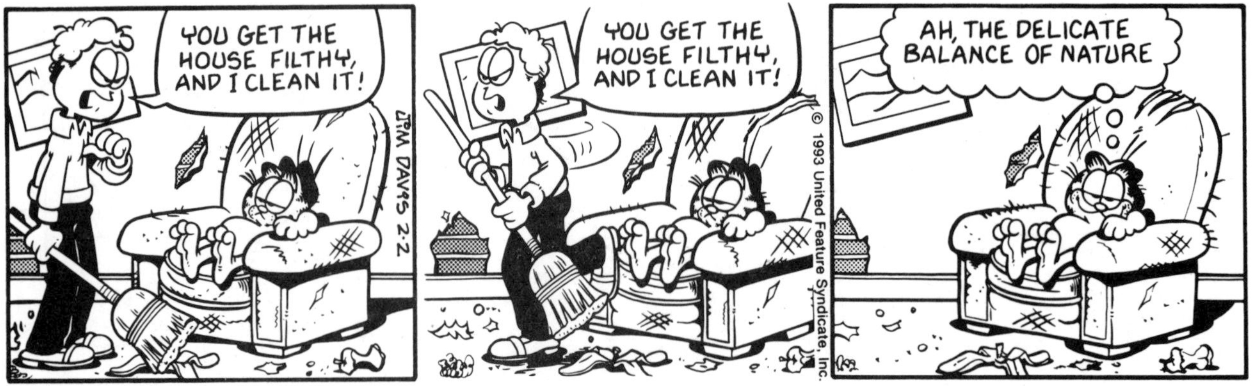
YOU GET THE HOUSE FILTHY, AND I CLEAN IT!
JIM DAVIS 2-2
YOU GET THE HOUSE FILTHY, AND I CLEAN IT!
AH, THE DELICATE BALANCE OF NATURE
© 1993 United Feature Syndicate, Inc.

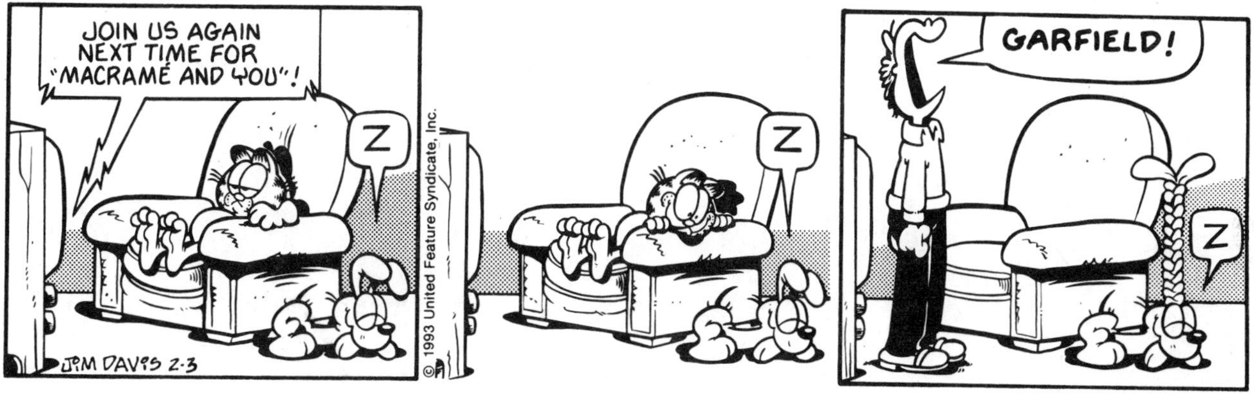
JOIN US AGAIN NEXT TIME FOR "MACRAMÉ AND YOU"!
Z
JIM DAVIS 2-3
© 1993 United Feature Syndicate, Inc.
Z
GARFIELD!
Z

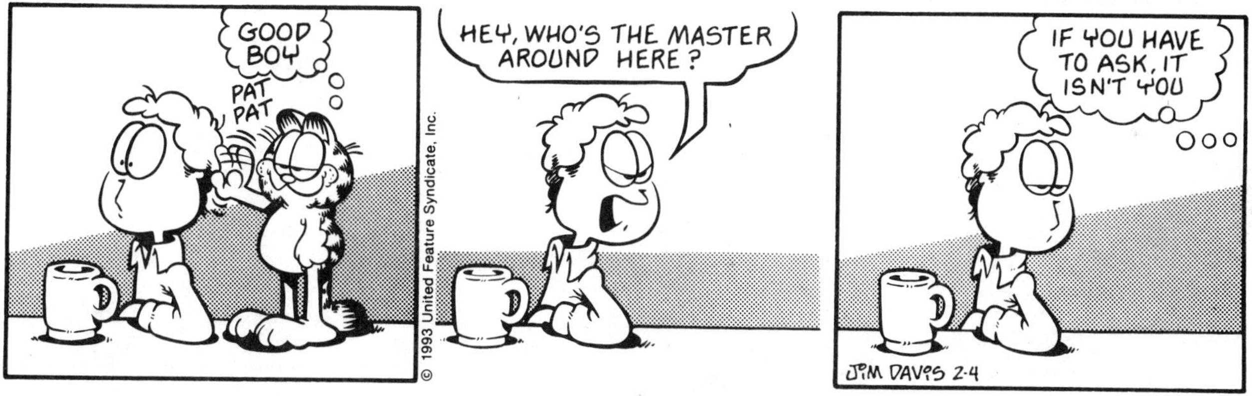
GOOD BOY
PAT PAT
© 1993 United Feature Syndicate, Inc.
HEY, WHO'S THE MASTER AROUND HERE?
IF YOU HAVE TO ASK, IT ISN'T YOU
JIM DAVIS 2-4

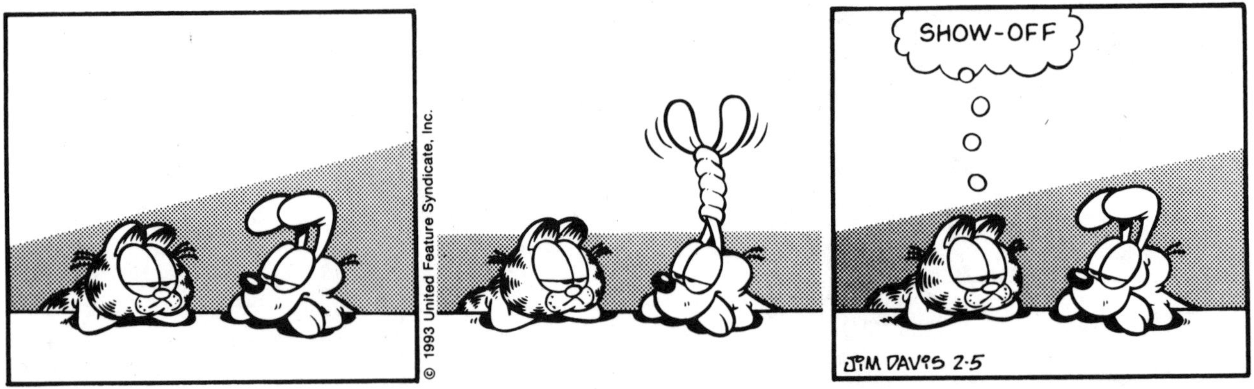
© 1993 United Feature Syndicate, Inc.
SHOW-OFF
JIM DAVIS 2-5

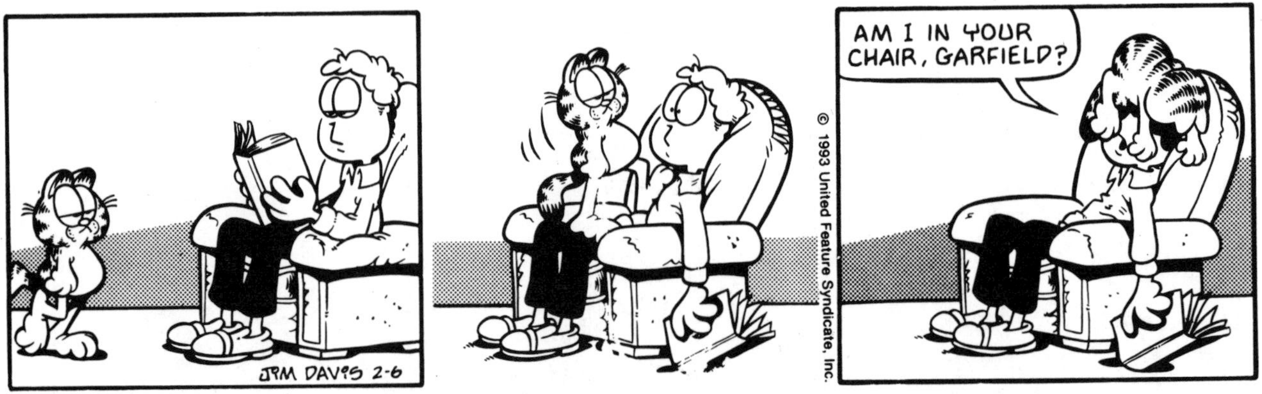
JIM DAVIS 2-6
© 1993 United Feature Syndicate, Inc.
AM I IN YOUR CHAIR, GARFIELD?

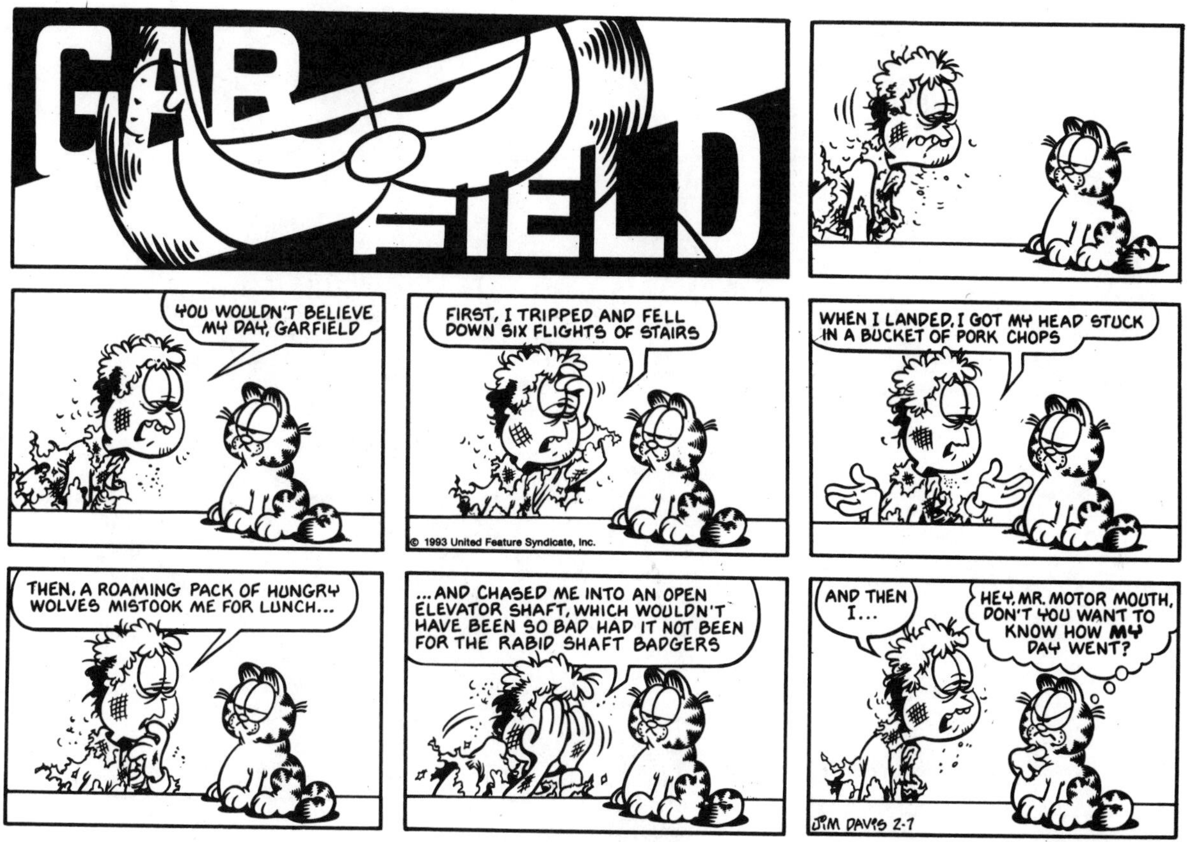
GARFIELD
YOU WOULDN'T BELIEVE MY DAY, GARFIELD
FIRST, I TRIPPED AND FELL DOWN SIX FLIGHTS OF STAIRS
© 1993 United Feature Syndicate, Inc.
WHEN I LANDED, I GOT MY HEAD STUCK IN A BUCKET OF PORK CHOPS
THEN, A ROAMING PACK OF HUNGRY WOLVES MISTOOK ME FOR LUNCH...
...AND CHASED ME INTO AN OPEN ELEVATOR SHAFT, WHICH WOULDN'T HAVE BEEN SO BAD HAD IT NOT BEEN FOR THE RABID SHAFT BADGERS
AND THEN I...
HEY, MR. MOTOR MOUTH, DON'T YOU WANT TO KNOW HOW MY DAY WENT?
JIM DAVIS 2-7

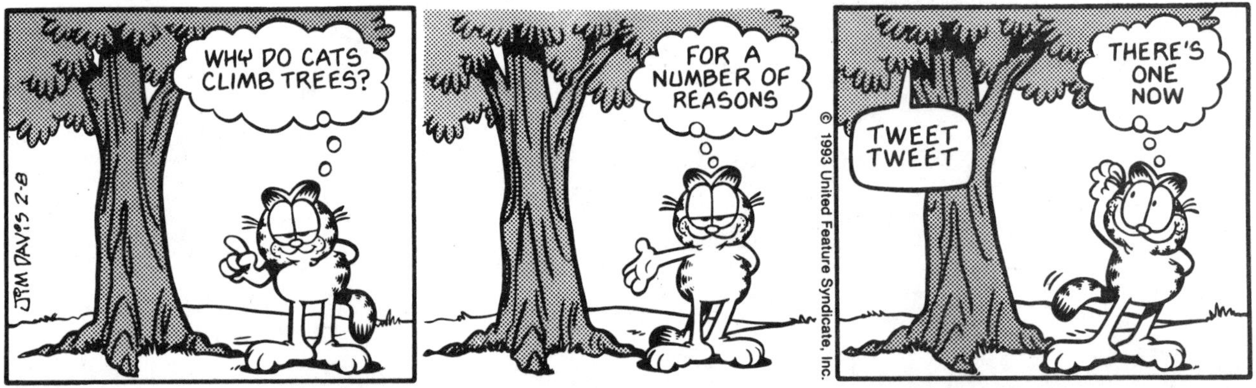
JIM DAVIS 2-8
WHY DO CATS CLIMB TREES?
FOR A NUMBER OF REASONS
TWEET TWEET
THERE'S ONE NOW
© 1993 United Feature Syndicate, Inc.

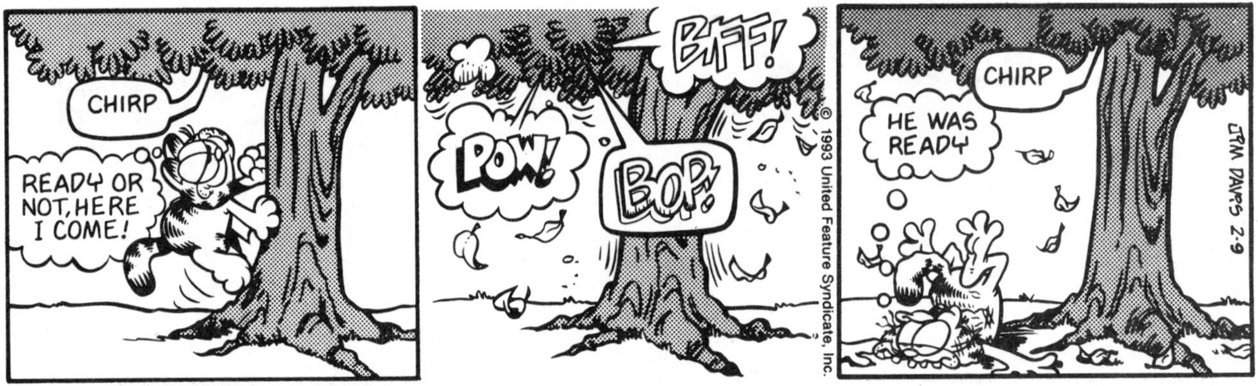
CHIRP
READY OR NOT, HERE I COME!
POW!
BIFF!
BOP!
CHIRP
HE WAS READY
JIM DAVIS 2-9
© 1993 United Feature Syndicate, Inc.

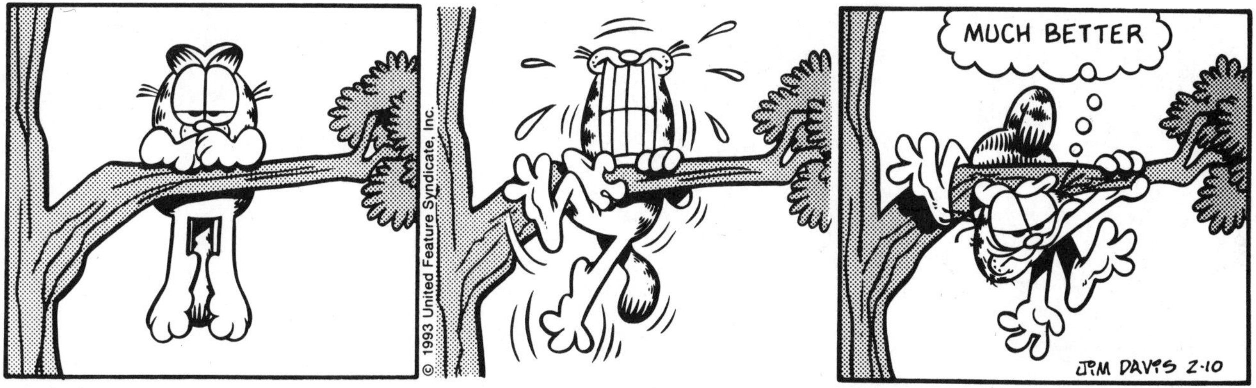
MUCH BETTER
© 1993 United Feature Syndicate, Inc.
JIM DAVIS 2-10

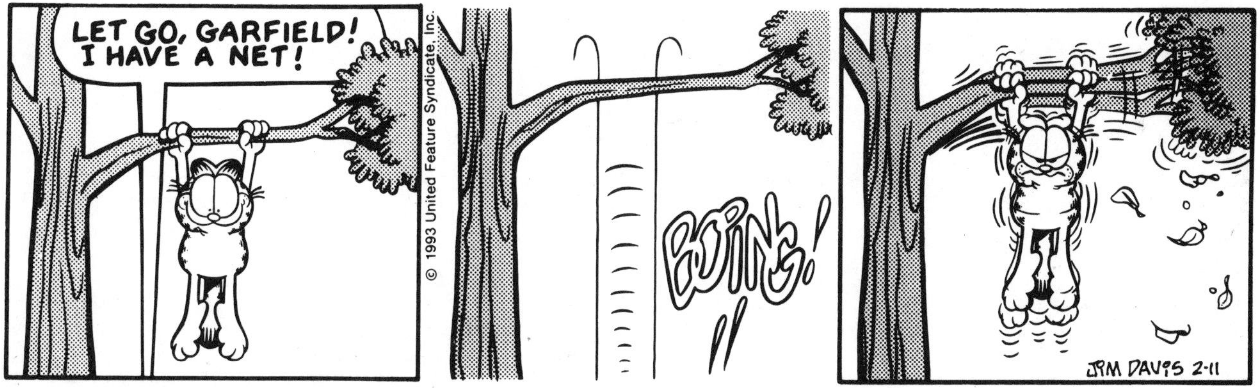
LET GO, GARFIELD! I HAVE A NET!
BOING!
© 1993 United Feature Syndicate, Inc.
JIM DAVIS 2-11

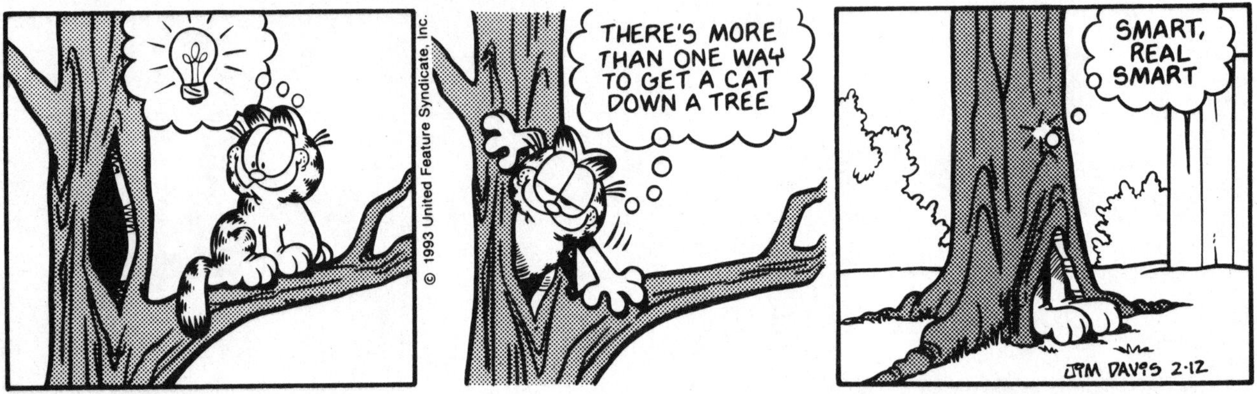
© 1993 United Feature Syndicate, Inc.
THERE'S MORE THAN ONE WAY TO GET A CAT DOWN A TREE
SMART, REAL SMART
JIM DAVIS 2·12

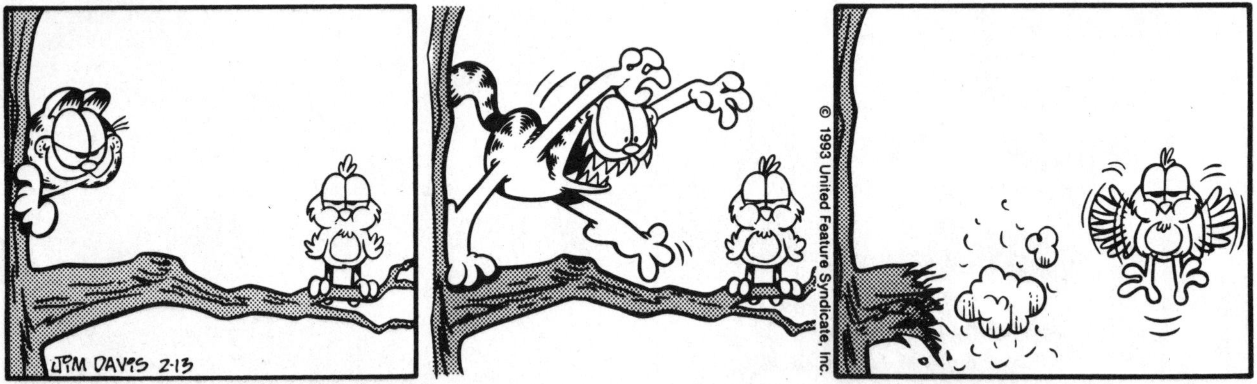
JIM DAVIS 2·13
© 1993 United Feature Syndicate, Inc.

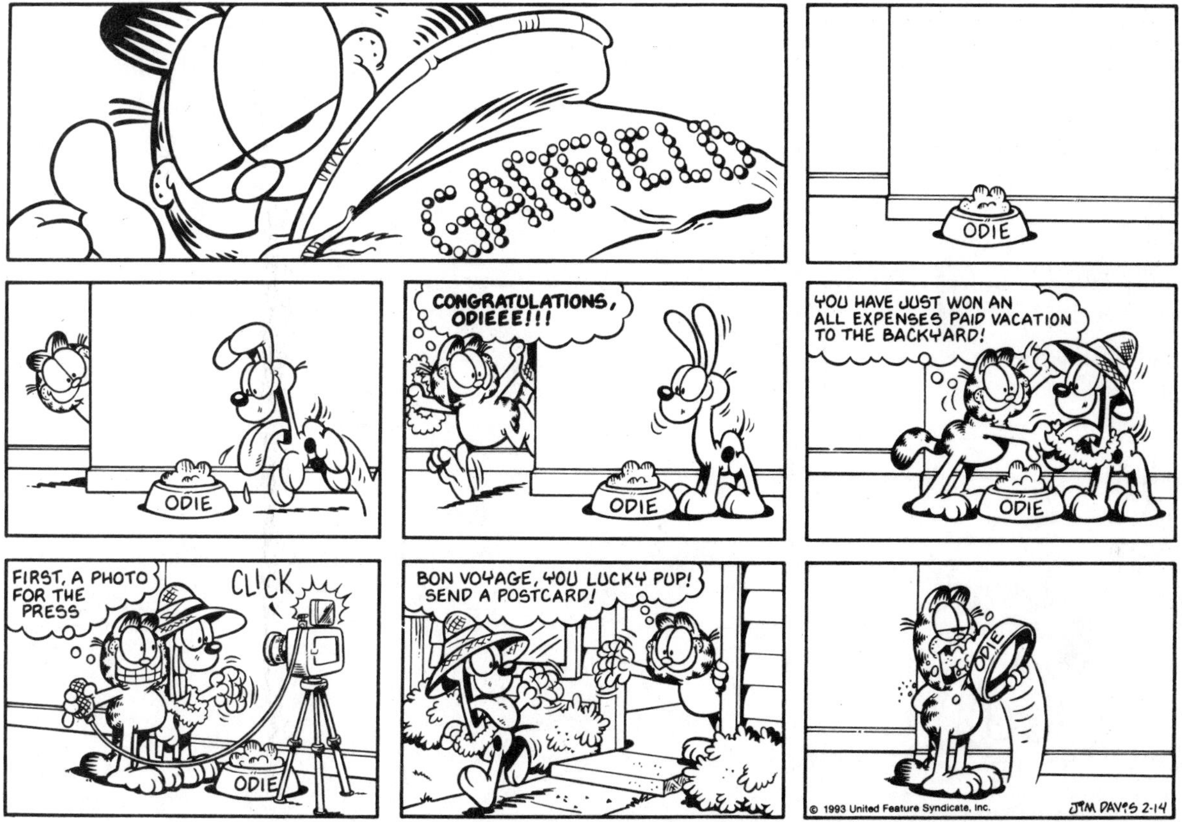
GARFIELD
ODIE
ODIE
CONGRATULATIONS, ODIEEE!!!
ODIE
YOU HAVE JUST WON AN ALL EXPENSES PAID VACATION TO THE BACKYARD!
ODIE
FIRST, A PHOTO FOR THE PRESS
CLICK
ODIE
BON VOYAGE, YOU LUCKY PUP! SEND A POSTCARD!
ODIE
© 1993 United Feature Syndicate, Inc.
JIM DAVIS 2-14

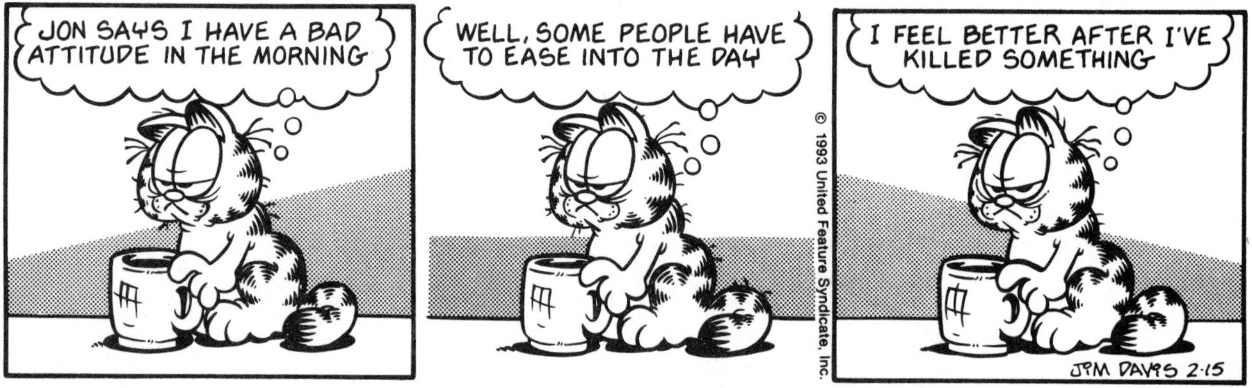
JON SAYS I HAVE A BAD ATTITUDE IN THE MORNING
WELL, SOME PEOPLE HAVE TO EASE INTO THE DAY
© 1993 United Feature Syndicate, Inc.
I FEEL BETTER AFTER I'VE KILLED SOMETHING
JIM DAVIS 2·15

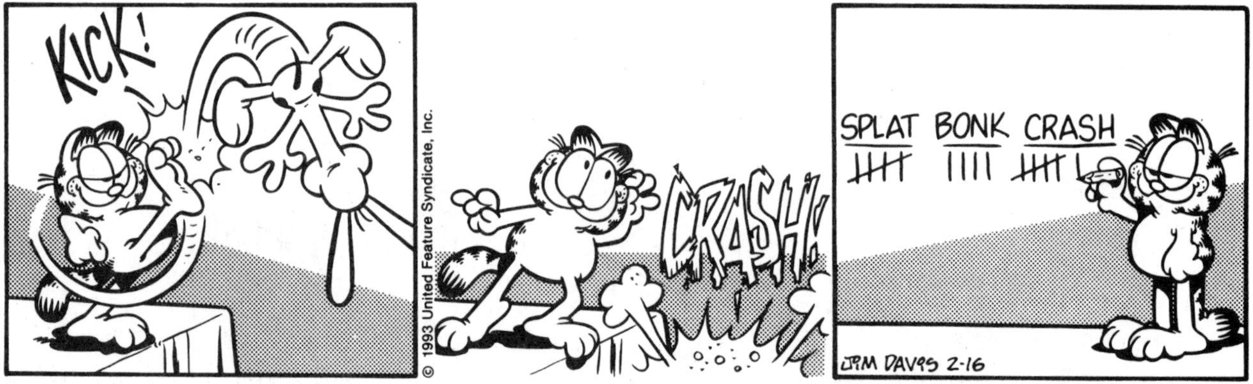
KICK!
© 1993 United Feature Syndicate, Inc.
CRASH!
SPLAT
BONK
CRASH
JIM DAVIS 2·16

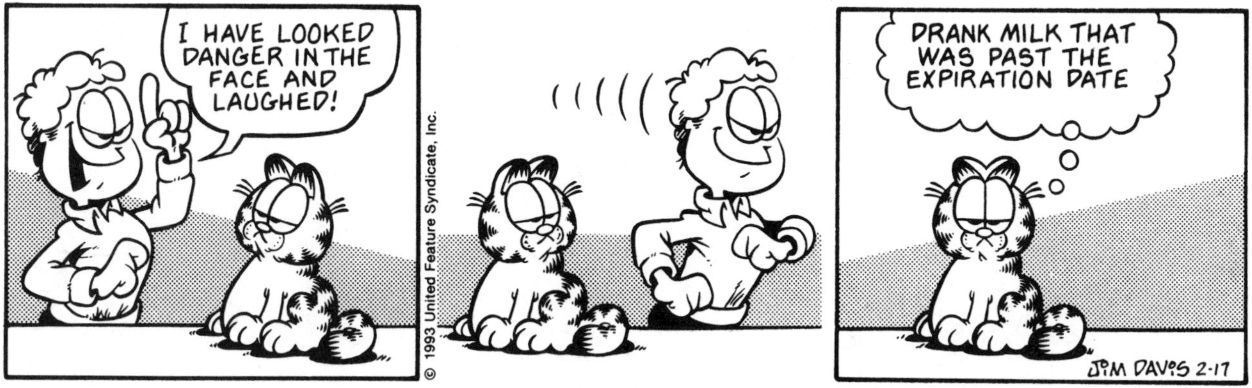
I HAVE LOOKED DANGER IN THE FACE AND LAUGHED!
DRANK MILK THAT WAS PAST THE EXPIRATION DATE
© 1993 United Feature Syndicate, Inc.
JIM DAVIS 2-17

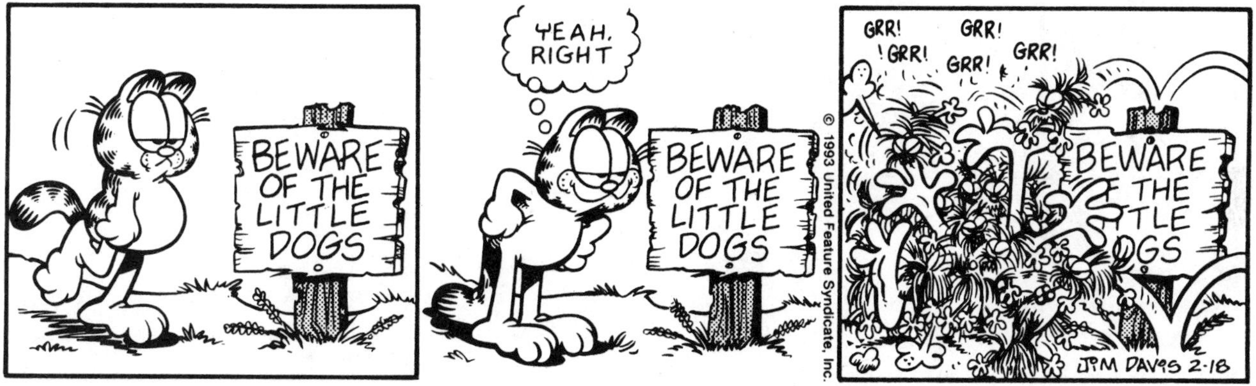
BEWARE OF THE LITTLE DOGS
YEAH, RIGHT
BEWARE OF THE LITTLE DOGS
GRR!
GRR!
GRR!
GRR!
GRR!
© 1993 United Feature Syndicate, Inc.
JIM DAVIS 2-18

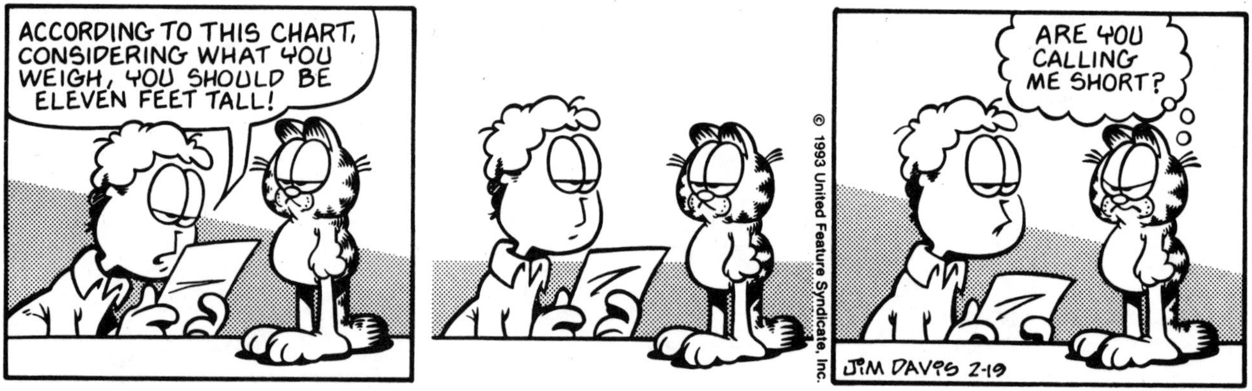
ACCORDING TO THIS CHART, CONSIDERING WHAT YOU WEIGH, YOU SHOULD BE ELEVEN FEET TALL!
ARE YOU CALLING ME SHORT?
© 1993 United Feature Syndicate, Inc.
JIM DAVIS 2-19

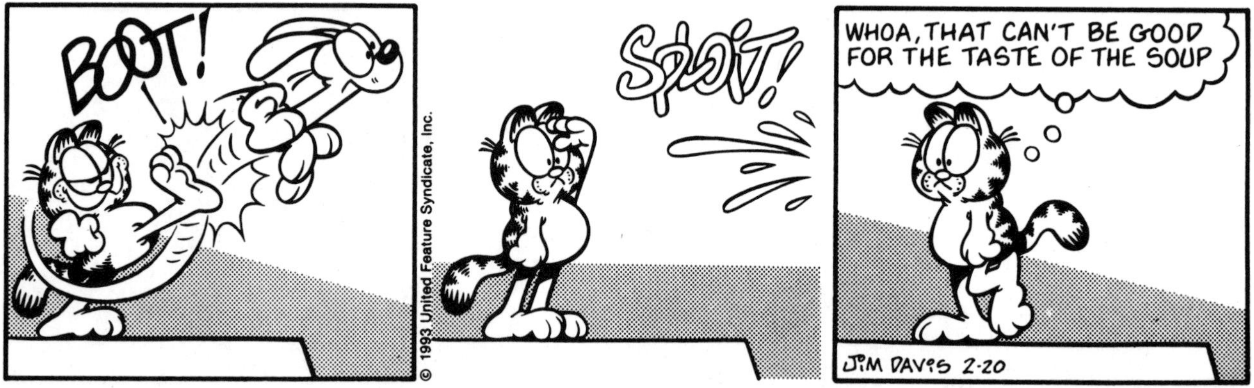
BOOT!
© 1993 United Feature Syndicate, Inc.
WHOA, THAT CAN'T BE GOOD FOR THE TASTE OF THE SOUP
JIM DAVIS 2-20

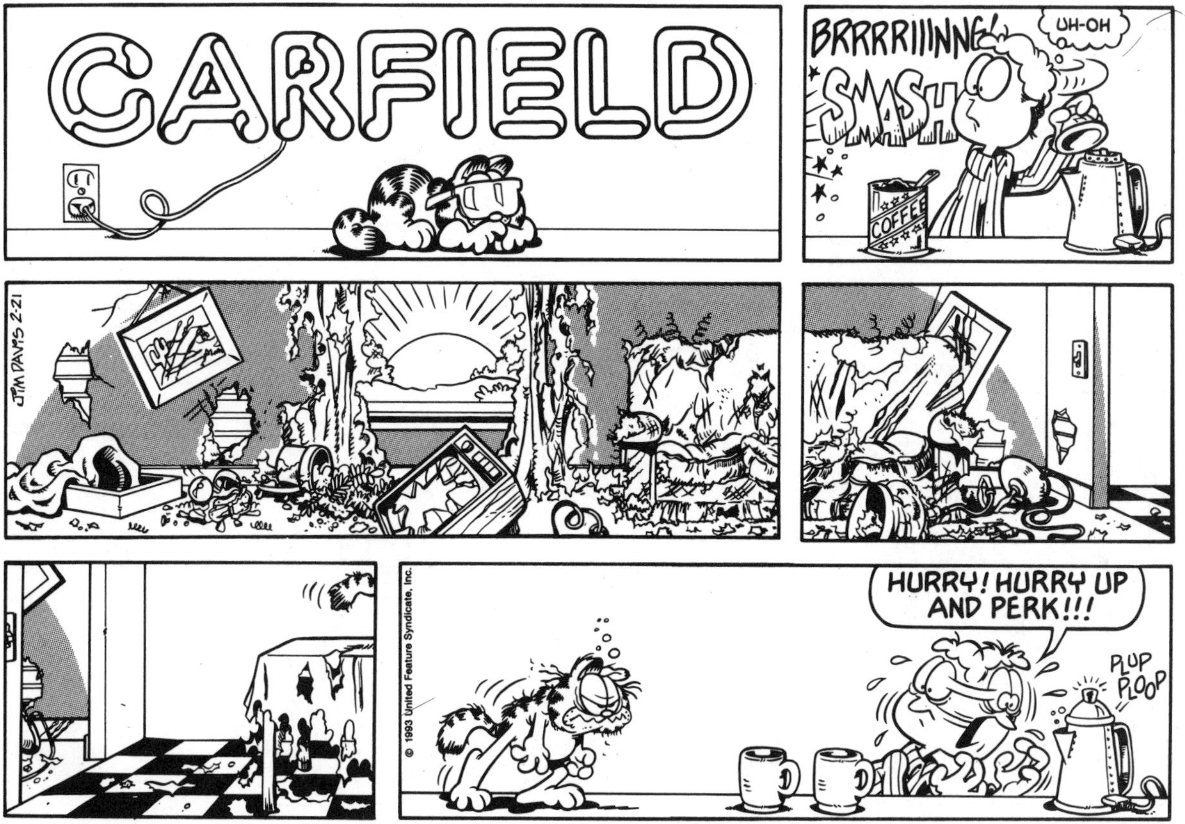
GARFIELD
BRRRRIIINNG!
UH-OH
SMASH
COFFEE
JIM DAVIS 2-21
© 1993 United Feature Syndicate, Inc.
HURRY! HURRY UP AND PERK!!!
PLUP PLOOP

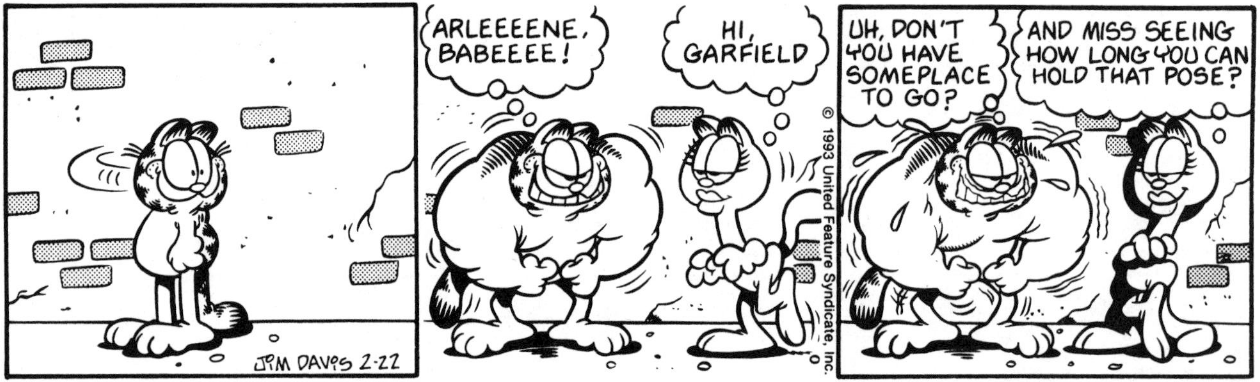
JIM DAVIS 2-22
ARLEEEENE, BABEEEE!
HI, GARFIELD
© 1993 United Feature Syndicate, Inc.
UH, DON'T YOU HAVE SOMEPLACE TO GO?
AND MISS SEEING HOW LONG YOU CAN HOLD THAT POSE?

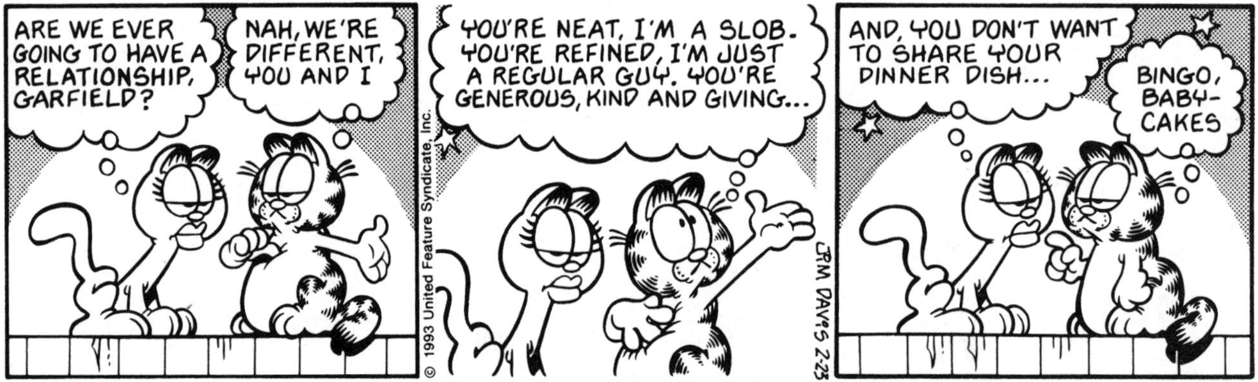
ARE WE EVER GOING TO HAVE A RELATIONSHIP, GARFIELD?
NAH, WE'RE DIFFERENT, YOU AND I
© 1993 United Feature Syndicate, Inc.
YOU'RE NEAT, I'M A SLOB. YOU'RE REFINED, I'M JUST A REGULAR GUY. YOU'RE GENEROUS, KIND AND GIVING...
JIM DAVIS 2-23
AND, YOU DON'T WANT TO SHARE YOUR DINNER DISH...
BINGO, BABY-CAKES

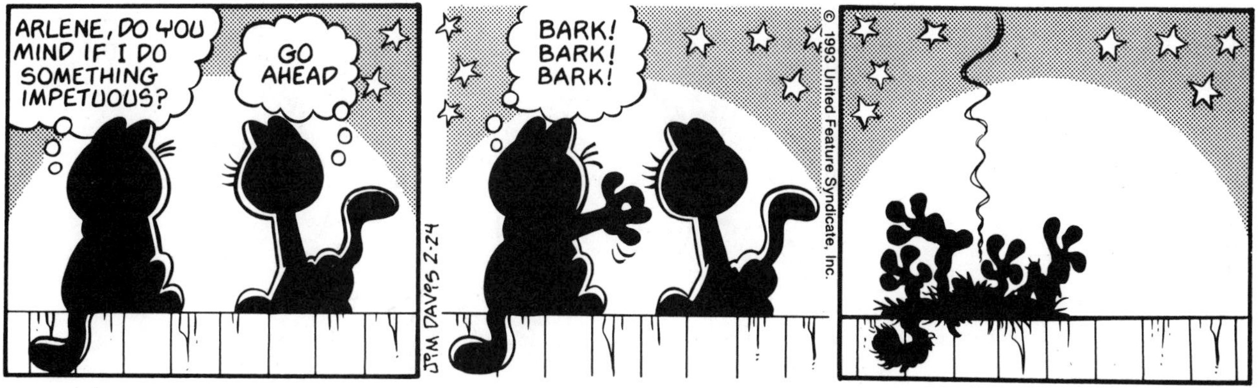
ARLENE, DO YOU MIND IF I DO SOMETHING IMPETUOUS?
GO AHEAD
JIM DAVIS 2-24
BARK! BARK! BARK!
© 1993 United Feature Syndicate, Inc.

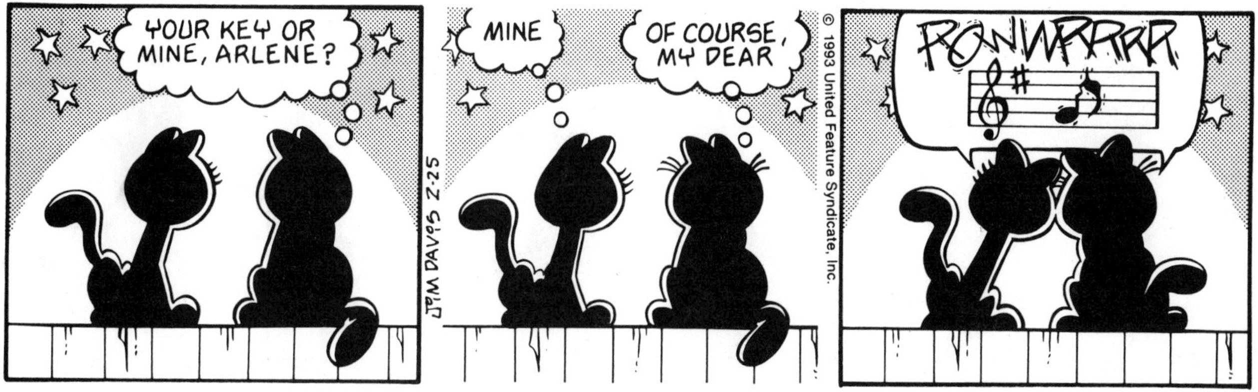
YOUR KEY OR MINE, ARLENE?
JIM DAVIS 2-25
MINE
OF COURSE, MY DEAR
© 1993 United Feature Syndicate, Inc.

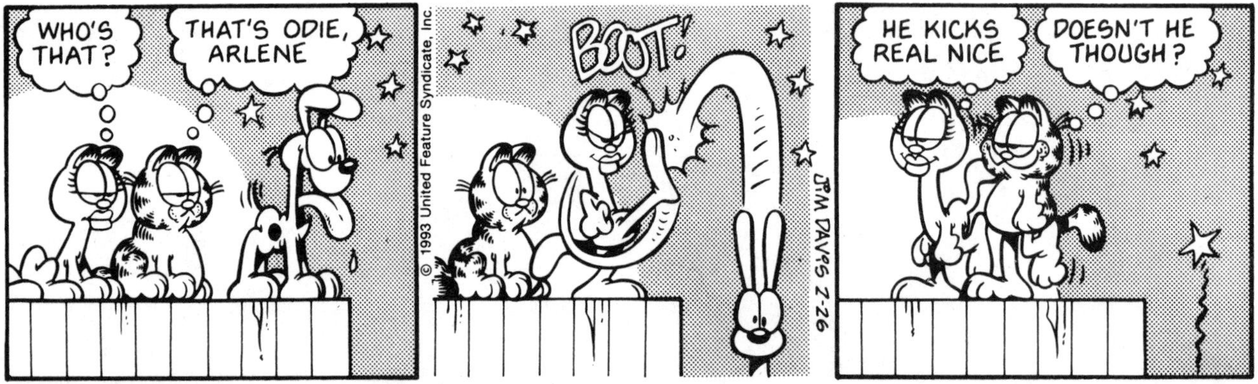
WHO'S THAT?
THAT'S ODIE, ARLENE
BOOT!
HE KICKS REAL NICE
DOESN'T HE THOUGH?
© 1993 United Feature Syndicate, Inc.
JIM DAVIS 2-26

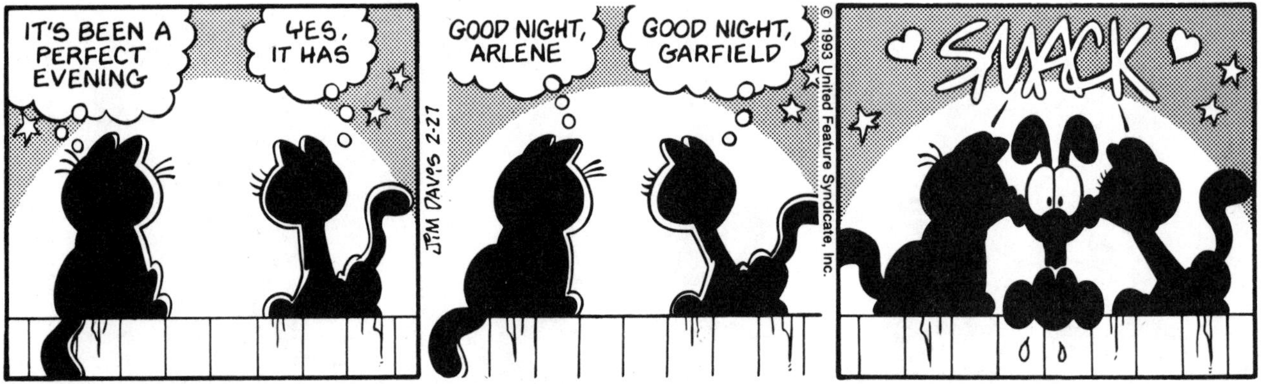
IT'S BEEN A PERFECT EVENING
YES, IT HAS
GOOD NIGHT, ARLENE
GOOD NIGHT, GARFIELD
SMACK
JIM DAVIS 2-27
© 1993 United Feature Syndicate, Inc.

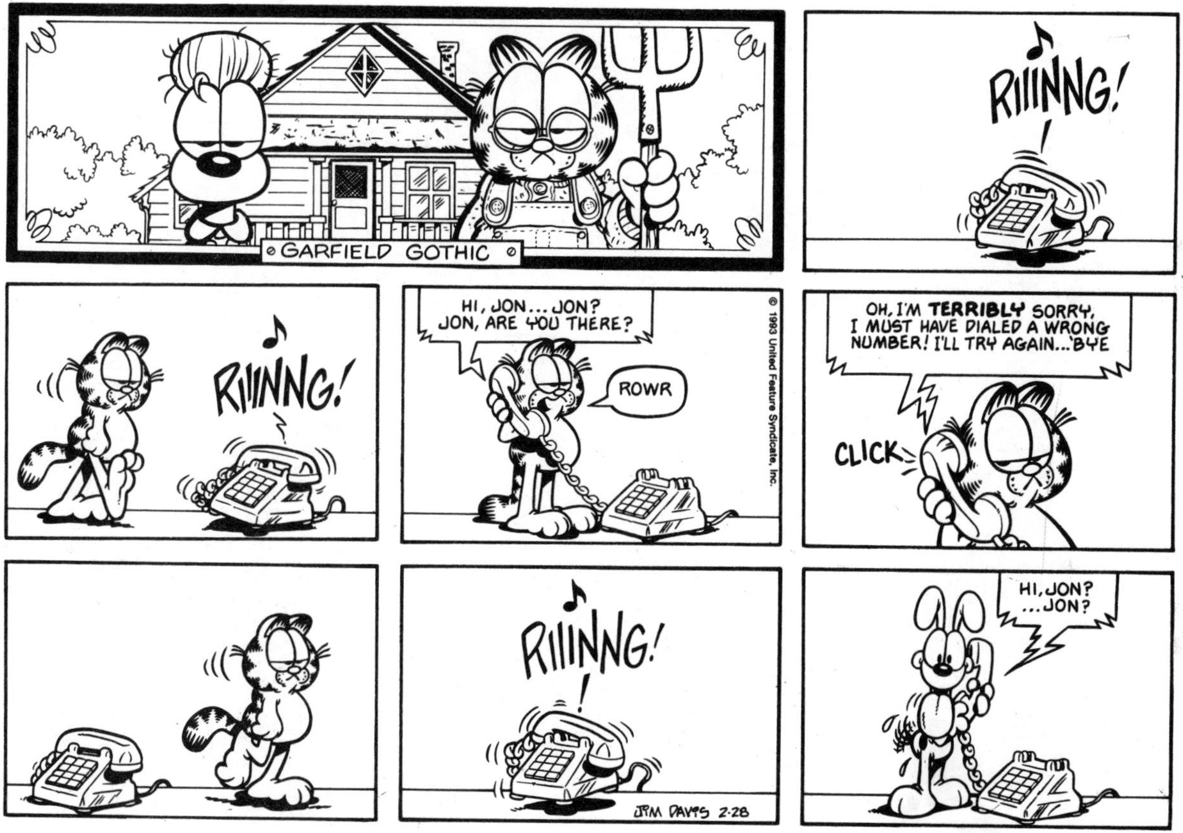
GARFIELD GOTHIC
RIIINNG!
RIIINNG!
HI, JON... JON? JON, ARE YOU THERE?
ROWR
OH, I'M TERRIBLY SORRY, I MUST HAVE DIALED A WRONG NUMBER! I'LL TRY AGAIN...'BYE
CLICK
RIIINNG!
JIM DAVIS 2-28
HI, JON? ...JON?

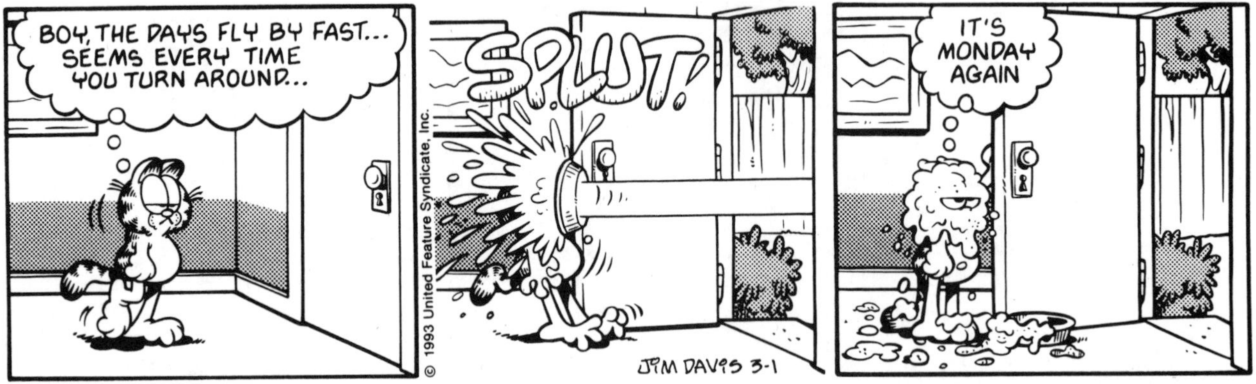
BOY, THE DAYS FLY BY FAST... SEEMS EVERY TIME YOU TURN AROUND...
SPLUT!
IT'S MONDAY AGAIN
© 1993 United Feature Syndicate, Inc.
JIM DAVIS 3-1

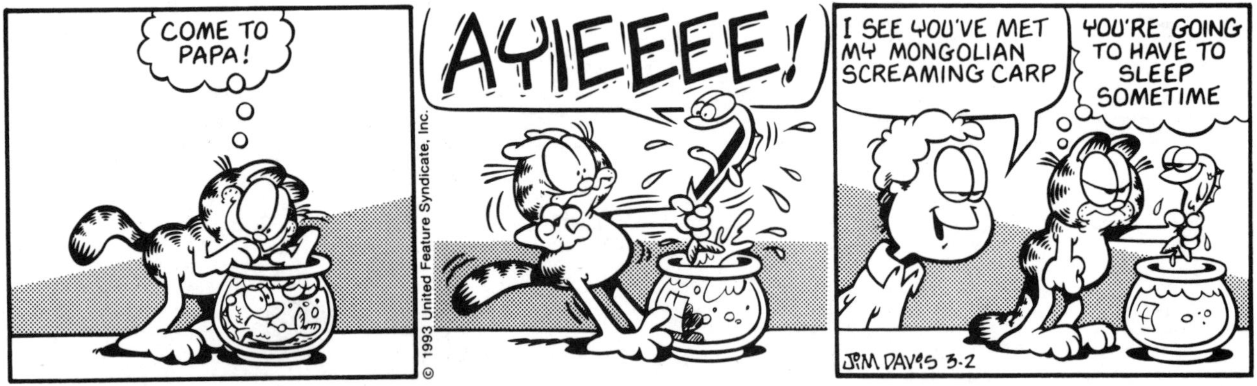
COME TO PAPA!
AYIEEEEE!
I SEE YOU'VE MET MY MONGOLIAN SCREAMING CARP
YOU'RE GOING TO HAVE TO SLEEP SOMETIME
© 1993 United Feature Syndicate, Inc.
JIM DAVIS 3-2

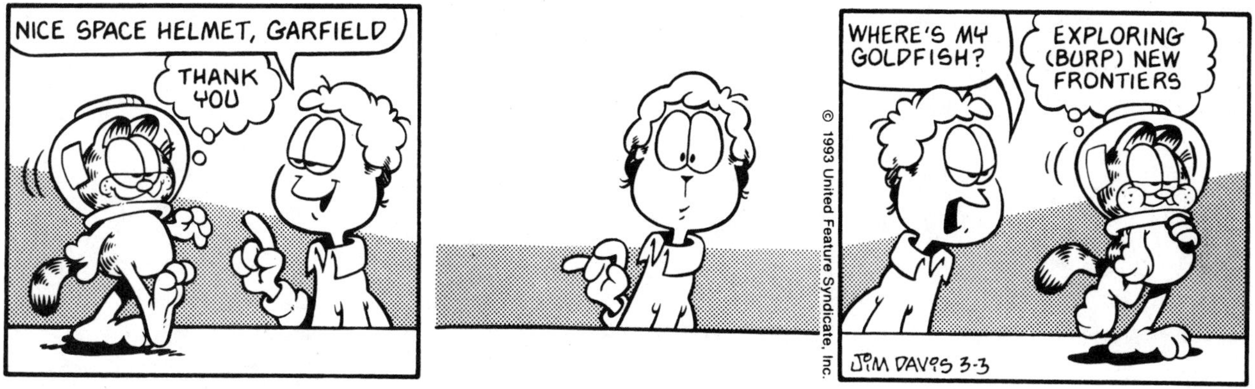
NICE SPACE HELMET, GARFIELD
THANK YOU
WHERE'S MY GOLDFISH?
EXPLORING (BURP) NEW FRONTIERS
JIM DAVIS 3-3
© 1993 United Feature Syndicate, Inc.

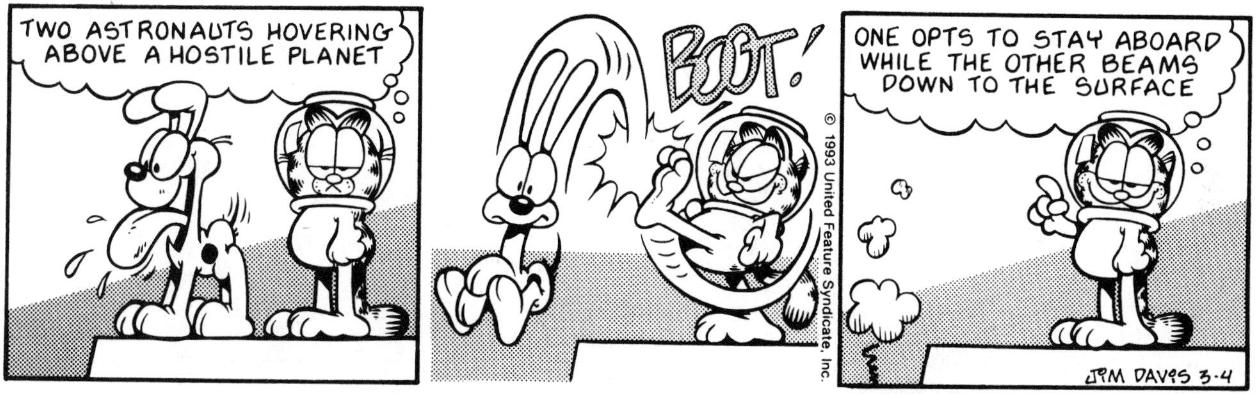
TWO ASTRONAUTS HOVERING ABOVE A HOSTILE PLANET
BOOT!
ONE OPTS TO STAY ABOARD WHILE THE OTHER BEAMS DOWN TO THE SURFACE
JIM DAVIS 3-4
© 1993 United Feature Syndicate, Inc.

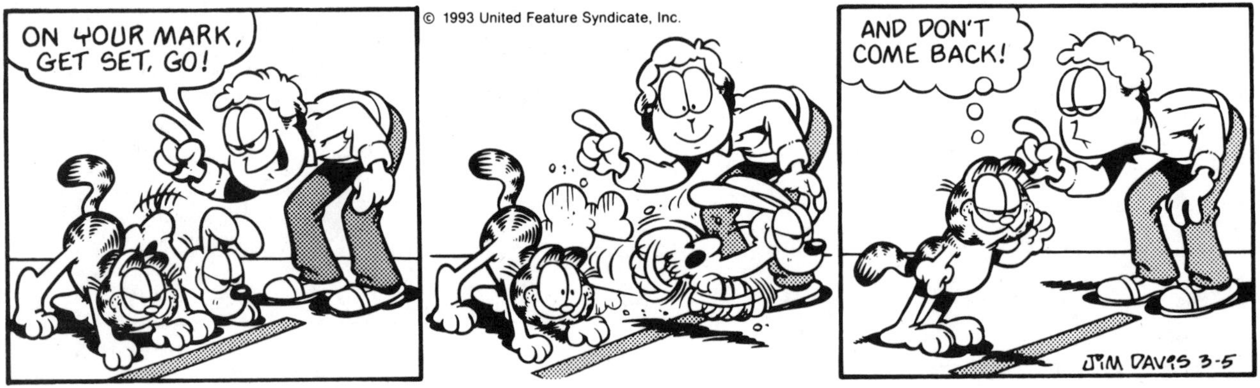
ON YOUR MARK, GET SET, GO!
AND DON'T COME BACK!
JIM DAVIS 3-5


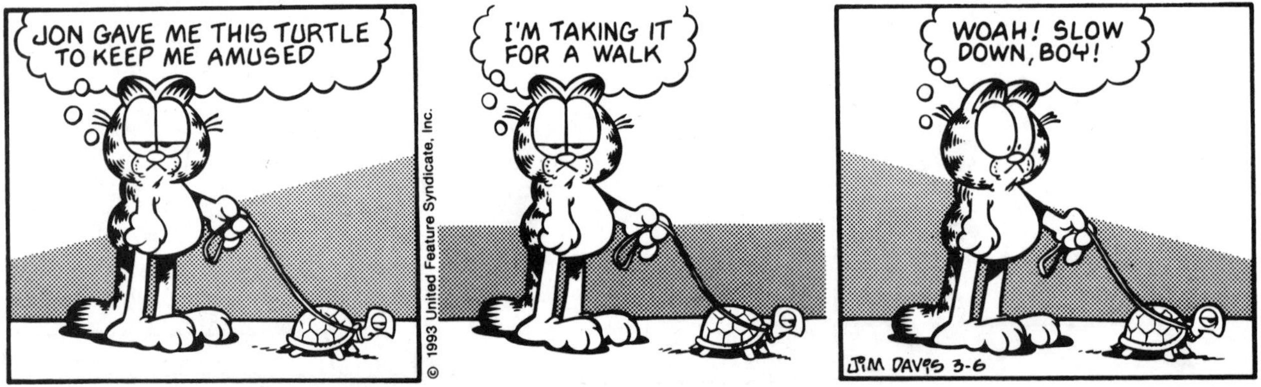
JON GAVE ME THIS TURTLE TO KEEP ME AMUSED
I'M TAKING IT FOR A WALK
WOAH! SLOW DOWN, BOY!
JIM DAVIS 3-6

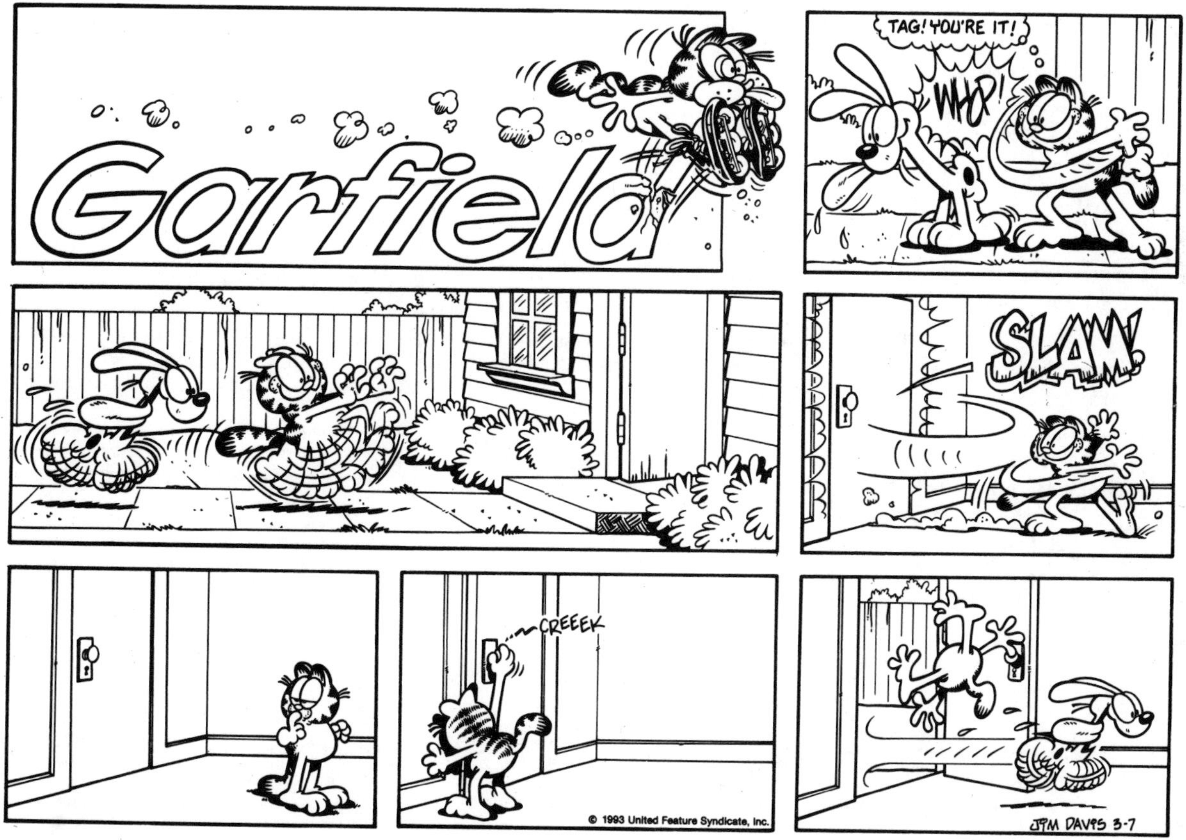

Garfield
TAG! YOU'RE IT!
WHOP!
SLAM!
CREEEK
© 1993 United Feature Syndicate, Inc.
JIM DAVIS 3-7

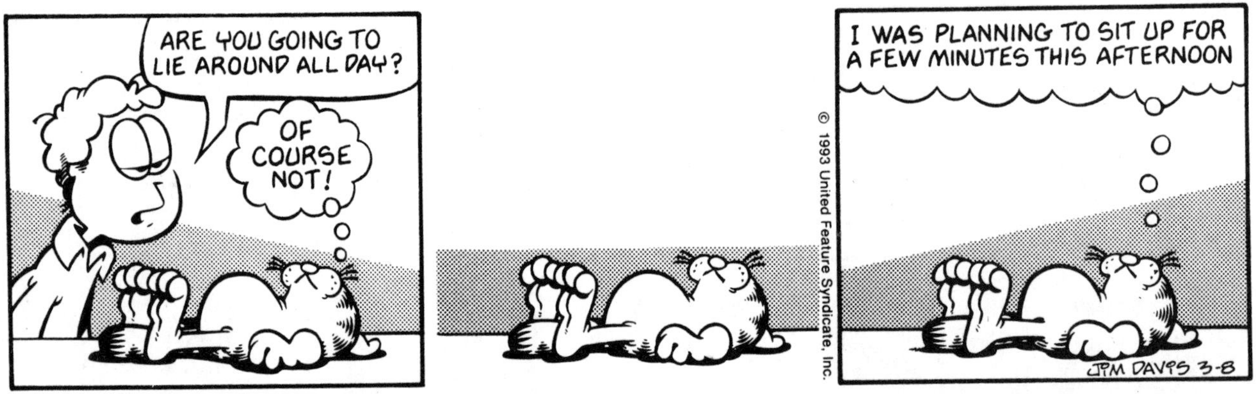
ARE YOU GOING TO LIE AROUND ALL DAY?
OF COURSE NOT!
I WAS PLANNING TO SIT UP FOR A FEW MINUTES THIS AFTERNOON
© 1993 United Feature Syndicate, Inc.
JIM DAVIS 3-8

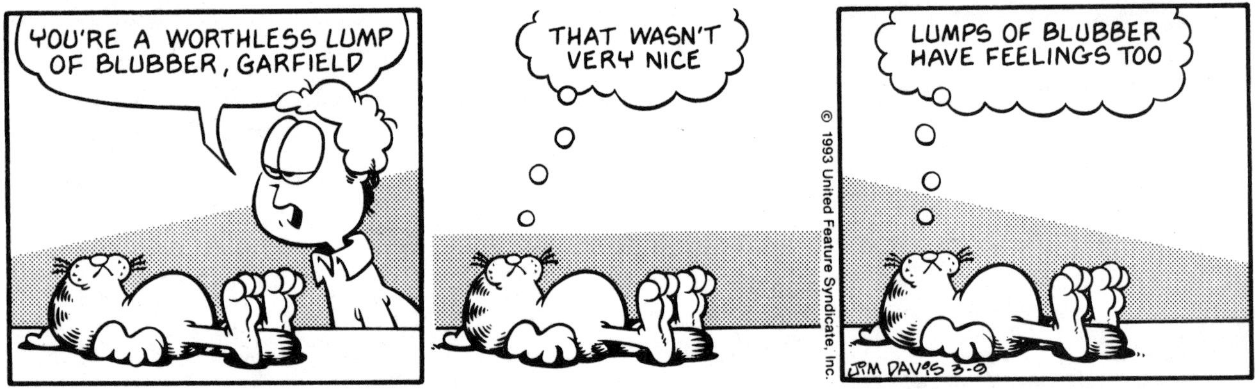
YOU'RE A WORTHLESS LUMP OF BLUBBER, GARFIELD
THAT WASN'T VERY NICE
LUMPS OF BLUBBER HAVE FEELINGS TOO
© 1993 United Feature Syndicate, Inc.
JIM DAVIS 3-9

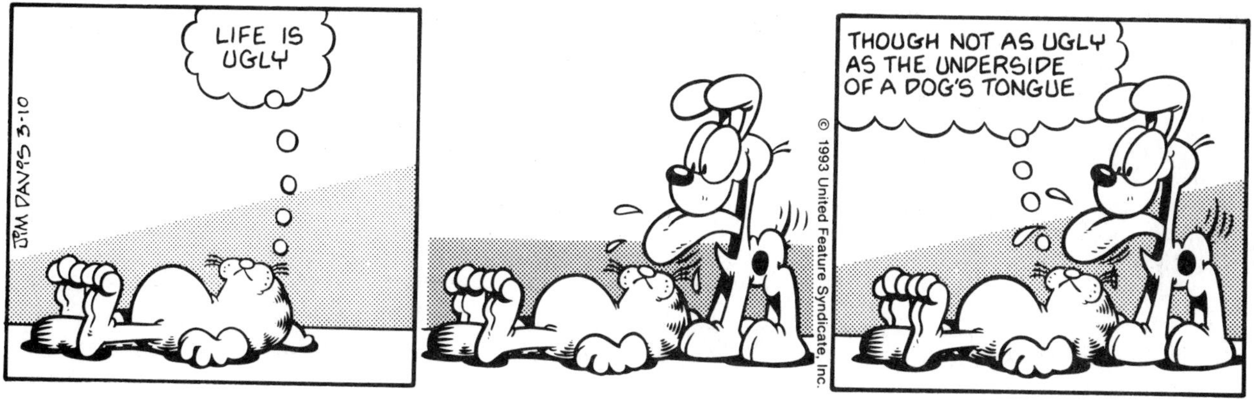
JIM DAVIS 3-10
LIFE IS UGLY
THOUGH NOT AS UGLY AS THE UNDERSIDE OF A DOG'S TONGUE
© 1993 United Feature Syndicate, Inc.

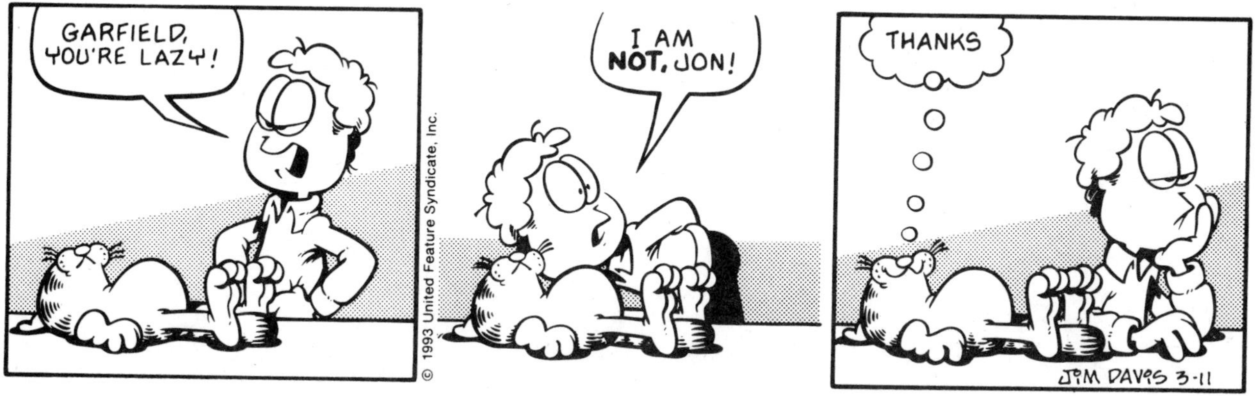
GARFIELD, YOU'RE LAZY!
© 1993 United Feature Syndicate, Inc.
I AM **NOT,** JON!
THANKS
JIM DAVIS 3-11

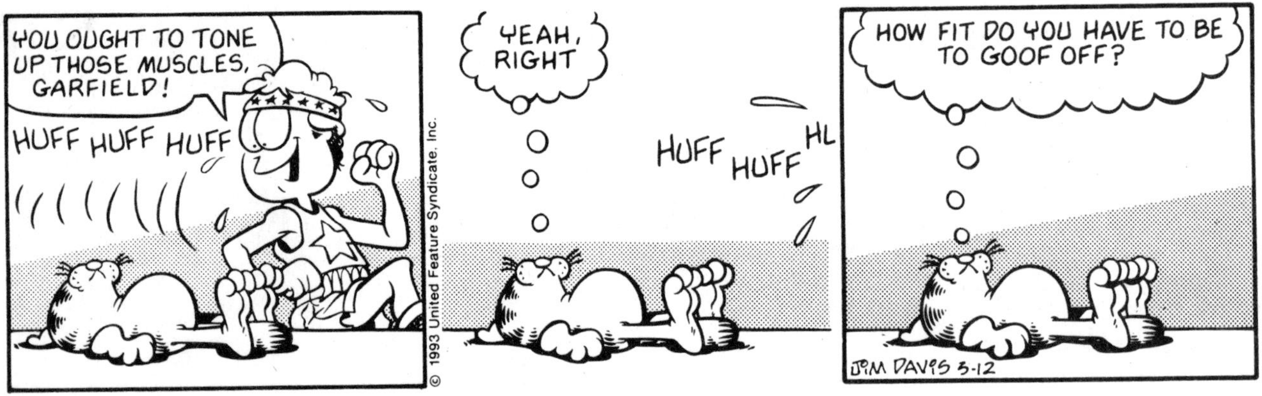
YOU OUGHT TO TONE UP THOSE MUSCLES, GARFIELD!
HUFF HUFF HUFF
© 1993 United Feature Syndicate, Inc.
YEAH, RIGHT
HUFF HUFF HL
HOW FIT DO YOU HAVE TO BE TO GOOF OFF?
JIM DAVIS 3-12

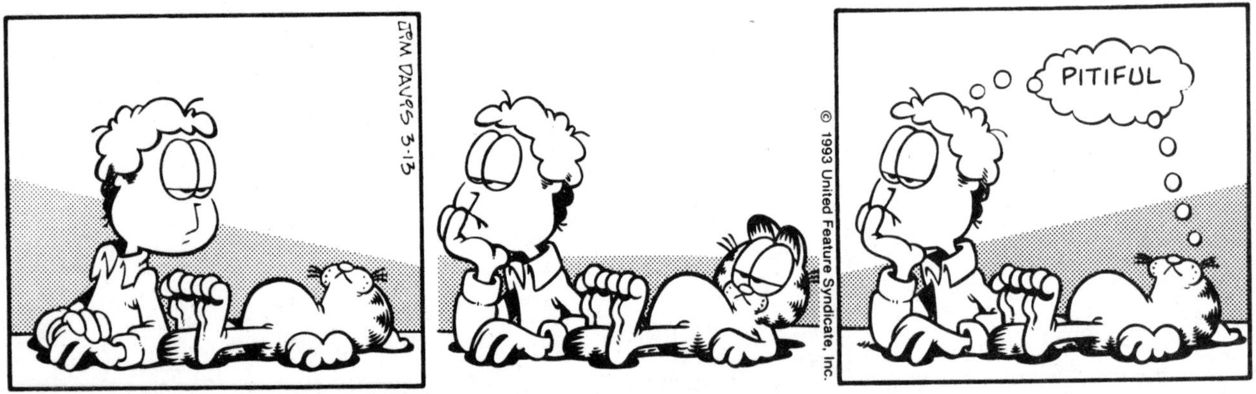
JIM DAVIS 3-13
© 1993 United Feature Syndicate, Inc.
PITIFUL

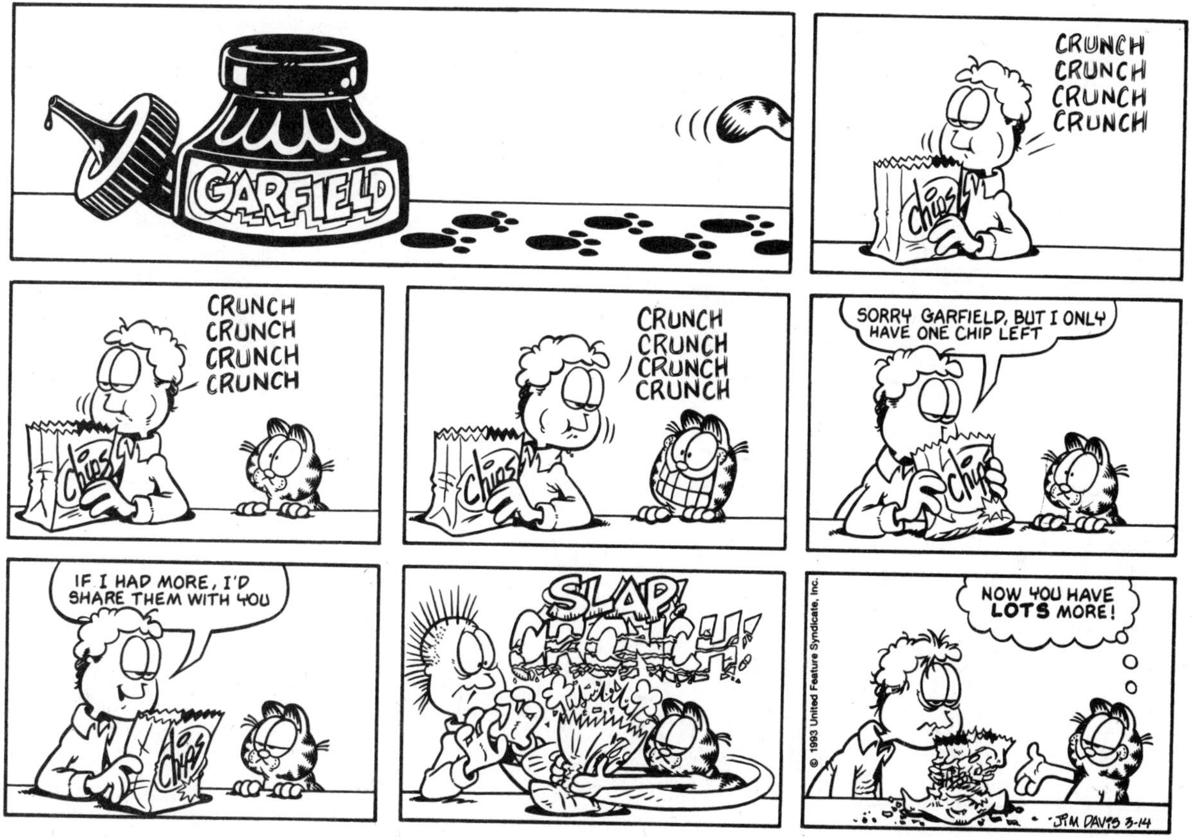
GARFIELD
CRUNCH
CRUNCH
CRUNCH
CRUNCH
Chips
CRUNCH
CRUNCH
CRUNCH
CRUNCH
CRUNCH
CRUNCH
CRUNCH
CRUNCH
SORRY GARFIELD, BUT I ONLY HAVE ONE CHIP LEFT
IF I HAD MORE, I'D SHARE THEM WITH YOU
SLAP!
CRUNCH!
NOW YOU HAVE **LOTS** MORE!
© 1993 United Feature Syndicate, Inc.
JIM DAVIS 3-14

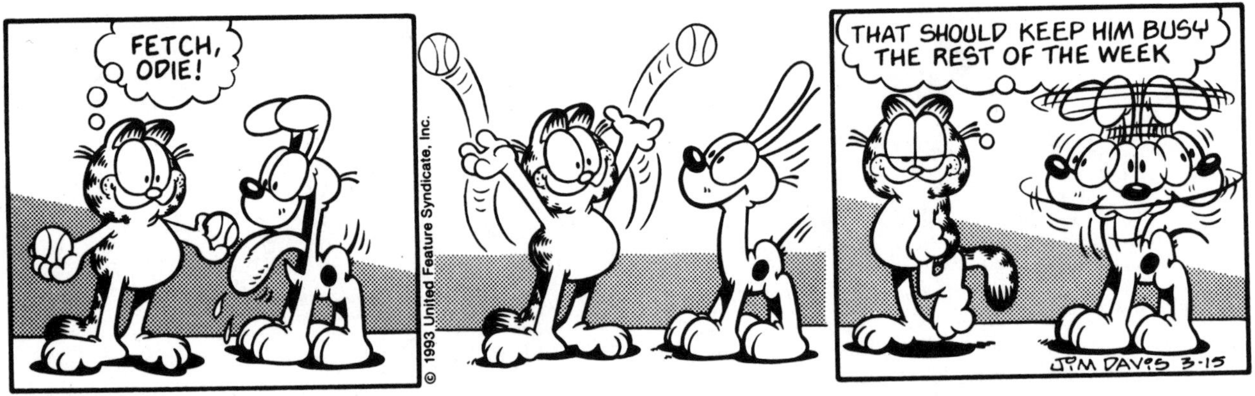
FETCH, ODIE!
© 1993 United Feature Syndicate, Inc.
THAT SHOULD KEEP HIM BUSY THE REST OF THE WEEK
JIM DAVIS 3-15

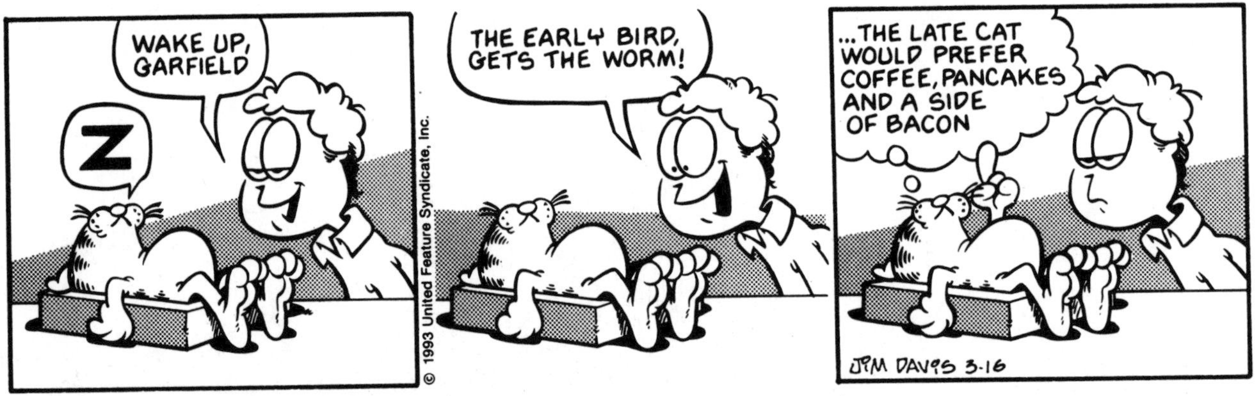
Z
WAKE UP, GARFIELD
© 1993 United Feature Syndicate, Inc.
THE EARLY BIRD, GETS THE WORM!
...THE LATE CAT WOULD PREFER COFFEE, PANCAKES AND A SIDE OF BACON
JIM DAVIS 3-16

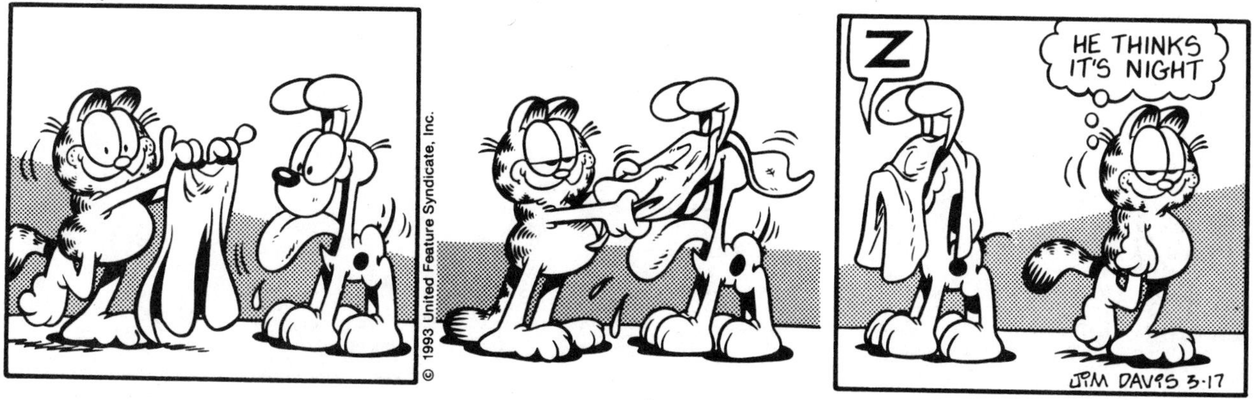

© 1993 United Feature Syndicate, Inc.
Z
HE THINKS IT'S NIGHT
JIM DAVIS 3-17


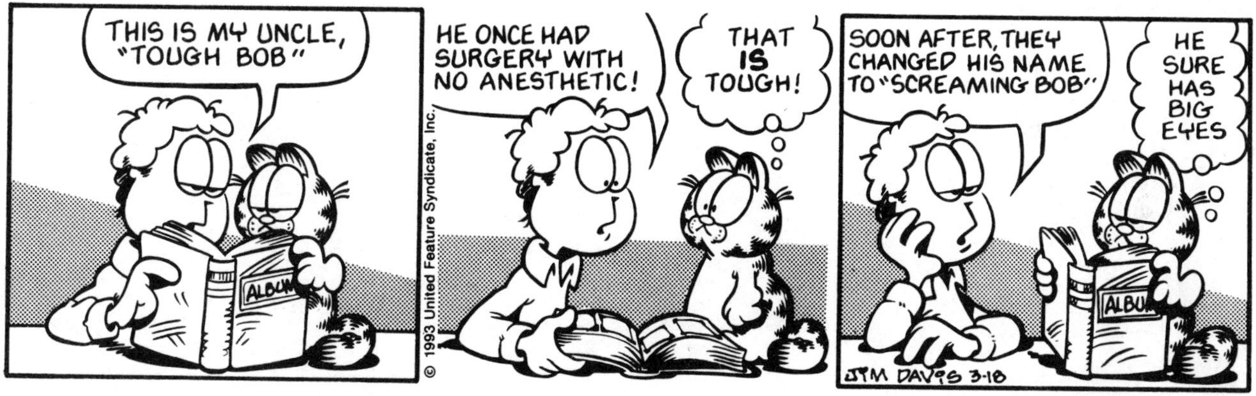

THIS IS MY UNCLE, "TOUGH BOB"
ALBUM
© 1993 United Feature Syndicate, Inc.
HE ONCE HAD SURGERY WITH NO ANESTHETIC!
THAT **IS** TOUGH!
SOON AFTER, THEY CHANGED HIS NAME TO "SCREAMING BOB"
HE SURE HAS BIG EYES
JIM DAVIS 3-18

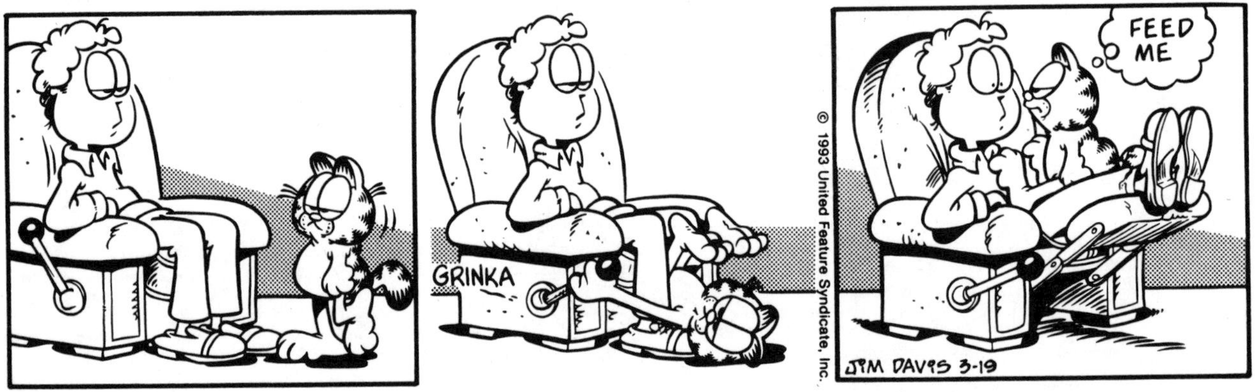
GRINKA
FEED ME
JIM DAVIS 3-19


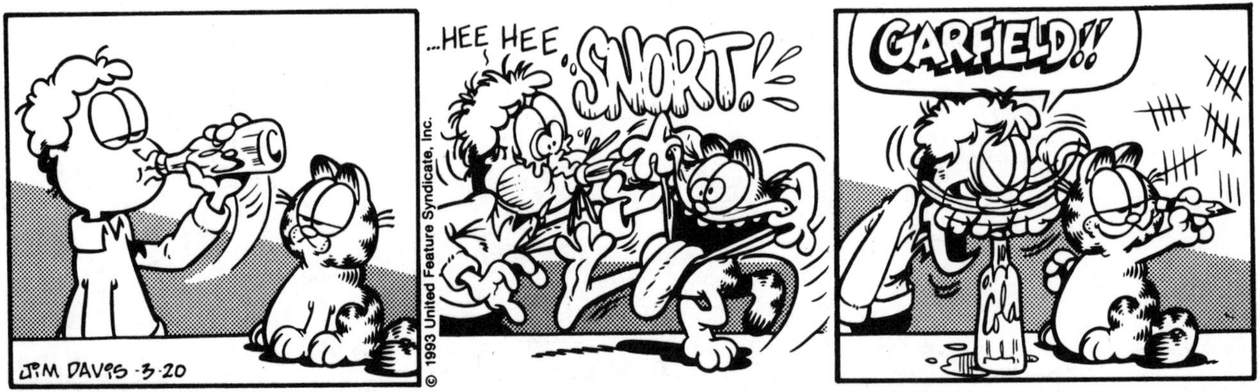
JIM DAVIS 3-20
...HEE HEE
SNORT!
GARFIELD!!
Cola

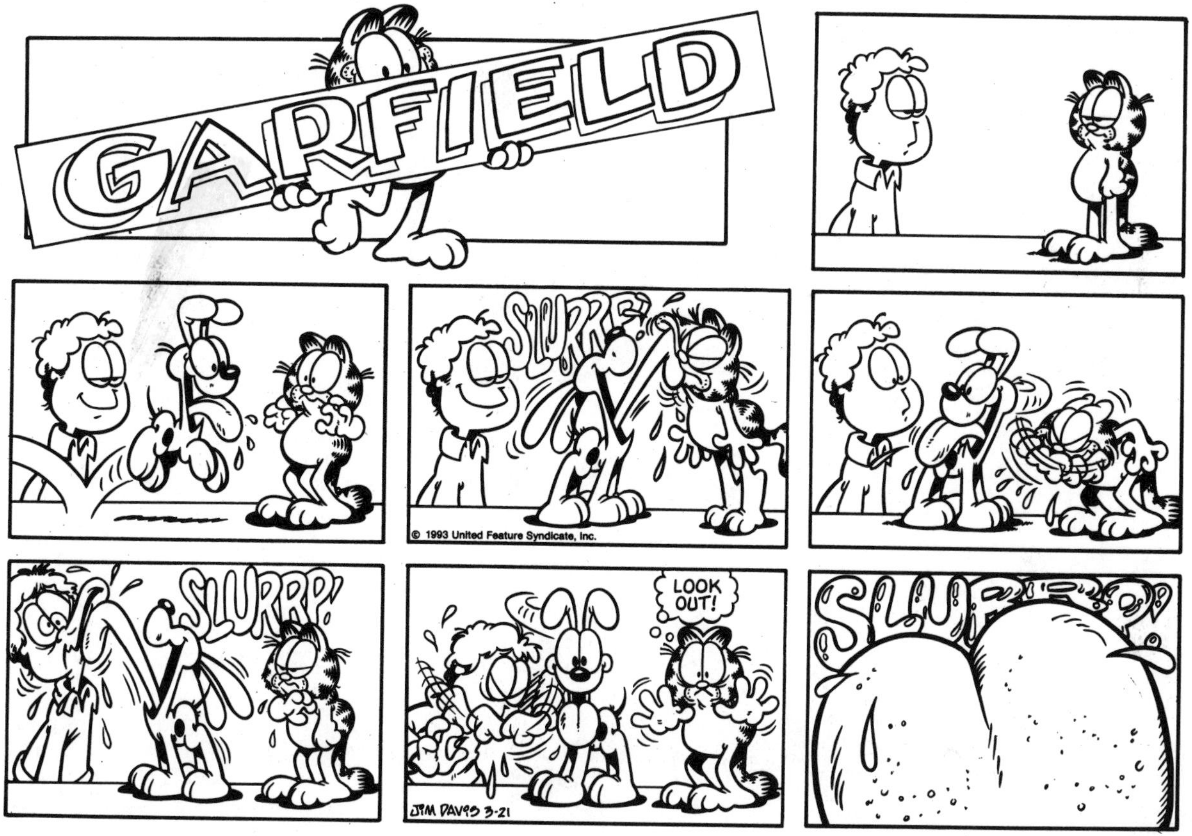

GARFIELD
SLURRP!
© 1993 United Feature Syndicate, Inc.
SLURRP!
LOOK OUT!
JIM DAVIS 3-21

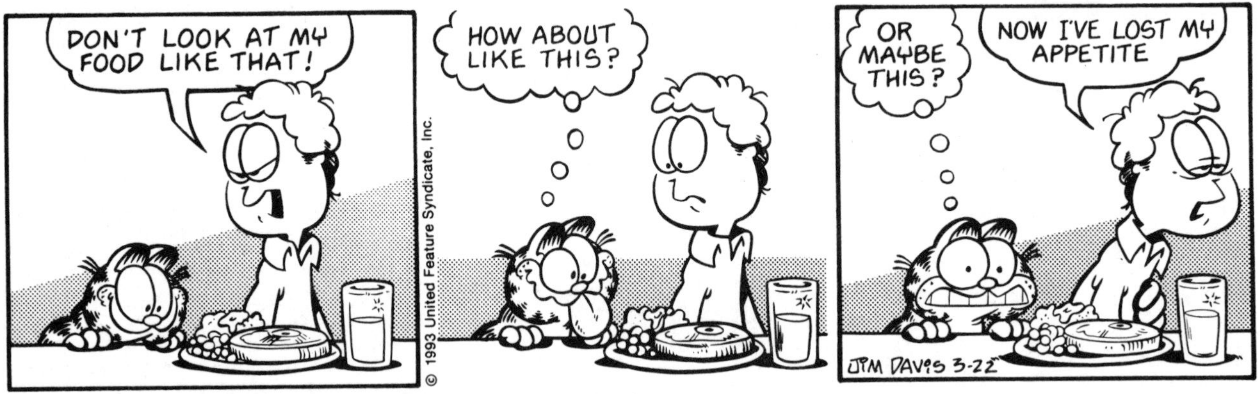
DON'T LOOK AT MY FOOD LIKE THAT!
© 1993 United Feature Syndicate, Inc.
HOW ABOUT LIKE THIS?
OR MAYBE THIS?
NOW I'VE LOST MY APPETITE
JIM DAVIS 3-22

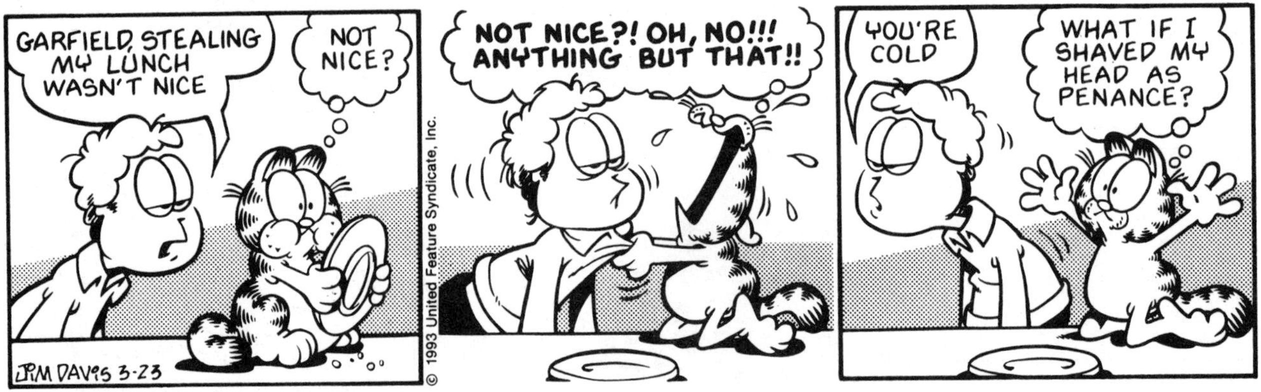
GARFIELD, STEALING MY LUNCH WASN'T NICE
NOT NICE?
© 1993 United Feature Syndicate, Inc.
NOT NICE?! OH, NO!!! ANYTHING BUT THAT!!
YOU'RE COLD
WHAT IF I SHAVED MY HEAD AS PENANCE?
JIM DAVIS 3-23

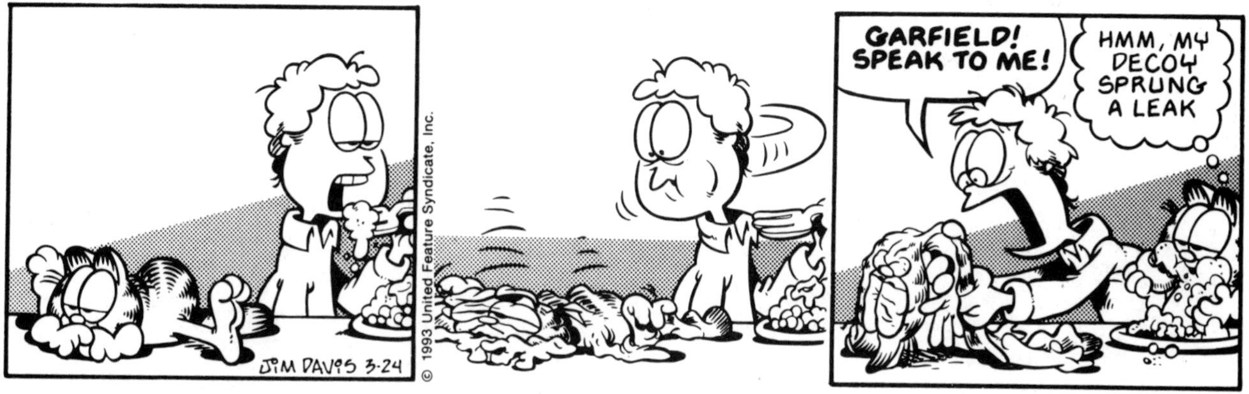
JIM DAVIS 3-24
© 1993 United Feature Syndicate, Inc.
GARFIELD! SPEAK TO ME!
HMM, MY DECOY SPRUNG A LEAK

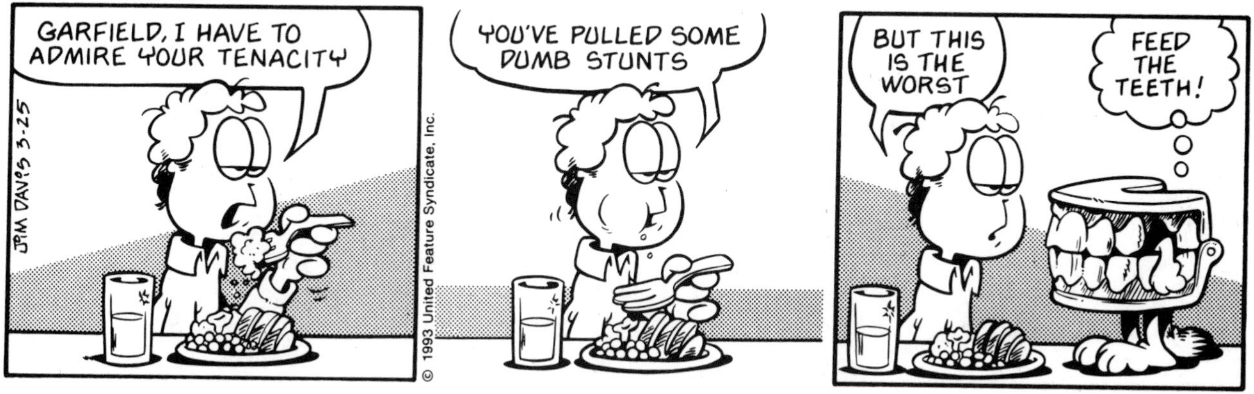
GARFIELD, I HAVE TO ADMIRE YOUR TENACITY
JIM DAVIS 3-25
© 1993 United Feature Syndicate, Inc.
YOU'VE PULLED SOME DUMB STUNTS
BUT THIS IS THE WORST
FEED THE TEETH!

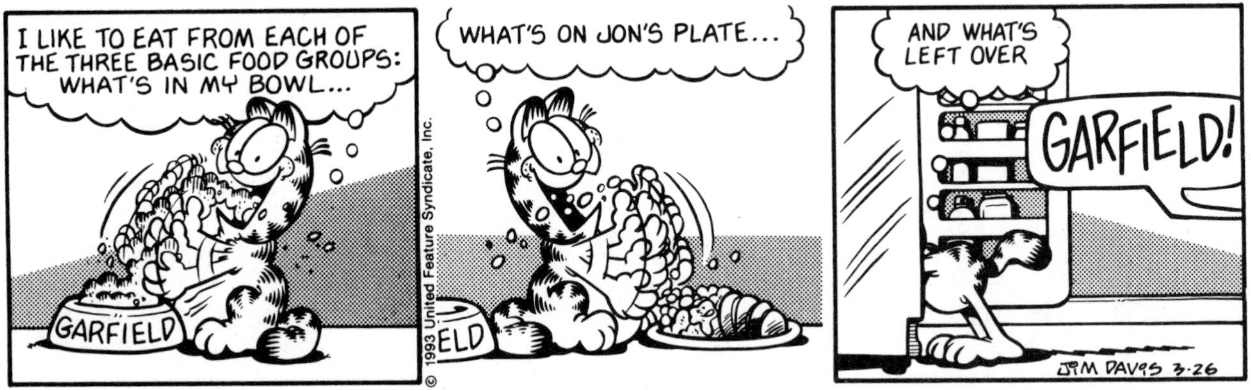
I LIKE TO EAT FROM EACH OF THE THREE BASIC FOOD GROUPS: WHAT'S IN MY BOWL...
GARFIELD
© 1993 United Feature Syndicate, Inc.
WHAT'S ON JON'S PLATE...
ELD
AND WHAT'S LEFT OVER
GARFIELD!
JIM DAVIS 3-26

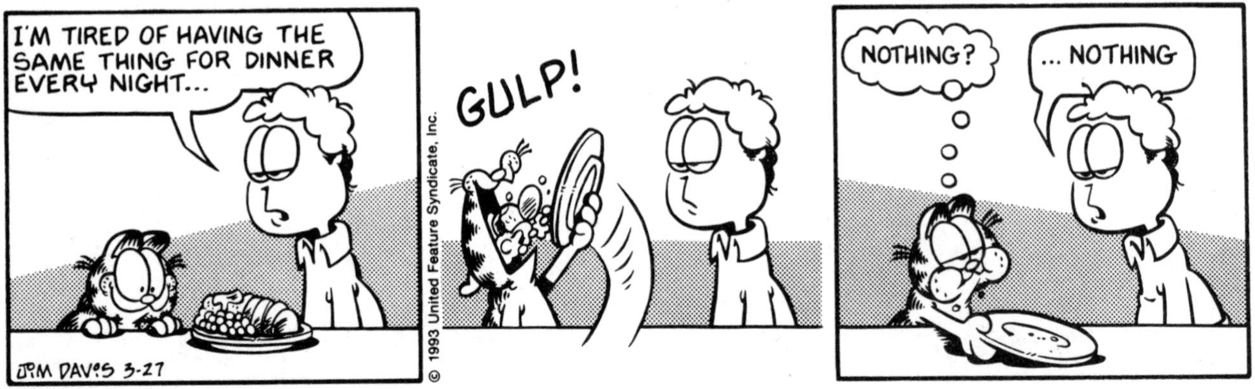
I'M TIRED OF HAVING THE SAME THING FOR DINNER EVERY NIGHT...
JIM DAVIS 3-27
© 1993 United Feature Syndicate, Inc.
GULP!
NOTHING?
... NOTHING

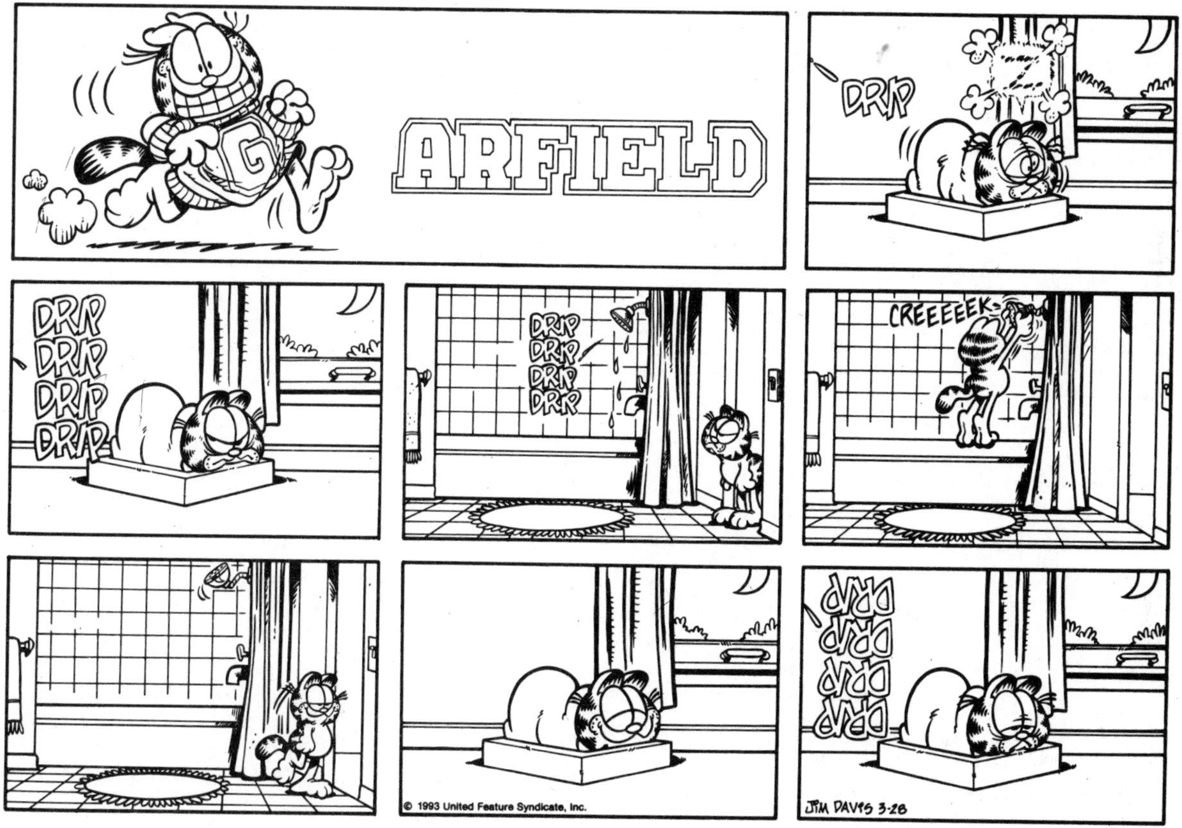
G
ARFIELD
DRIP
DRIP
DRIP
DRIP
DRIP
DRIP
DRIP
DRIP
DRIP
CREEEEEK
© 1993 United Feature Syndicate, Inc.
DRIP
DRIP
DRIP
DRIP
JIM DAVIS 3-28

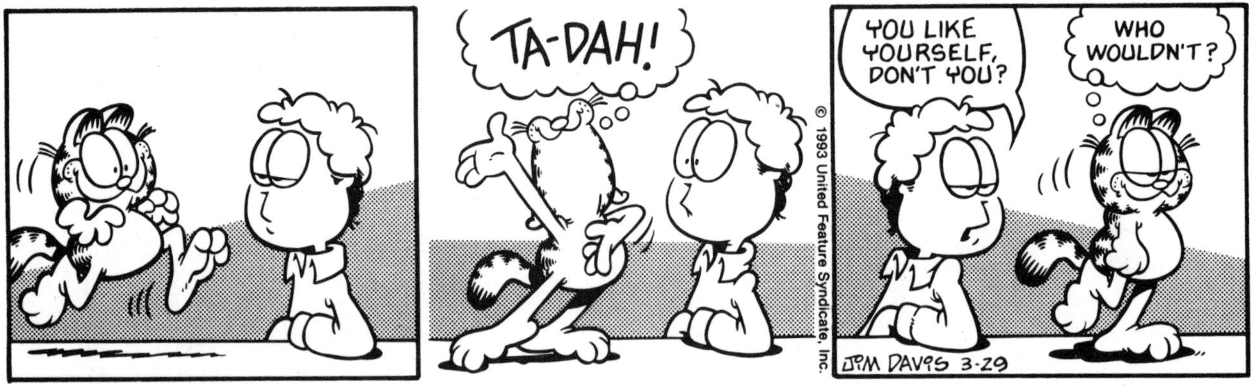
TA-DAH!
YOU LIKE YOURSELF, DON'T YOU?
WHO WOULDN'T?
JIM DAVIS 3-29
© 1993 United Feature Syndicate, Inc.

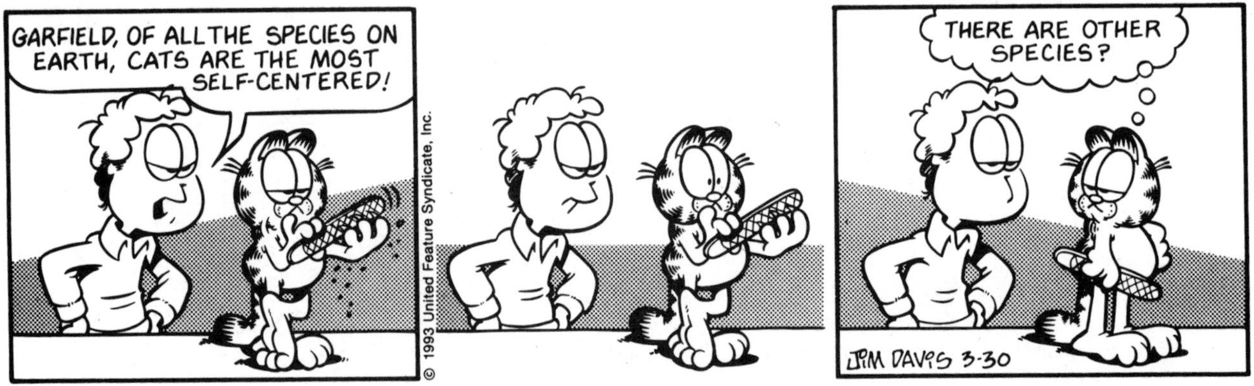
GARFIELD, OF ALL THE SPECIES ON EARTH, CATS ARE THE MOST SELF-CENTERED!
© 1993 United Feature Syndicate, Inc.
THERE ARE OTHER SPECIES?
JIM DAVIS 3-30

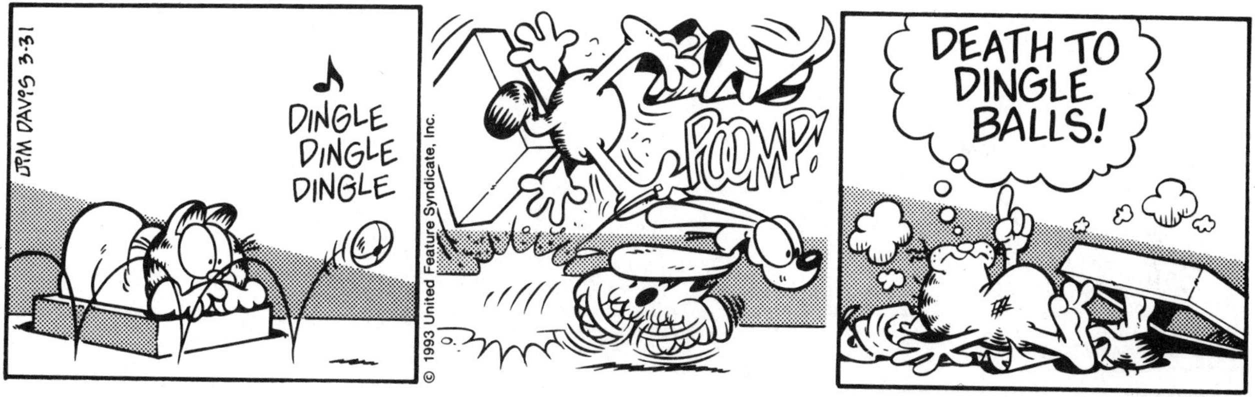
JIM DAVIS 3-31
DINGLE DINGLE DINGLE
POOMP!
DEATH TO DINGLE BALLS!


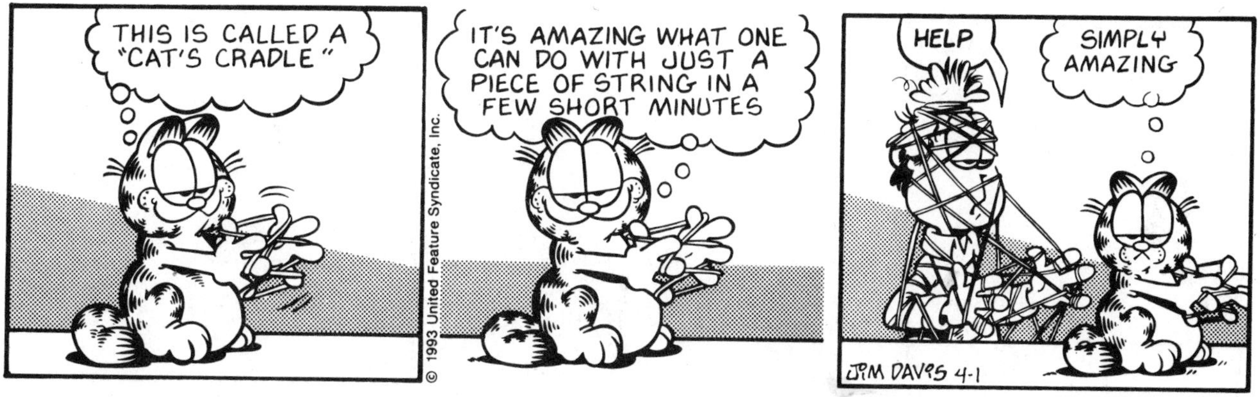
THIS IS CALLED A "CAT'S CRADLE"
IT'S AMAZING WHAT ONE CAN DO WITH JUST A PIECE OF STRING IN A FEW SHORT MINUTES
HELP
SIMPLY AMAZING
JIM DAVIS 4-1

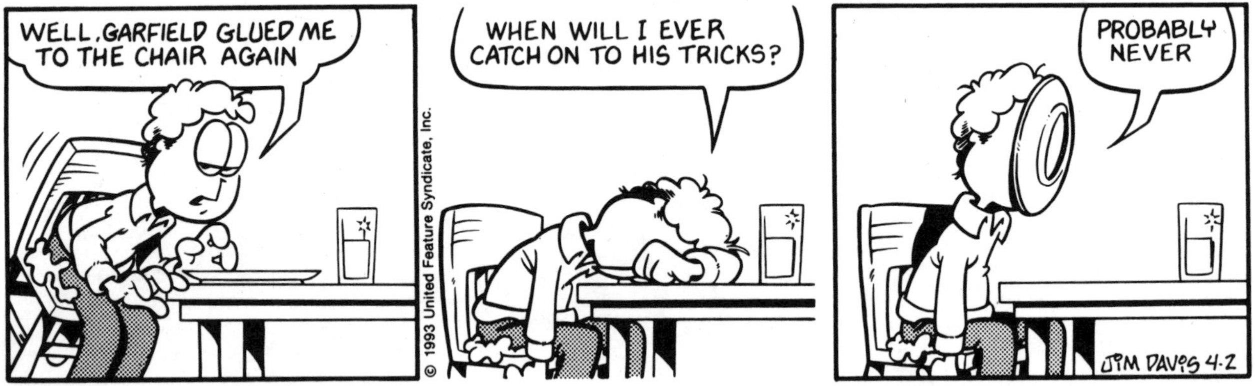
WELL, GARFIELD GLUED ME TO THE CHAIR AGAIN
WHEN WILL I EVER CATCH ON TO HIS TRICKS?
PROBABLY NEVER
© 1993 United Feature Syndicate, Inc.
JIM DAVIS 4-2

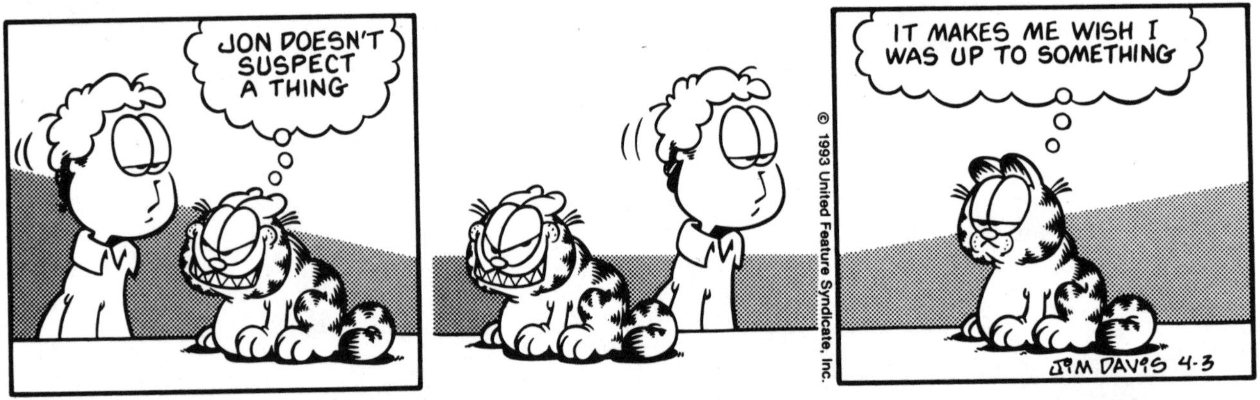
JON DOESN'T SUSPECT A THING
IT MAKES ME WISH I WAS UP TO SOMETHING
© 1993 United Feature Syndicate, Inc.
JIM DAVIS 4-3

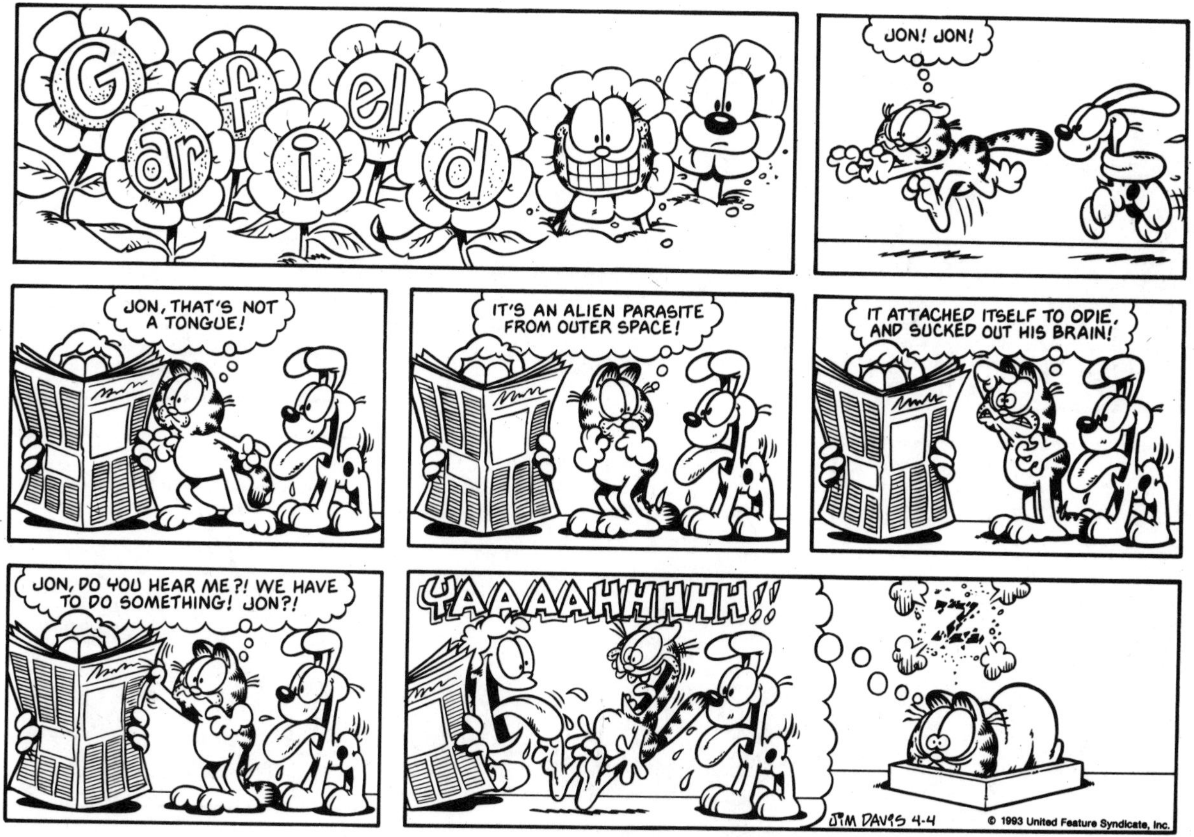
Garfield
JON! JON!
JON, THAT'S NOT A TONGUE!
IT'S AN ALIEN PARASITE FROM OUTER SPACE!
IT ATTACHED ITSELF TO ODIE, AND SUCKED OUT HIS BRAIN!
JON, DO YOU HEAR ME?! WE HAVE TO DO SOMETHING! JON?!
YAAAAAHHHHH!!
JIM DAVIS 4-4
© 1993 United Feature Syndicate, Inc.

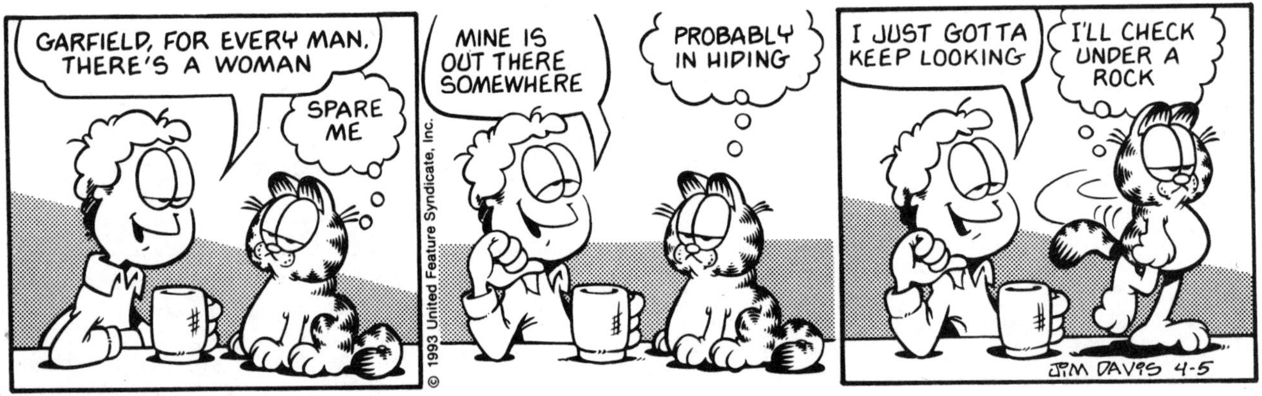
GARFIELD, FOR EVERY MAN, THERE'S A WOMAN
SPARE ME
© 1993 United Feature Syndicate, Inc.
MINE IS OUT THERE SOMEWHERE
PROBABLY IN HIDING
I JUST GOTTA KEEP LOOKING
I'LL CHECK UNDER A ROCK
JIM DAVIS 4-5

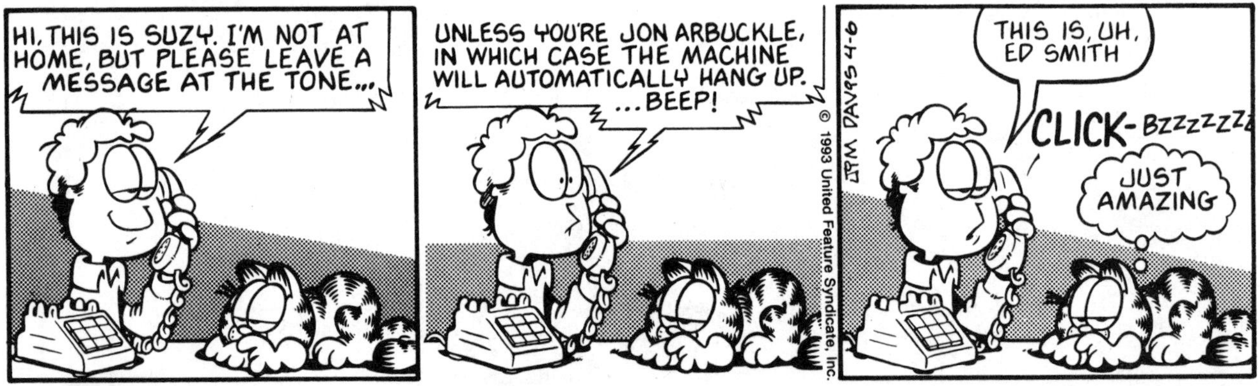
HI, THIS IS SUZY. I'M NOT AT HOME, BUT PLEASE LEAVE A MESSAGE AT THE TONE...
UNLESS YOU'RE JON ARBUCKLE, IN WHICH CASE THE MACHINE WILL AUTOMATICALLY HANG UP. ...BEEP!
© 1993 United Feature Syndicate, Inc.
JIM DAVIS 4-6
THIS IS, UH, ED SMITH
CLICK-BZZZZZZ
JUST AMAZING

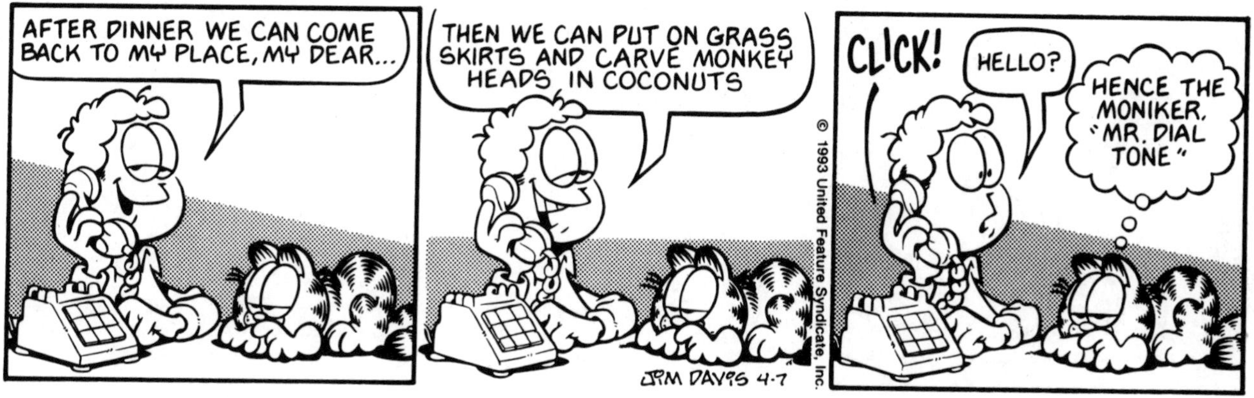
AFTER DINNER WE CAN COME BACK TO MY PLACE, MY DEAR...
THEN WE CAN PUT ON GRASS SKIRTS AND CARVE MONKEY HEADS IN COCONUTS
CLICK!
HELLO?
HENCE THE MONIKER, "MR. DIAL TONE"
JIM DAVIS 4-7
© 1993 United Feature Syndicate, Inc.

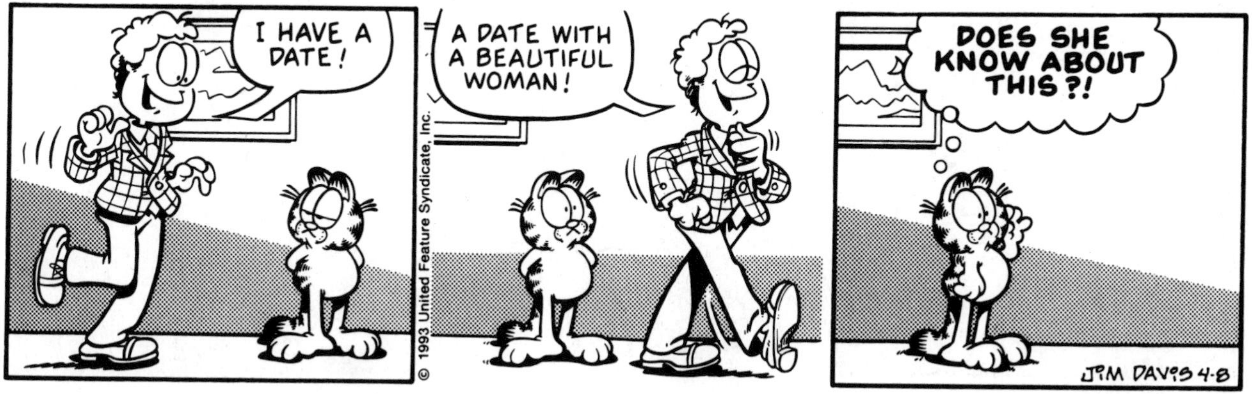
I HAVE A DATE!
A DATE WITH A BEAUTIFUL WOMAN!
DOES SHE KNOW ABOUT THIS?!
JIM DAVIS 4-8
© 1993 United Feature Syndicate, Inc.

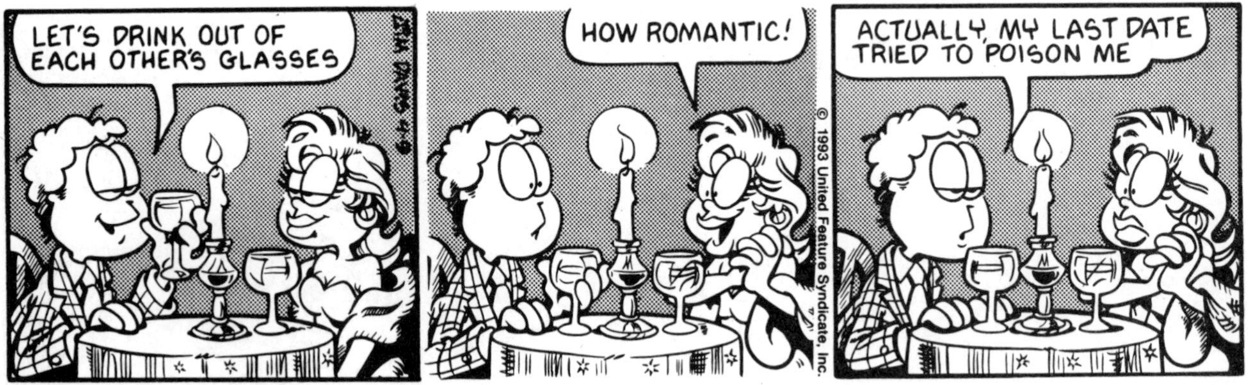
LET'S DRINK OUT OF EACH OTHER'S GLASSES
HOW ROMANTIC!
ACTUALLY, MY LAST DATE TRIED TO POISON ME
© 1993 United Feature Syndicate, Inc.

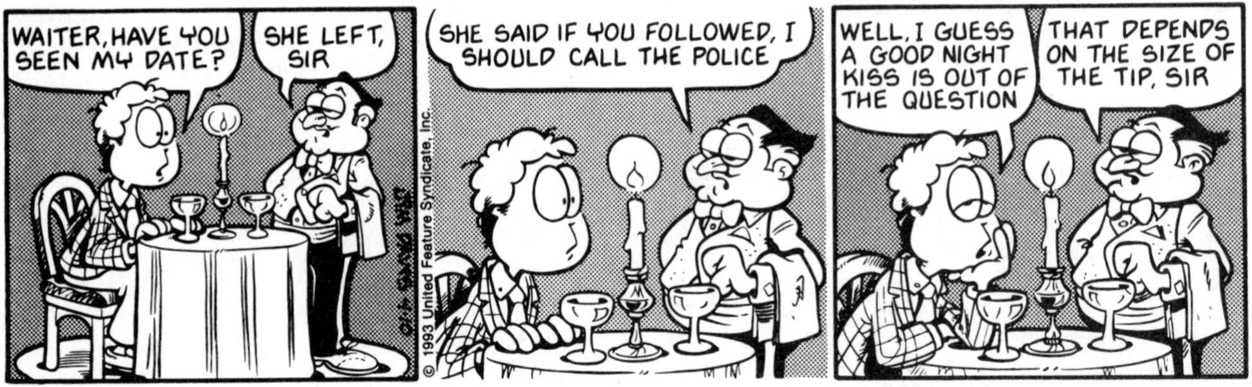
WAITER, HAVE YOU SEEN MY DATE?
SHE LEFT, SIR
SHE SAID IF YOU FOLLOWED, I SHOULD CALL THE POLICE
WELL, I GUESS A GOOD NIGHT KISS IS OUT OF THE QUESTION
THAT DEPENDS ON THE SIZE OF THE TIP, SIR
© 1993 United Feature Syndicate, Inc.